DATE DUE

GAYLORD			PRINTED IN U.S.A.

Divided Cities

The City in the 21st Century
Eugenie L. Birch and Susan M. Wachter, Series Editors

A complete list of books in the series is available
from the publisher.

Divided Cities

Belfast, Beirut, Jerusalem, Mostar, and Nicosia

Jon Calame and Esther Charlesworth

PENN

University of Pennsylvania Press
Philadelphia

Published by
University of Pennsylvania Press
Philadelphia, Pennsylvania 19104-4112

Printed in the United States of America on acid-free paper
10 9 8 7 6 5 4 3 2 1

Library of Congress Cataloging-in-Publication Data

Calame, Jon.
  Divided cities : Belfast, Beirut, Jerusalem, Mostar, and Nicosia / Jon Calame and Esther Charlesworth.
     p. cm. — (The City in the 21st Century)
  ISBN: 978-0-8122-4134-1 (alk. paper)
  Includes bibliographical references and index.
  1. City and town life. 2. Urban violence. 3. Urban warfare. 4. Persecution.
5. Population transfers. 6. Beirut (Lebanon)—History. 7. Belfast (Northern Ireland)—
History. 8. Jerusalem—History. 9. Mostar (Bosnia and Hercegovina)—History.
10. Nicosia (Cyprus)—History. I. Title. II. Charlesworth, Esther Ruth
HT153.C24 2009
307.76—dc22   2008035354

Contents

Foreword by Lebbeus Woods   vii

Preface   ix

1   Warning Beacons   1

2   Cities and Physical Segregation   19

3   Beirut   37

4   Belfast   61

5   Jerusalem   83

6   Mostar   103

7   Nicosia   121

8   Breaching the Urban Contract   143

9   Professional Responses to Partition   167

10   Patterns   205

Epilogue: Jerusalem Redivided   237

Works Cited   243

Index   255

Acknowledgments   261

Foreword

Lebbeus Woods

The five cities under study in this book are vitally important to an understanding of the contemporary world. Each is different, in that each emerges from a unique historical background, belonging to a quite particular and localized set of cultural conditions. Yet, each shares with the others a common set of existential factors, belonging to what we might call an emerging global condition. Prominent among these is sectarianism—a confrontation of differing, though not necessarily opposed, religious beliefs, leading to widespread violence—and a stopgap solution focused on the physical separation of conflicting parties and communities. The other feature shared by the cities under study is that the stopgap solution of separation, intended as an emergency measure to prevent bloodshed and disorder, turns into more or less persistent, if not permanent, division. No one intends to create divided cities as a long-term solution to sectarian violence; rather, such cities emerge from the seeming intractability of the conflicts and their causes.

The story of the present is increasingly being written in terms of religious conflicts. The secularism of the West is exposed through globalization to the sectarian quarrels that bedevil many regions of the world. Western institutions of government and commerce, which operate according to democratic processes or market-savvy principles, are no match in single-minded determination for those elsewhere driven by religious fervor. On the defensive, they have hardened their own positions accordingly. At the same time, Western politicians are not above exploiting religious differences to disguise neocolonial ambitions.

Going against two centuries of growing liberalism in the West, there are many new walls—physical, legal, psychological—being hastily thrown up in the interests of "security" to separate "us" from "them." This goes beyond realities of gated communities for the rich, and restrictive, ethnically biased immigration laws, extending to attempts to seal entire national borders. If the perceived threat of religious warfare increases dramatically, it is conceivable that, not only in the West, ghettoes and internment camps may be deemed necessary. Looking to the future, this is the worst-case scenario. Can things possibly get that bad, in this information-enlightened age?

To insure they will not, it is necessary to understand not only the tragic mistakes of the past, but also the dynamics of the present in terms of the polarization of peoples and their communities. Critical aspects of these dynamics are revealed in this book, for in the physical divisions of Beirut, Nicosia, Belfast, Mostar, and Jerusalem the means by which fear and misunderstanding are given physical form are revealed in all their dimensions. Once in place, the barriers separating disputing groups become the mechanisms for sustaining the urban pathology of communities at war with themselves. The right thing, as this book inspires us to imagine, is to remove the barriers and replace them with new openings for dialogue and exchange. The best thing, however, is never to build the barriers at all. It is to that distant, but attainable, goal that I believe this book is dedicated.

Preface

This book is the result of research conducted between 1998 and 2003 in five ethnically partitioned cities: Belfast, Beirut, Jerusalem, Nicosia, and Mostar. As it went to press in 2008, Beirut still smoldered in the wake of new clashes between Hezbollah and Israel, Baghdad neighborhoods were partitioned according to religious sect, and racial divisions in New Orleans following the Katrina hurricane were still starkly unmended. Though old divisions persist and new ones emerge, fresh insights about how and why urban partitions happen remain in short supply.

The effort to isolate patterns that could provide such insights began in 1996 with our involvement in a reconstruction planning workshop in the Bosnian city of Mostar. The capacity of the divided administration there to coordinate an effective response to social and physical crises in the postwar context was severely limited. Many capable foreign experts stayed away, too, emphasizing the need for a political settlement before revitalization could progress. Investment prior to unification would effectively sanction ethnic segregation, they argued. Still, foreign professionals of all types poured into this vacuum to provide humanitarian assistance, funding, and advice of all kinds.

We were among the dozens of foreign architects, planners, and conservators who visited Mostar with the intention to work despite the political stalemate. We saw that important decisions regarding reconstruction were being left to self-anointed foreign donor agencies working, for the most part, in an isolated and unregulated fashion. It was clear that preliminary consideration of long-term impacts, tradeoffs, and models for successful post-conflict development was rare. Even if those involved had wanted to plot their moves more systematically, the kind of documentation and analysis needed to support such considerations simply did not exist.

A credible response to the questions we encountered in Mostar required close examination of other cities polarized by ethnic conflict. This book summarizes the patterns and insights that emerged in relation to pre- and post-partition phases of urban development. We conclude that divided cities are not aberrations. Instead, they are the unlucky vanguard of a large and growing class of cities. In these troubled places, intercommunal rivalry seems inevitably to recommend physical segregation.

Our discussions with urban professionals, politicians, policymakers, cultural critics, and residents in these five cities suggest that mistakes could have been avoided if decision makers had possessed a broader understanding of urban partition's causes and consequences. We learned that symptoms of discord in the urban environment—in particular, physical partitions—often affirm local assumptions about persecution and encourage one ethnic community to antagonize another. In this sense, they are a self-fulfilling prophecy of involuntary separation and militancy between urban neighbors with a history of mutual distrust.

By way of disclaimer, this study does not attempt to offer theoretical remedies, physical plans, or practical recommendations for divided cities. The histories of conflict and division in each city are long and well documented by others (in particular Scott Bollens, Meron Benvenisti, Samir Khalaf, and Fred Boal). This exploration of the spatial and functional anatomy of divided cities complements extensive scholarship already completed on failed policy and governance, borrowing only as far as necessary to summarize the broadest causes and circumstances of partition. Our ambition was to isolate and begin to explain the patterns linking five divided cities. We are now convinced that recognition of pre-partition development patterns can contribute to more effective management in cities where physical segregation is deepening.

In order to undertake comparative work on such an ambitious scale, we have grounded our arguments in direct observation and large quantities of original interview material. In each city, conversations were documented with local residents on both sides of the partition: cab drivers, politicians, policymakers, architects, planners, and journalists. In many cases, the interviewees rejected the very notion that their native cities were dysfunctional, while others urged wider comparisons to understand the magnitude of the problems they encountered, invoking the notions of "urban apartheid" (Ervine 2001) and "anti-urban" (Pašić 2003) sentiment to explain the impulse toward partition.

The need for better answers to some key questions, many of which are largely neglected in the existing literature on urban partition, guided this inquiry. Regarding agency, we asked who actually drew the lines, who produced the resulting partitions, and who paid for them. Regarding the social and physical impacts of division, we tried to understand how life proceeds in the wake of partitioning, what penalties and profits accompany it, and whether forcible ethnic segregation serves any legitimate purpose in light of its enormous social and material costs. Regarding the affected stakeholders, we sought to identify the primary actors in the divided city drama along with their motivations. Regarding function, we explored how partition relates to notions of land, property rights, security, collective security and sovereignty. In each case, we proceeded on the assumption that developmental patterns illustrative of a generic divided city phenomenon might emerge. Regarding space, documentation of the partitions' scale, structure, and porosity allows the reader to appreciate how intentional, sophisticated, and oppressive they can be for local residents.

Our findings allow us to sketch a generic profile of the divided city, found in Chapter 10. Rarely a senseless and spontaneous convulsion, urban partitioning may be like a fever: the unhappy but strategic response of an organism to a threat encountered within its own body. Still, a fever is not productively sustained for long; our systematic exploration of five divided cities suggests that partition is not an effective long-term reply to discrimination and violence. The insights that resulted from this study will serve to strengthen future efforts to protect vulnerable communities with measures that are more effective and less burdensome than the barricade.

The summaries of historic urban development for the cities discussed here are drawn from the work of specialized scholars to provide the reader with insights regarding the evolution of physical partitions. They examine events and situations with specific relevance to the process of physical partition along ethnic lines. They are not intended to be comprehensive or to rationalize the political conflicts leading to division.

Figure 0.1. Multiple layers and generations of defensive screens dominate the backyards of thousands of residents living near interface areas in Belfast, contributing to an oppressive physical atmosphere and a cynical social climate. Authors.

Chapter 1
Warning Beacons

I would describe the Northern Ireland problem as probably not much different than anywhere else. The more and more I try to understand conflict, the more and more I find resonances in other places and with other people . . . So can we have a single facet that is stark and in front of us that says: 'Let's deal with the problem'? Well, of course we do. It's fear. Emotion. The intimacy of fear. So we try to remove the fear by creating the self-imposed apartheid that people demand. But none of it deals with the historical, the cultural, the economic, the social, none of it deals with any of those, so unless we have a multi-faceted approach to what our problem is, I don't think we can remotely begin to deal with our problem.

(David Ervine, former Member of the Legislative Assembly, Belfast, 2001)

This book compares five internally partitioned cities: Belfast, where "peacelines" have separated working-class Catholic and Protestant residents since "the Troubles" began in 1968; Beirut, where seventeen years of civil war and a volatile "Ligne de demarcation" made the city into a sectarian labyrinth; Jerusalem, where Israeli and Jordanian militias patroled the Green Line for nineteen years; Mostar, where Croatian and Bosniak communities split the city along an Austro-Hungarian boulevard into autonomous halves beginning in 1992, and Nicosia, where two walls and a wide buffer zone have segregated Turkish and Greek Cypriots since 1974.

In each city, urban managers under-estimated growing interethnic tensions until it was so late that violence spread and resulted in physical segregation. Though the walls, fences, and no man's lands that resulted were generally designed to be temporary, they have considerable staying power, forcing divided residents to grapple with life "under siege." Unlike regular soldiers, destined to leave the battlefield in one condition or another, the inhabitants of wartorn cities confront their terrors at home without the means of retreat or escape. Even after politicians have secured a peace, the citizens struggle with losses and missed opportunities that are beyond compensation. Along the path to urban partition, a social contract between municipal government and residents is broken. The costs of rene-gotiation tend to be high.

Five Warning Beacons

Partitioned cities act as a warning beacon for all cities where intercommu-nal rivalry threatens normal urban functioning and security. Every city con-tains ethnic fault-lines or boundaries that give shape to "good" and "bad" neighborhoods and lend local meaning to "the other side of the tracks." Since all cities reflect local demographics in spatial terms, each can be lo-cated somewhere on a continuum between perfect spatial integration and complete separation.

Evidence gleaned from the five cities examined here suggests that, given similar circumstances and pressures, any city could undergo a compa-rable metamorphosis. Accordingly, this comparative study offers guidance to urban managers who seek to avoid the enormous costs of physical segre-gation. Extreme case studies are useful because they reflect accelerated cause and effect dynamics that might otherwise require decades to observe (Ben-venisti 1982: 5). Divided cities expose what lies in store for a large, and per-haps growing, class of cities on a trajectory toward polarization and parti-tion between rival communities. In the early twenty-first century, this class includes Montreal, Monrovia, Dagestan, Washington, D.C., Baghdad, Dili, Bunia, Novi Sad, Kigali, Singapore, Cincinnati, Kirkuk, and Oakland.

Divided cities are generally linked with civil wars in which group iden-tity is threatened. This type of war dominated the late twentieth century, leaving many cities vulnerable. Indeed, since World War II there has been a marked shift in global warfare trends from inter- to intrastate conflict: of 64 wars between 1945 and 1988, 59 were intrastate or "civil" wars, and about 80 percent of those who perished were killed by someone of their own na-tionality. During this same period, 127 new sovereign states were created and 35 new international land boundaries have been drawn since 1980 (Strand, Wilhelmsen, and Gleditsch 2003).

This splintering trend peaked around 1990 with the height of what has been called the "Third World War"—the systematic and violent disintegra-tion of weak states into statelets controlled by regional ethnic rivals (Mar-shall 1999). As of 2007, about 23 protracted non-state, civil conflicts were ongoing, down from about 38 in 2003 and more than 90 in 1990. Of these, approximately 80 percent were grounded in contested group rights or threatened collective identity. Examples include recent hostilities in Sudan, Afghanistan, Angola, East Timor, Chechnya, Dagestan, Iraq, Ethiopia, Kosovo, India, Democratic Republic of Congo, Nigeria, the Philippines, Ivory Coast, and Rwanda.

Civilian urban populations have been severely affected by this surge of interethnic warfare. Their burdens in relation to warfare appear to be growing. In World War I, for example, about 43 percent of all battle-related deaths were civilian. That figure rose to around 59 percent in the course of World War II, and since then—during a period when the number of intrastate conflicts surpassed the number of interstate conflicts—civilian deaths constituted approximately 74 percent of the wartime totals (White 2003). The scale and intensity of psychological trauma suffered by noncombatants has risen proportionately. Divided cities are emblems of this overwhelming loss, dislocation, and prolonged anxiety.

These trends appear to be borne out by Israel's unilateral partitioning program, which broke ground in 2002 amid escalating friction with Palestinian civilians. A sophisticated physical partition, called a "security fence" by its proponents and a "separation barrier" by critics, was about 60 percent complete in late 2007. The barricade's proposed length is 723 km along a new Israel-West Bank border, including up to 167 km sealing off the vulnerable eastern and northern flanks of Jerusalem.

The Symptom and the Illness

There has been symbiosis between cities and walls since the emergence of occidental urban culture. In divided cities, that relationship has deepened so much as to become dysfunctional. Internal partitions can be seen as causes, symptoms, or cures with respect to chronic urban problems.

The five divided cities examined here share more than fortified ethnic enclaves. Each was renowned for ethnic diversity and successful cohabitation prior to the outbreak of intergroup violence and the appearance of physical barricades. Though an ethnically mixed population is a prerequisite for urban partition, rival ethnic groups still manage to cooperate admirably in cities like Bombay, Phnom Penh, Mombassa, Kuala Lumpur, Kumasi, Jos, Bangalore, and Kinshasa. Why, then, do some cities resort to physical partition while others do not? One important factor may be the degree to which ethnicity conditions political affiliation:

in some places, identity politics came to define the logic of the political game, and in other places, it did not. In those places where it did, the odds of violence were higher. . . . The incentives and constraints offered by political institutions, and the strength of those institutions to follow through, largely determined those odds. (Crawford and Lipschutz 1998: 3)

The ethnic rivalries governing urban partitions often obscure more fundamental social tensions, like those felt between the professional and working classes, indigenes and settlers, or powerful minorities and marginalized majorities. Some scholars have even suggested that ethnically motivated discrimination and violence are provoked by "sectarian political entrepreneurs" whose political fortunes rely on intergroup competition and antagonism (Crawford and Lipschutz 1998). Indeed, ethnic conflict may appear intractable more because it is artificial than because it is endemic.

Scholars of ethnic conflict in Lebanon, Israel, Bosnia, Northern Ireland, and Cyprus debate whether partition is the result of conspiratorial politics or homegrown prejudice. (Of special usefulness are the works of Henderson, Lebow, and Stoessinger 1974; Horowitz 1985; Schaeffer 1990; Crawford and Lipschutz 1998; Cleary 2002.) The problem of false dichotomies is an important one in most divided cities, since a failed cure is certain to follow a faulty diagnosis.

One Belfast politician described a common anxiety:

We are destined to get worse, not better, for as long as there is the concept of fear and siege. So if fear is, at the core, the most dangerous emotion . . . then remove the fear. Now, how do you do that? Is it done by walls? Is it done by education? Is it done by being inventive about how you share the land? I'm not sure that I have any of the answers—plenty of the questions. (Ervine 2001)

What can urban managers do when a group of Belfast teenagers light a bonfire of trash and wood in an empty lot along one of the city's many Protestant-Catholic interfaces? Their excitement grows if members of a rival group from the adjacent neighborhood appear at the scene. Alcohol is consumed, taunts are exchanged, and someone throws a stone. When a riot ensues, older community members on both sides are summoned in a ritualized chain reaction. As confrontation escalates slowly over weeks and months, the stakes are gradually raised and houses on one or both sides are attacked, terrorizing the inhabitants, who typically have no connection with the violence outside. These victims are innocent but are simply too close to the interface, so they bear the brunt of social, physical, and psychological traumas. Faced with such a chronic problem, the citizens petition their parliamentary representative for an interface wall. If their case is sound, the municipal government allocates the necessary funds and commissions another peaceline. Typically, the restless teenagers at the center of the drama move on to the next empty pocket and the cycle begins again. As a result, more than thirteen major barricades have been erected between Catholic and Protestant residents in Belfast, and none have yet been dismantled.

This Belfast scenario illustrates a common concern among the managers and besieged residents of divided cities: the need to stem physical violence at hostile interfaces. Policymakers often feel compelled to provide protection in the form of barricades once conventional approaches fail. In many instances, threatened citizens or paramilitary groups have already erected ad hoc barriers. Whether unofficial or sanctioned, the physical partition is employed to contain a crisis that has overwhelmed existing systems designed to maintain order and protect urban residents in an evenhanded way.

One reason municipal governments are hesitant to address the subject of partition is that the barricades are a measure of their own failure to fulfill a basic political mandate. Another is that the walls, whether illicit, scandalous, or ugly, tend to curb intercommunal violence more cheaply and effectively in the short term than police surveillance. They solve a profound, longstanding problem in a superficial, temporary way.

If such partitions worked over the long haul, urban dividing walls could be considered an unfortunate but effective response to ethnic conflict. However, as passive security devices they are a failure for the municipal government, and this is just one of many reasons why their construction should be questioned. In many cases, these partitions also postpone or even preclude a negotiated settlement between ethnic antagonists because they create a climate of dampened violence, sustained distrust and low-grade hostility. Urban partitions seem to reduce violent confrontation while justifying fear and paranoia. If there were no actual danger, this logic suggests, the walls would no longer be standing. In this way, the partition becomes the emblem of threat as much as a bulwark against it. The communities behind these walls often witness their neighborhood evolve from an arena of violent conflict into an insulated pressure cooker.

Voluntary and involuntary habits of segregation, with visible and invisible forms, become mutually reinforcing. In Nicosia, even the anger of older Cypriots that has been generated by their personal knowledge and history seems preferable to the idle prejudice of younger citizens whose cynicism is inherited and untested by direct contact. The ignorance of the

Figure 1.1. Ethnic partitions in Belfast, like this one near Grosvenor Road, govern everyday relations between neighbors and create dangerous, wasted spaces. Authors.

unknown but stereotyped "other" behind urban partitions is a core ingredient for future conflict, and its toxic effects on the social atmosphere of the city must be weighed in relation to the short-term benefits of division, most of which accrue to the city's managers rather than its citizens. If instances of interethnic violence were rare or isolated, these concerns would be of merely anecdotal value. However, the statistics related to intergroup conflict on a global level point in the opposite direction.

Long treated as anomalies, divided cities are linked to each other by clear and coherent patterns. Some of these are summarized in Chapter 10. Urban partition results from concerns found in almost every city, such as ethnicity tied to political affiliation, institutional discrimination, physical security, fair policing, and shifting relations between majority and minority ethnic communities.

Even a casual scan of international affairs this early in the twenty-first century reveals that urban communities torn and traumatized by physical segregation are multiplying quickly. Brussels remains the would-be trophy of separatist parties in Wallonia; Montreal could be caught in a similar tug-of-war in Quebec; Los Angeles has yet to confront the racial fractures exposed by popular violence in the 1990s; the Serbian and Albanian residents of Mitrovica have split themselves on either side of the Ibar River; riots between the Hausas and Yorubas of Nigeria have ravaged Lagos; Hindus and Muslims clash routinely in Ahmedabad, though they dispute the Ayodhya religious complex hundreds of miles away; sovereignty in Baghdad is contested by several ethnic and religious groups in the current wave of instability there; in 2001 Cincinnati's racial fault-lines were activated in the wake of discriminatory police brutality. These are but a few of many examples worldwide.

In reply to such lapses in traditional urban peacekeeping, urban communities resort to riot, revolt, threats of succession, and paramilitary activity. New walls between rival ethnic groups are constantly emerging, while old scars are stubborn in healing. The causes for rivalry, along with the evidence of forsaken alternatives, generally go unrecognized or are long forgotten.

Politicians—both those embroiled in the ethnic conflicts and those who attempt to intercede on behalf of the international community—often become mired in short-term policy fixes that are designed in response to a crisis. Official advocacy of urban partition as a reply to ethnic conflict was once shunned but is now common. Physical segregation has emerged over the last fifty years as one of the most popular and most myopic solutions to intergroup violence in the urban environment.

Chinagraph Frontiers

Cities can be divided in many ways. Some have been shattered by a wax pencil in the space of an hour, remaining split for decades by a "chinagraph frontier," as in Nicosia. Others are restless battlegrounds scored by informal boundaries of varying degrees of permanence. Some cities develop sealed, semipermeable boundaries in response to particular episodes, seasons, or political events. In Belfast it has been shown that "movement patterns and feelings of threat depended on the level of tension or violence locally" and that "the level of tension or violence increased at different times of the year" with special concerns centering on traditional anniversaries, marches and parades (Murtagh 1995: 217). All such cities use roads, mountains, rivers, and open spaces to reinforce informal systems of physical segregation, sometimes complemented by engineered barricades.

Arbitrary lines drawn on a map—due to the urgency of a compromise, the necessity of war, or the tremor of a human hand—result in urban minefields navigated daily by residents who are unable to avoid them. In Jerusalem, the arbitrary "thickness" of the Green Line, as drawn on the armistice map of 1948, generated confusion that persisted for many months after the formal division of the city, and several people were wounded after wandering by accident inside the "width of the line" (Benvenisti 1996: 61). These boundaries isolate communities that know each other, rely on each other and overlap with one another.

Cities are rarely divided by their own citizens in isolation. They are typically the product of external forces acting on a city with the intent to protect it, save it, claim it, demoralize it, or enlist it in a larger struggle from which it cannot benefit. Lines become walls and walls govern behavior. Total separation ultimately makes bigotry automatic, functional division habitual, and deepening misunderstandings likely. Walls are both a panacea and poison for societies where intergroup conflict is common, but over time it is their toxicity that tends to prevail in social relations. The Green Line in Nicosia was called an "unremitting obstacle to progress toward normalization between the two communities" (Harbottle 1970: 67) by one observer, and this characterization can be applied to all five cities examined here.

Although their social impacts are nearly identical, urban partition lines bear little outward resemblance to one another because their origins differ greatly. Some dividing lines, like those in Jerusalem and Nicosia, were hand-drawn on a map by appointed negotiators. These lines generally require physical barricades, since they often carve their way through shared spaces and seem arbitrary or counterintuitive in their meanderings through contested urban territory. Being the result of "rational" design, such partitions are typically constructed as parallel barricades that separate a barren neutral zone in the city center. Others, like the dividing lines in Belfast, Mostar, and Beirut, are place-specific remnants of interethnic violence, often lacking walls and fences. These demarcations tend to be slow to emerge, slow to disappear, and unofficial. Local residents are conditioned by habit and painful experience to avoid them. Belfast provides a good example of a city where the municipal government has yet to represent the peacelines separating Catholics from Protestants on any map, though millions of dollars are appropriated to construct, enlarge, and maintain these walls in response to public petitions.

In Beirut, the Green Line was an official military boundary that proved quite inadequate to create protected zones for urban residents, since paramilitary warlords swiftly subdivided larger Christian and Muslim sectors with their own boundaries determined by the shifting location of snipers' nests. In Mostar, the largest north-south street became the front line between military and paramilitary forces. A wall was never erected: open space, uniquely hazardous in a dense Ottoman city fabric, constituted the primary barricade along the line. Had this front line slipped slightly eastward to the natural partition—the Neretva River gorge—the elimination of the city's native Muslim population would have been assured.

Lending additional urgency to the study of divided cities is the predictable nature of their transition from healthy, integrated places to physically partitioned ones. While sudden and unexpected episodes of violence often herald the final stages of intercommunal isolation, the fault-lines activated during these cataclysmic periods are rarely unfamiliar to residents. Still, the divided cities examined here were not destined for partition by their social or political histories; they were partitioned by politicians, citizens, and engineers according to limited information, short-range plans, and often dubious motivations.

Until the onset of its crippling civil war in 1991, Mostar was an emblem of interfaith tolerance in the Balkans, representing the educated observer's last guess for the city most likely to erupt into sectarian violence.

Beirut was viewed by some as a Paris of the Middle East, a seat of international banking, and an exemplar of secular and cosmopolitan life. Proud of their central role in the business culture of the region, Beirutis held a strong faith in the unifying power of entrepreneurship and prosperity over the divisive influence of their inherited culture.

Jerusalem and Nicosia had long been crossroads of belief, politics, and commerce. They were cities defined by exceptional ethnic diversity, which had been absorbed successfully for hundreds of years prior to their episodes of partition.

Belfast, sacrificed by Dublin's independence movement in 1920 and a stronghold of British influence, was the one contested city in Ireland that seemed to guarantee strong, centralized social control. It was reasonable to assume that peace could be maintained there by Westminster, one of the most seasoned democracies in the world.

Forks in the Road

In each divided city examined here, the tide of social unrest and institutional discrimination could have pushed in a different direction. The paths that eventually led to physical partition were determined both by long-standing habits of segregation and by the vicissitudes of political fortune, making the final outcomes neither random nor irrational.

The narratives of partition presented here support the assertion that partition was not inevitable for the five cities examined. There were many junctures along each path toward physical and involuntary urban segregation. At each juncture, the actions of a handful of individuals determined whether a city would seek a detour. Though these five did not manage to avoid division, they might have done so. At the same time, it is likely that many others confronted equally stark challenges but managed to conclude their conflicts without resorting to physical barricades.

Embedded in each narrative of partition were moments when segregation shifted from a habitual and voluntary phenomenon to an obligatory one. There were moments when municipal governments chose to prioritize hereditary affiliations above merit and need. There were moments when institutions and laws that upheld conditions of relative deprivation with respect to a beleaguered minority population were not questioned, or were strengthened by decision makers with the power to alter them. There were moments when organized labor movements, for example, might have unified underprivileged members of rival ethnic communities in a coordinated and legitimate struggle against the sources of a common discontent. There were junctures where new residents could have been absorbed by the city rather than marginalized by it. For example:

- The Catholic and Muslim defenders of Mostar could have celebrated the eventual repulsion of the Yugoslav National Army in 1992, using their victory and the international sympathies accompanying it to revitalize their city.
- In the 1920s and 1930s shipyard and factory workers in Belfast could have joined the labor unions that promised to channel their frustrations toward productive political ends, instead of pouring them into paramilitary violence.
- Decisive measures undertaken by the central Cypriot government in the late 1950s might have foreseen and extinguished the early stirrings of violence provoked by the Ethnic Organization of Cypriot Fighters and prevented the campaign for *enosis* that eventually prompted foreign intervention from both Britain and Turkey.
- In Beirut, student protests and Communist Party demonstrations during the late 1960s offered the government a chance to address the basic social injustices that later fueled popular rebellion. Diplomatic engagement with the leadership of the Palestinian Liberation Organization during the initial stages of its operations in Lebanon, along with effective use of the Lebanese army to diffuse and dampen paramilitary operations in Beirut, could have significantly weakened incentives associated with random sectarian violence.
- British Mandate officials in Palestine could have eliminated all references to ethnicity in the public sector bureaucracy in order to establish a tradition of meritocracy prior to their pullout in 1948, thereby leaving a legacy of interdependence, rather than one of mutual resentment between Jewish and Arab citizens.

Choices made along these forking paths eventually led to the imposition of ethnic partitions between urban neighbors. The conditions of physical segregation in turn initiated a chain reaction of political decisions that led to social hardship in the cities in which they occurred.

Related Crises

As with any problem linked to widespread and recurrent social trauma, divided cities cannot be successfully appraised in isolation. Though their episodes of violence may be contained in time and space, they are rarely a product of local forces alone. More often, they provide a battle zone for larger proxy wars initiated and orchestrated by agents whose interests extend beyond the municipal boundaries. On an even more fundamental level, the demise of a city cannot be separated from a failure of the social institutions and political systems of which it is an extension. In the case of divided cities, these systems include new and old nationalisms, liberal democracy, and mechanisms of social justice.

Decision makers who look on as the cities under their jurisdiction slide toward ethnic apartheid are quick to point out that their hands were tied by external powers, or that the violence was imminent, or that their attempts at rapprochement were in earnest. The result observed in Belfast is nearly identical to that in the other divided cities under examination here: "sustained violent conflict has infused decision makers in a range of policy sectors with a sense of hopelessness that has allowed them to draw limits on the impact of their brief" (Murtagh 1995: 210).

The record shows that many municipal politicians were willing to ally themselves with national or foreign interests at the expense of disenfranchised minority communities within their sphere of responsibility. On the road to partition, examples of intercommunal cooperation and pluralism are frequently ignored and discounted. Even before politically weak communities are antagonized, their desires for fair treatment and police protection by municipal authorities are often frustrated.

In response, urban residents whose best interests are routinely disregarded sometimes choose to abandon the systems that no longer serve them. They typically replace their allegiance to the police with their own paramilitaries and their faith in political representation with the decision to take direct action. Under extreme circumstances, one of the first projects of such a group is to erect barricades between themselves and their immediate enemies. Citing threats to their physical well-being both real and presumed, these communities call the bluff of politicians who defend failed systems of social control or claim impartiality with respect to the rights of minority groups. From this first moment of abandonment, all other episodes of urban division follow according to a rational sequence. It remains only to isolate and understand the steps that lead up to this initial break in order to characterize the process of urban partition in general terms.

The Cost of Partition

The negative impacts of urban division are legion. Even where political advantages accrue to rival communities seeking isolation, voluntary and involuntary partitions have brought death, suffering, disorientation, loss, and social anemia wherever they appear.

Composite estimates for loss of life in relation to interethnic violence are varied and difficult to confirm, and figures tied to specific cities are even less common. The most explicit statistics have been generated for Belfast; most studies cite around 1,500 Troubles-related deaths there out of a total of 3,500 in Northern Ireland during the years 1969–2001. In Israel, the total deaths from the first and second *intifadas* (2000–2003) are estimated at around 2,700. In Cyprus approximately 6,300 deaths have been unofficially linked to civil unrest during 1955–1985. In Lebanon, where war deaths were largely centered in Beirut, most estimates hover around 150,000 civilian deaths during 1975–1990. In Bosnia-Herzegovina, civil war estimates of military and civilian dead range between 60,000 and 250,000 in total during 1992–1995.

Urban apartheid schemes generally signal a failure of governance and diplomacy because their success relies on violence, avoidance, and intimidation for success. The construction of isolated ethnic clusters defies liberal principles of tolerance and pluralism in favor of rudimentary group survival. Walls at an urban scale are expensive to build, maintain, and monitor. In some cases, elaborate no man's lands must be constructed and patrolled, while in others checkpoints and transit stations track movements at each crossing. New physical and institutional infrastructure must be built on both sides of an urban partition to replace what was left behind, and whole bureaucracies blossom to address problems of jurisdiction, compensation, and encroachment. Rather than investing in the growth or prosperity of an urban community, partition-era administrations must spend lavishly to resist the back-sweeping tide of intercommunal violence.

While political struggles determine the behavior of the city as a whole, residents with little stake in the negotiations pay a high price for long-term destabilization and violence. Family members and friends are often wounded or killed. Property is lost, social networks are shattered, and opportunities are forfeited. Psychological trauma is often suffered by those who had least to do with partition: the student, the mother, the pensioner, the soldier. A resident of Beirut recalled that civilians living near the Green Line were especially vulnerable: "We used to see death in front of us. This is how we lived: shells, theft, murder, sniping. . . . No one protected us. I'll tell you again that those who paid the price are the Lebanese citizens" (Salma T., 2000).

A cab driver in Belfast noted that now-dangerous boundaries used to seem benign: "We used to walk across onto the Falls Road and nobody said 'boo' to you. You know what I mean?" (Sean R., 2000). The evolution of benign urban thresholds into treacherous ones is a hallmark of urban partition.

A resident of Turkish Nicosia commented on the frustration of postponed political settlement in a divided city:

For almost thirty years I am thinking that tomorrow I am going to have peace, tomorrow I am going to have peace: every day I said; tomorrow, then the coming year, the coming year, the coming year—like that, and you are not thinking of anything else for your life. (Öznel 2001)

A journalist from Mostar shared this frustration and lamented the loss of opportunity that came along with urban apartheid:

My memories have been destroyed. . . . I am forty-one now. When this war started, I was a bit over thirty. I see myself as a person from whom somebody has stolen those eight years. (Marko V., 2000).

There is no simple way to inventory the losses and deprivation that accompany urban partition. Long after war and partitions fade, as they have in Beirut, countless individuals still find their sense of belonging shaken and their prospects dimmed. For many divided-city residents, partition corresponds with a sense of lost time and opportunity that may never be regained.

In Northern Ireland, a landmark study quantified the impact of a shattered economy and fractured social networks in a series of reports regarding the cost of the Troubles (Fay, Morrissey, and Smyth 1999). This research—by far the most comprehensive of its kind in any divided city to date—confirms the notion that physical partitions generate a host of social problems that are separate and distinct from the ones that prompted their construction. The parameters of these costs included deaths related to sectarian violence (assessed according to location, religion, age, and gender); health problems (including post-traumatic stress disorders, sleep disruption, alcoholism, depression, and involuntary recall); unemployment above the norm, public housing occupation above the norm, benefit dependency above the norm, and pervasive feelings of fear outside one's residential neighborhood. Key variables throughout were proximity to areas of intense violence and disturbance, religion, gender, age, and income level (Fay, Morrissey, and Smyth 1999).

Divisions, while often beneficial to interface residents in the short term, typically become a self-fulfilling prophesy of exclusion and resentment in the long term.

The Logic of Partition

The process of urban partition is rational, predictable, and patterned. It marks the failure of traditional urban security infrastructure from the perspective of at least one resident group, often a minority ethnic community. If it provides a short-term solution to intercommunal violence, it also typically creates a long-term impediment to intercommunal cooperation and normal urban development.

Divided cities, already physically tailored for ethnic apartheid, foster social and institutional structures to suit their requirements. Services are rerouted and improvised, resources become atrophied and duplicated, streets and buildings are appropriated, ruined, or rendered obsolete, and relationships are severed. The divided city becomes a war metropolis and a warren of claustrophobic ethnic enclaves.

The inversion of normal, cohesive social inclinations in cities obsessed with fortification and security can be nearly fatal:

The city arose as a special kind of environment, favorable to co-operative association, favorable to nurture and education, because it was a protected environment . . . . Plainly, a civilization that terminates in a cult of barbarism has disintegrated as civilization; and the war-metropolis, as an expression of these institutions, is an anti-civilizing agent: a non-city. (Mumford 1960: 278)

An Alternative View of the City

The hypocrisies embedded in a portrayal of the divided city as marginal and anomalous to the concerns of healthier societies were not lost on one Lebanese observer:

Outsiders look at Beirut from a wary distance, as though it had nothing to do with them; as though, through a protective glass partition, they were watching with immunity a patient thrash about in mortal agony, suffering a ghastly virus contracted in forbidden and faraway places. (Makdisi 1990: 20)

Onlookers who characterize ethnic conflict as virulent and exotic can dismiss the relevance of divided cities, but chauvinism has always accompanied urban development, as illustrated in chapter two. On a more fundamental plane, conflict and anxiety are seen by some as baseline conditions of urban life:

If by the "good city" is meant one in which a person crosses from one distinct neighborhood to another without knowing precisely where one ended and the other began, then Beirut has never enjoyed this good fortune. (Khalaf 1993: 83)

Do cities as a whole constitute a social experiment writ large that has run its course, a living contradiction of their own formative principles? If so, the divided city may represent a movement away from and beyond an exhausted social structure that has reigned for nearly 2,500 years in the western tradition.

It will be profitable to inquire further about the system that seems to be undermined by urban partition: the whole, integrated city as a unit. What is sacrosanct about the unified city? Is the notion of an unimpeachable, indivisible model part of the problem? Could it be that physical partitions in the service of ethnic cohesion constitute a kind of solution?

Hundreds of experts have attempted to characterize the healthy city, emphasizing the robust circulation of people, goods, vehicles, ideas, and money. Standard urban development theory assumes that the western city should evolve toward a state of cohesion, equilibrium, and integration consistent with principles of liberal democracy. Progressive urban strategists promise to help city managers succeed in their pursuit. Raw scale is not normally treated as a mitigating factor in this theoretical framework: urban complexes of vastly different scales are categorized uniformly as cities, and are presumed to follow the same rules of growth or degradation.

For instance, Portland (Maine, population 64,000), Porto (Portugal, population 264,200), Portland (Oregon, population 568,000), and São Paulo (Brazil, population 9.84 million) are each called a "city," though their sizes differ by a ratio of 1:4:27:153. The secession of an entire Porto's worth of disenchanted São Paulo residents would hardly be noticed at home, though if that band of pilgrims landed on the rocky shores of Maine they would swamp their adopted city demographically, converting the primary language in schools and buses to Portuguese. If, in turn, Portland, Maine's English-speaking minority migrated to their namesake city in Oregon, they might be greeted with signs like "Yankees Go Home." If a Portland,

Maine's, worth of Portland, Oregon, then decided to build a wall around itself, would that enclave constitute a city, a ghetto, or something else?

If the unitary city is a fiction, if it has become a political entity estranged from the organizational principles of its constituent communities, then conventional approaches to the logic of the divided city are also brought into question. If a community finds solace in partition, it is reasonable for its members to prioritize their own well-being above the integrity of the city—which is a mere abstraction in relation to their everyday concerns. A constructive critique of the divided city scenario would embrace the same priorities and recognize the benefits of urban barricades.

Subsequent chapters of this book address many of these issues by drawing on anecdotal evidence and noting common spatial and political features of all five case studies. Chapter 2 examines the historic relationships binding cities and walls together, with an emphasis on the legacies of internal ethnic boundaries. Chapters 3 to 7 track the precursors and emergence of partitions in each of the fives cities examined in detail by the authors. Chapter 8 examines how trust between minority citizens and urban managers breaks down, generating the preconditions for physical segregation. Chapter 9 explores professional responses to partition in each of the five case studies, and Chapter 10 attempts to isolate the key characteristics of all divided cities.

The catalyst for urban wall-building is sustained vulnerability. For most urban evolutionary history, this vulnerability was shared in the urban domain because it stemmed from a common fear of discrete foreign enemies that generally represented cultures without a prominent urban tradition. These threats encouraged solidarity between heterogeneous social groups in the city. Security requirements also forged important bonds between residents and city managers, and such bonds were repeatedly tested as the economic and technological burden of collective defense grew heavier. As early as 1225, murage taxes were widely levied throughout Europe to support the construction and maintenance of city walls, which were constantly in need of upgrading. Occasionally, cities starved and bankrupted themselves in the process of protecting their dwindling assets from attack.

The benefits of the walls for defense, built at enormous material and social cost to urban residents, were frequently offset by unintended social and psychological effects:

As in a ship, the wall helped create a feeling of unity between the inhabitants: in a siege or famine the morality of the shipwreck—share and share alike—developed easily. But the wall also served to build up a fatal sense of insularity: all the more because of the absence of roads and quick means of communication between cities. (Mumford 1960: 54)

Heir to the mural tradition of urban fortification, the divided city bears a strong likeness to its ancestors. It is not difficult to identify similarities linking traditional "defining" and contemporary "dividing" city walls: the intensification of group solidarity, the promotion of a siege mentality, and the deepening commitment to a moribund insularity. Medieval walled cities in the western tradition reinforced an urban singularity in the process of defending citizens against a shared threat, so that internal quarrels were overshadowed by the prospect of collective defeat.

Divided cities seem to have inverted this dynamic: partitions reinforce social difference and weaken the city's capacity to contend with larger forces external to itself. Walls are the product of a diverse vulnerability that erodes traditional forms of urban solidarity while multiplying the ills and rewards of insular behavior. The physically partitioned city has many cousins: the racial ghetto, the abandoned core, the neighborhood "redlined" by lending banks, and the increasingly popular gated residential community. Its barricades assert what seems to be a natural, preordained principle of mutual incompatibility that, for those residents affected directly by it, becomes very difficult to test or resist.

In Search of a Pattern

The stark realities of life in divided cities indicate how the social contract joining the interests of city managers and urban residents since the Middle Ages can become dangerously frayed. No longer a sure respite from external perils or a reliable reservoir of opportunity, the city offers diminishing benefits to a growing number of frustrated subscribers. Some of them attempt to renegotiate their urban contract, and one result of such efforts is the divided city. There, boundaries and loyalties are adjusted by means both legitimate and illegitimate until a threatened community achieves a tolerable level of security. This process can take decades, and in many instances it is ongoing. Interethnic violence and physical separation reflect a collective desire to reduce vulnerability.

In telling the stories of five divided cities in depth, this book sets out to show that a discernable logic guides the formation of divided cities not only in individual cases, but also in general terms that affect a large class of cities in tension.

Chapter 2
Cities and Physical Segregation

Introduction

Cities and walls have a long, intertwined history. Physical barricades have historically provided a functional separation between civilized and uncivilized domains for resident communities. Following the disintegration of the Roman Empire in medieval Europe, for instance, it was generally better for the traveler to be inside the city walls when the sun set and, as a rule "one was either in or out of the city . . . one belonged or one did not belong" (Mumford 1960: 54). Walls ensured collective security: this was a fundamental part of the early urban contract. The city was a social fortress filled with allies in league against a common enemy: raiders from the hinterlands in search of the resources stockpiled within.

As long as cities have contained such stockpiles, walls and the collective security they afford have been central to urban development. Physical barricades have defined the density, size, and social character of cities. For hundreds of years, outer fortifications have constituted legal and administrative boundaries as well as a hedge against the constant fear of attack. Issues of protection, separation, identity, siege, and social unity in the face of recurrent threats have long been linked to the presence of such physical barricades. In this context divided cities do not present an exception to the rule of urban development, but rather offer a variation on the theme of urban fortification. They are only the latest reminder that the prosperity of cities has always relied on exclusion and fortification. Wall building is frequently inseparable from city building. Cities were often shaped by a survival instinct resulting in a tendency to exclude weak minorities, a need to reinforce group identity, and a desire for collective, passive defense. Urban development strategies isolated from one another by space and time addressed these concerns in roughly the same way. They employed physical partitions to protect the precious resources that aggregated as the urban population grew.

The perimeter wall circumscribing an urban nucleus that had the form of a stronghold or sacred precinct was the first and most common form of urban barricade. These city walls provided the traditional infrastructure and constituted the primary urban amenity: passive, reliable protection for the people and goods within. Besides providing an essential form of physical protection against the external threats that multiplied as the city prospered, partitions also asserted social distinctions and controlled access to the city's nonmaterial resources.

Enhanced security provided unprecedented stability in the face of assorted and vexing external predations. Intramural life proceeded in this way toward greater prosperity, becoming increasingly distinct from rural life and increasingly dependent on the institutions and mechanisms that guaranteed the conditions of its prosperity—protective walls being prominent among them. Strict boundaries lent a clear meaning to citizenship, since the rules governing social, political, economic survival inside the city walls were unmistakably distinct from those shaping the rural tradition.

Distinct urban identities flourished along with inter-urban rivalries and jealousies. The apotheosis of the Greek city state, for instance, owed much to the efficiency of fortification walls. The shared benefits and deprivations of intramural urban life allowed residents to develop and sustain a strong sense of solidarity—a characteristic of healthy cities that also underlies many of the more brutal and morbid aspects of everyday life in divided cities.

Walls have been an important factor in the evolution of cities since the third millennium B.C. or before. Where they were erected, they were designed to address at least one of two distinct goals: to counteract external threats by providing passive security or to counteract the social assimilation that usually accompanies a dense and cooperative urban environment. The human and material resources that generally accrued to the city required increasingly specialized forms of protection. Where this defensive project was successful, group identity among urban residents was consolidated. Social development patterns in Jericho, Athens, Rome, Venice, and Sienna, among countless others, bear out this generalization.

From their first appearance in the archaeological record, it is likely that city walls provided more than passive protection from external attack. They were also an armature for the regulation of people, goods, and disease. They sometimes defined an autonomous political unit like the city-state. Urban walls were a source of symbolic and psychological pride for residents, providing a reliable container for the specific meaning of local citizenship. This book attempts to place recently partitioned cities in the broadest possible historic context, accepting the premise that city building from its inception has been shaped by "a paranoid psychal structure . . . preserved and transmitted by the walled city" (Mumford 1960: 39).

The internally and ethnically divided city, primarily a phenomenon of the twentieth century, has a highly evolved urban lineage. Ancient prototypes for the ethnically partitioned city may be visible in the Egyptian archaeological record. At the workers' village of Kahun, constructed around 2670 B.C., the efficiency of gridded housing was compounded by a perimeter wall (Morris 1972: 13), perhaps to exert control over a vital but underprivileged social class. A similar arrangement is seen at a workers' village in Amarna that appeared with a nearly identical plan about 1,300 years later. The laborers and artisans obliged to live in these cramped places—distinct in organization and scale from the regular citizens' residential districts— were essential to the physical growth of the adjacent urban complexes, but probably subject to racial discrimination by political elites. In these early instances of urban partition, ethnic segregation was accomplished spatially without sacrificing the vital economic contributions of an officially subordinate group; walls may have reconciled contradictory urban tendencies toward economic cooperation and social separation by allowing for simultaneous proximity, security, interdependence, and isolation. Their bold appearance on the urban stage at Kahun provides a vivid legacy for later partitioning projects carried forward purposefully or spontaneously up to the present day. The physical record in Egypt suggests that many of the motives for urban partitioning have changed little since the third millennium B.C.

The Legacy of Nonphysical Partitions

Although less obvious to the eye than perimeter walls, several separate trends in urban partition further demonstrate the utility of formalized thresholds within cities. Most of these underscore disparities in wealth between neighboring communities, and many of these, in turn, reflect prevalent ethnic prejudices. In the United States, where liberal democratic ideals were officially held in high esteem, institutionalized racial segregation took complex forms. For example, Chinatowns and Little Italies emerged in many cities to receive new immigrants in an environment familiar to them. These ethnic enclaves, although rarely the result of coercive legislation, reflected a mutual interest in living separately held by new immigrants and more powerful Americans belonging to majority ethnic groups of less recent arrival. The residents of ethnic neighborhoods often created their own institutions and support networks while the governing majority gladly ceded tax revenue in a climate of benign neglect.

In other instances, a desire to live separately was not shared by majority and minority groups. Several landmark studies document a longstanding practice of mortgage "redlining" in America. When African American homebuyers sought to purchase properties in predominantly and traditionally Caucasian neighborhoods, many lending banks refused to offer them loans even though Caucasian applicants with equivalent qualifications were accepted as borrowers. In many cases, city maps showing the boundaries of class and race were drawn up and maintained by banks for their internal guidance during the lending process. These maps have a durable legacy of semipermeable, customary, and institutionalized ethnic enclaves that sometimes lack only a wall to separate them completely from the surrounding urban environment.

Perimeter Walls and the Urban Nucleus

To understand the legacies to which divided cities fall heir, the observer should take a step backward and examine the relationship of the earliest urban settlements to walls, fortifications, and institutionalized social exclusion. While many notable exceptions can be found, the kernel of many early and prototypical urban development processes was the citadel, or castle keep. Archaeological records have shown that perimeter fortification played important role in the first cities of Mesopotamia and Europe, and, as late as 1914, the physical defenses of Paris were activated against German advances; yet Morris notes that "the role of fortifications as an urban form determinant has been largely neglected by urban historians" (Morris 1972: 111).

It can be assumed that the earliest urban walls surrounded relatively small areas containing the citadel or residential enclosure of a local ruler. Beginning around the third millennium B.C., the earliest cities grew out from these fortified precincts, and urban expansion is clearly marked by mural rings at Ur, Erbil, Babylon, and Uruk. Good examples dating to the premedieval period include Turin, Rome, and Milan. Urban expansion and wall building occurred in synchrony over the course of centuries, a pattern legible in the archaeological remains diagrammed in Figure 2.1 and in nu-

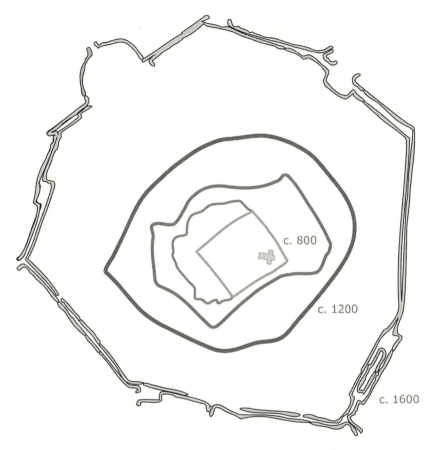

Figure 2.1. A diagram of the expansion of defensive perimeter walls around a Roman nucleus in the early development of Milan, 800–1600 A.D. shows the fortified character of much early urban development in Europe. Authors based on A. E. J. Morris, *History of Urban Form: Prehistory to the Renaissance* (New York: Wiley, 1972), 110.

merous written accounts of siege, municipal expenditure, and land expropriation dating to the earliest eras of urban development.

During times of crisis, war, or an imminent threat from external sources, the tenants of a local landowner would congregate inside a fortified compound. Once inside, their common fate encouraged everyone to combine forces for a common defense. Typically, citizens would volunteer to defend the walls whenever the city came under siege. Presumably, as these proto-urban communities grew and prospered, attacks increased in frequency. During these crucial and dramatic moments in a city's development, heavy emphasis on hierarchical and hereditary distinctions of race, status, and individual cultural identity between citizens would have been disastrous. Instead, everyone with a stake in the prosperity and progress of the city would be called on to make sacrifices in its defense.

This arrangement, which served all urban interests well, forged a kind of urban contract. An understanding between urban managers and residents affirmed that special sacrifices would be made by all the citizens in exchange for access to special resources and the passive quotidian protection offered by the perimeter wall. Solidarity between members of this collective—spanning, to some degree, lines of wealth, heredity, and social status—was cemented by external threats. These crucial episodes of collaboration may have been the kernel of what would later become the urban ideal of liberal social exchange and cooperation across class lines.

One of most remarkable achievements of the city as a social construct was its capacity to incubate a powerful, metacultural identity. The size of early urban collectives was small enough for bonds of trust and familiarity to grow between members in an unencumbered manner, further strengthening the notion that the most important elements of individual identity were derived from membership in the city as a whole.

The success of cities required increasing vigilance to protect amassed wealth. As hinterland attackers on horseback became more formidable and confident, the prospect of permanent residence within the walls for a majority of members of the economic collective appeared ever more desirable. In Europe and elsewhere, these developments may have accelerated the gradual demise of feudal regimes, so that social liberalization often developed in step with the emergence of more permanent urban settlements. As the perimeter walls surrounding the citadel or castle were expanded, property in the surrounding agricultural zones was abandoned and permanent residence inside the walls supported by nonagricultural professions became routine. In the Greco-Roman tradition of urban development, this shift was evident by about the sixth century B.C.; in Mesopotamia it occurred at least 1,000 years earlier.

This trend in early European urban development—defined by a gradual shift from occasional to full-time existence behind fortified walls—was a rational reply to incessant attacks and a swing toward a permanent urban siege mentality. From this point forward, the growth and material success of urban settlements accelerated. The stability afforded by a permanent and passive defensive system in the midst of external threats allowed commercial and professional endeavors to proceed with unprecedented efficiency. The resources stockpiled in the city demanded political systems to support the rising merchant class and its burgeoning investments. By the end of the medieval period in Europe, the rapid flourishing of urban centers had engendered new political and economic classes whose sole arena was the city and the urban network to which it belonged.

In its earliest manifestations, the perimeter urban wall was a simple masonry structure much like any other used for construction. These plain, thick partitions could be constructed inexpensively by common masons in any city. They could be modified, demolished, or extended according to the needs of the urban people or the will of their managers. Wherever a small fortified urban settlement succeeded, new perimeter walls were likely to trace the expansion of the population outward beyond the original enclosure.

These simple examples demonstrate two important principles linking early urban development with physical partitions: upgrading the perimeter defense remained in step with growth for centuries, and distinctions between life inside and outside the city walls grew increasingly sharp.

The Demise of the Medieval Walled City

If these urban envelopes provided reliable protection for a busy and industrious urban population, they also underscored the high value of the resources that were accruing within, encouraging increasingly determined assault. Hinterland attacks were not the only concern: cities launched campaigns to conquer other cities, and the threats to collective security for urban residents multiplied. Bloody urban narratives crowd the annals of European history since the era of the Roman legions. In this hostile climate—scorned by rivals and envied by hinterland tribes—particular urban identities became increasingly refined and public investment in physical fortifications rose to astronomical levels.

City walls came under siege by a new generation of armies whose weapons were much more sophisticated than those of their predecessors. Eventually, the simple masonry wall could no longer effectively serve defensive needs. In response, urban managers were required to create and support a standing army whose only function was to prevent the hostile penetration of their costly and crucial urban envelope. As part of the same project, architects and military engineers were enlisted to redesign perimeter barricades in accordance with the latest theories and practices of defensive architecture.

Other investments followed. In the attempt to equalize military conditions, towns from this point on were compelled to abandon their old system of simple walls, defended for the most part by a citizen soldiery. They were forced to hire soldiers who could sally forth and engage the enemy in open battle, and after the successful defense of Milan by Prospero Colonna in 1521 they were forced to adopt the new methods of fortification that had been worked out there by Italian military engineers (Mumford 1960: 84). These designs bore little resemblance to their homespun precursors; they were precise, complicated, and expensive.

In the early sixteenth century—coincidentally, about the time Sir Thomas More published *Utopia*—the complexity and expense of urban wall construction reached suffocating levels in Europe. Following the construction of complex new bastion systems around Milan, "ingenious defenses . . . cast a dreadful social burden upon the protected population" (Mumford 1960: 84). The notion of a "dreadful social burden" imposed by urban walls upon resident groups is central to the assessment of divided cities undertaken in subsequent chapters.

Besides claiming ever-larger portions of the municipal budget, the new "fortress" walls were neither flexible nor expandable. Their massiveness, cost, and formal precision meant that the city could no longer expand quickly or easily beyond them. The natural expansion of cities, which had long accompanied their social and cultural development, was now stunted. At this developmental juncture, outward growth was for the first time hindered by forces other than topography and demography, resulting in socially oppressive forms of inward expansion as the city conformed to its newly militarized straitjacket.

At the same time, upgrading the hygienic infrastructure in response to increasing demographic pressures was hampered by municipal budgets that were increasingly devoted to military expenditure, and municipal politicians were corrupted by the costs of mural upgrade and the maintenance of the standing army required to defend city walls against sophisticated attackers. Even when a city was successful in defending itself, the burden of that defense weighed so heavily on its inhabitants that their loyalty and solidarity were severely strained.

The price of upgrading defense eventually became insupportable under any circumstances, and in the later phases of their development many walled cities failed to protect their residents against the ever-widening array of military devices used to attack them. Even the most costly and innovative fortress cities ultimately lost their battle with improved artillery technologies. The chain reaction begun by the need for a stable passive protection of urban resources commonly resulted in density, destitution, and martial governance at scales previously unimaginable. The defensive value of living within the city walls was lost and eventually overturned: cities in the next era would become epicenters of violence and insecurity.

The success of the urban project—dependent in large part to maintenance of expensive perimeter walls—generated new forms of social conflict that would erode the strength of the unitary city from within. Long after cities had firmly established their ascendancy over their hinterland rivals and outgrown their farthest perimeter wall, city managers continued to refine the politics of exclusion and the art of engineering physical enclaves. They used every strategy at their disposal: construction of both visible and invisible barricades, activation of voluntary and involuntary boundaries, and exacerbation of real and imaginary intergroup antagonisms. The logic of this shift in concentration from external to internal threats contributes significantly to a broader understanding of the divided city phenomenon to be examined in later chapters.

Scale and Group Identity

A city's scale, infrastructure, and material resources do not have to limit the number of different belief systems or distinct social networks that coexist within its boundaries. All the same, theoretical models of integrated, healthy urban life place a heavy emphasis on both size and scale. Foremost among these is the Utopian model, first devised by Thomas More in 1516. More's account is especially instructive because it is the original intellectual formulation of Utopia in the western tradition and because it offers firm specifications for the shape and function of an ideal city.

While rivalry existed between cities even in More's *Utopia*, in each city harmony was found among inhabitants. More asserted that this social equilibrium correlates strongly with urban scale, which was carefully monitored and controlled in his imaginary world. In short, Amaurot's maximum and minimum population sizes were prescribed, and

lest any city should become either too great, or by any accident be dispeopled, provision is made that none of their cities may contain above six thousand families, besides those of the country around it. No family may have less than ten and more than sixteen persons in it. (More 1516 [1914: 22])

With this decisive stroke, More established the maximum size for his ideal city at 96,000 adults. Beyond this point, administrators were to siphon surplus families to less populous cities, or establish new ones, in order to maintain the desired equilibrium.

How arbitrary was this designation? While the demands and capacities of the sixteenth-century city differ widely from those of the twenty-first century, it would be a mistake to disregard More's emphasis on raw population scale altogether in relation to contemporary urban partitioning. The size of an ethnic cluster in a segregated urban environment may matter in ways that have not yet been adequately measured.

Questions of absolute scale lead to more questions about the way cities are designated in the first place. Do the populations within the administrative boundaries of a city actually comprise multiple, autonomous social units? Are these units subject to innate and self-regulating laws of expansion and contraction? Do relations between rival ethnic communities function successfully below certain population thresholds, but stop functioning above them? Is urban partition a natural process of urban downscaling driven by the social need to maintain manageable, healthy, and defensible ethnic clusters? Should the physical and functional integrity of a city be sacrificed to the needs of constituent communities?

Where traditional forms of intergroup collaboration faded, the notion of a shared fate within the urban community must have suffered as well. This dissipation revealed fractures and antagonisms between groups in the city that may have been previously overshadowed by mutual interests tied to collective survival. Rapid urban growth and diversification may have forced the scale of primary group identification to shift downward from the urban unit as a whole to the smaller unit of neighborhood, enclave, class, or clan.

The institutionalization of ethnic discrimination was a predictable product of these shifts of scale. The expression of prejudice and hostility toward fellow members of the urban collective, antithetical to the psychology that had governed successful urban growth for centuries, became common. Solidarity was no longer conditioned simply on membership in the urban community, which had grown too large, complex, and generally prosperous to support the notion that everyone's interests were somehow bound together regardless of class or ethnicity. Rather, solidarity became increasingly grounded in ethnic group identity. Free from substantial threats to its sanctity as a social and economic unit, the city gradually became an arena ripe for competition among these groups.

The Ethnic Urban Ghetto

Employed as peripheral barriers, urban walls historically ensured the survival and continued prosperity of citizens. Employed as internal barriers, urban partitions become a substitute for urban policing and equitable governance between weaker and stronger resident communities. Despite chronic episodes of violence and bigotry between rival ethnic groups, their economic interdependence often makes it difficult for urban managers to exclude politically weak minorities altogether. Rigorous ethnic segregation is often consistent with popular sentiment, but it is contrary to the best economic interests of a growing city. This tension, intensifying with rapid demographic change, routinely confronted urban managers with a challenging question. How far can exclusion be carried without forfeiting the advantages of minority group participation in the urban economy?

Their reply, in part, was the invention of the urban ghetto. Ghettos were used to systematically disenfranchise an ethnic group on which the urban economy depended. They were created by passing laws, building walls, or generating conditions of intimidation so severe and constant that laws and walls become unnecessary. They imposed limited restraints designed to retain dispossessed classes and ethnic groups in the economic collective while excluding them from the social and political collectives. Voluntary and involuntary systems of urban segregation resulted.

The majority of ethnic ghettos in Europe were the byproduct of customary and institutionalized racial prejudice: urban communities held apart by choice, convenience, and coercion. Most were not strictly controlled or partitioned due to the cost and difficulty of limiting circulation in crowded, unplanned cities. This pragmatic and customary approach to ethnic segregation is consistent with the traditionally organic character of urban development, but in some cities—Venice, Rome, Krakow, Lodz, Tripoli, and Prague are useful examples—it gave way to more draconian strategies.

The first planned, involuntary, physical ghettos appeared in European cities in the sixteenth century. The Third Lateran Council edict of 1179 had imposed excommunication on Christians who "presume to live with" Jews.

Emboldened by this and other similar canons of the period, it was common-place for urban managers to designate a Jewish ghetto on undesirable land with its own boundaries, laws, taxes, deprivations, and social norms. One of the earliest ghettos was created in Venice, where the term was coined—appropriately enough—with reference to an island formerly used for the production of iron where Jews were compelled to live. (Italian *geto* means foundry and the verb *gettare* to cast iron.) The association of the ethnic en-clave with heavy or noxious industry, though largely coincidental, recurs in Nicosia, where small-scale industry has taken over the streets that are nearest to the buffer zone and thus considered undesirable by the residents.

Following Venice's defeat in the League of Cambrai war, economic revitalization was urgently needed. Jews were welcomed into the city by vir-tue of their professional skills in medicine, commerce, and banking. These waves of immigration collided with longstanding racial stereotypes of the Jew as dirty, depraved, and naturally inhabited by "corrupting bodily vices":

A formal solution was proposed to the Doge in 1515 by Zacaria Dolfin: "Send all of them to live in the Ghetto Nuovo which is like a castle, and make drawbridges and close it with a wall; they should have only one gate, which would enclose them there and they would stay there, and two boats of the Council of Ten would go and stay there at night, at their expense, for their greater security." (Sennett 1994: 235)

This prescription is especially illuminating in the broader context of urban partitioning. For purposes of persuasion Dolfin borrowed the familiar meta-phor of the castle, emphasizing the seemingly natural efficiency and simplic-ity of his scheme. Permanent collective protection would be offered to Jews within a fortified enclave, like those to which the earliest urban residents re-treated. Dolfin's concerns regarding the safety of the Jews of Venice was not altogether disingenuous, since Christian mobs frequently targeted them in the throes of the murderous riots accompanying Lent and other important religious holidays. Partition was mutually beneficial in numerous ways:

The existence of the ghetto did not have only negative consequences for its resi-dents: not only did a rich culture flourish, in part protected from dilution by the outside world, but in some cases the ghetto was deliberately established and walled in as a matter of purportedly benevolent concern by a lord, in order to protect its Jewish residents from anti-Jewish actions, and ultimately from the pogroms. (Mar-cuse and van Kempen 2002: 20)

Still, there is no mistaking the primary objective of the plan: to formalize racial prejudice in ways that benefited the city much more than the Jews forced to cope with recurrent hostility.

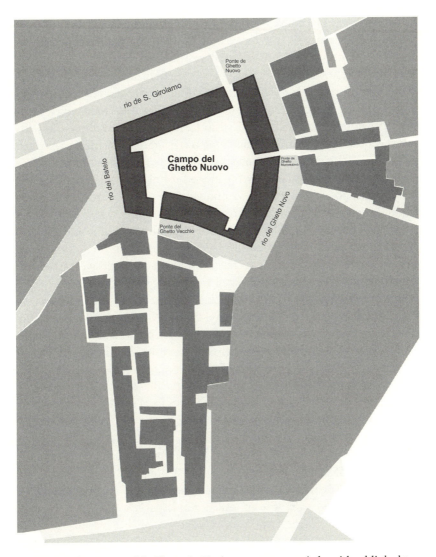

Figure 2.2. The New Jewish Ghetto in Venice, c. 1550, occupied an island linked to the city by three easily defended bridges. It was carefully engineered to protect the city from the Jews and the Jews from the city. Authors.

An abandoned foundry in the form of a rhomboid island was converted for the purpose, and by 1516 more than 700 Jewish Venetians had moved in as tenants of Christian landlords there. Perimeter canals isolated the site much like a moat, with two drawbridges that sealed the enclave after dark by converting it into an island. It is also notable that residential structures forming the ghetto's continuous external façade were shuttered at night, with their balconies removed to form an impenetrable aspect "like the sheer walls of a castle" (Sennett 1994: 234). Special municipal ordinances did the rest: residents of the ghetto were obliged to be inside between sunset and sunrise, and Christian guards patrolled the exterior in accordance with Dolfin's proposal. This routine continued until 1797, when Napoleon bestowed equal rights upon Jews throughout the empire.

The Venetian example, having proved to be both viable and advantageous from the point of view of urban managers, caught on quickly in Europe. Many other cities came to rely on walled ethnic enclaves as the cornerstone of systems that minimized the privileges and benefits owed to minority groups while still insuring their contribution to the urban economy. The persistence of anti-Semitic violence provided a useful pretext for the construction or formalization of ghettos. These forms of coercive segregation in turn confirmed the prejudices through which institutionalized exploitation was sustained—a self-fulfilling prophecy of ethnic rivalry in the urban domain that was newly asserted with the divided cities of the twentieth century. It will be seen subsequently that several defining characteristics of the early European ghetto were inherited by the ethnically divided city, often finding unmatched expression there.

Since its invention, the ghetto model of internal segregation has been popular, flexible, and successful. Though post-Enlightenment European societies favoring democracy and individual human rights generally could not continue to support the idea of walled ethnic enclaves within their cities, other physical instruments have been used to similar effect in the urban environment in recent centuries. Highways, railroad tracks, fences, and polluted river banks have all provided distinct physical boundaries separating urban elites from disenfranchised minority groups.

Suburban Models for Ethnic Segregation

Ethnically homogeneous islands, ghettos, or enclaves at the margins of mainstream urban life often evolve into semi-autonomous urban settlements, closely resembling small freestanding cities. The ghettos of South Africa created during the apartheid era (c. 1948–1994) provide a good example of this phenomenon. Barred from normal access to the resources of the major cities, which were reserved for whites, black, Indian, and other groups were forced into large quasi-urban settlements adjacent to restricted urban centers. Many of these arrangements were formalized and legalized with the Group Areas Act of 1950. Buffer strips 100 m wide were created to separate white and non-white communities. These no man's lands were essential for policing the "townships" and minimizing social contact, and useful for industrial and transport functions. Often large dormitory cities were constructed for black men who worked in the white cities and returned to their suburban encampments at the close of the day. Socially isolated female workers were often employed as servants in wealthy white residences, and likewise obliged to live in back rooms far away from their community or family. In South Africa, gender and racial discrimination was shaped by physical boundaries separating black from white residents by sector and within individual structures.

Larger South African townships like Soweto and Alexandria contained commercial and transportation facilities built exclusively for Black citizens, similar to the city centers built for White citizens. The dormitory cities and townships were carefully guarded, patrolled, and physically barricaded to prevent trespass. Physical restrictions were compounded by laws and policies that made any attempt to function outside the apartheid system dangerous. All the formative principles of the Venetian ghetto were carried into the twentieth century at an unprecedented scale and degree of organization.

Another example of the autonomous suburban ethnic enclave is found in Lebanon, where Palestinian refugee camps have grown alongside Beirut's eastern flank. Seeking asylum from the violence and persecution in the West Bank and Israel since the departure of the British, Palestinians in large numbers have migrated north into Lebanon since 1948 and the outbreak of hostilities. Denied full citizenship and access to normal municipal services in Beirut, many of these families first settled in suburban camps that were designed to be temporary.

At the time of their relocation, it was assumed by the Palestinian refugees and others that a settlement between the Israeli and Lebanese governments would allow for early return home or full integration into Beiruti society. Neither scenario came to fruition. Instead, the temporary camps became permanent parasitic fringe settlements neither embraced nor outlawed by their reluctant urban host. Refugee families residing in the camps were forced to live in conditions considered unacceptable to native Beirutis just a few kilometers away. Though refugees provided a vital influx of manual labor for the Lebanese economy, they have yet to be granted citizenship rights or to enjoy most of the privileges associated with normal membership in Lebanese society. In Beirut, but not of it, the refugee camps have crafted their own rules and institutions, augmented by meager subsidies from the Lebanese government and small-scale efforts of foreign nongovernmental organizations.

Perimeter walls were invoked for purposes of protection in the twentieth century, enclosing elite gated communities designed to insulate affluent suburban residents from crime, especially in countries with large gaps separating poor and wealthy citizens. In some cases, the fortification scheme is elaborate:

Walls are only the beginning. Inside may be surveillance cameras, infrared sensors, motion detectors and sometimes-armed guards. St. Andrew's, a gated community in Boca Raton, Florida spends over a million dollars a year on helicopters and canine patrols. (Dillon 1994: 4)

Census records from 2000 indicate that more than seven million American households—about 6 percent of the national total—were part of residential collectives protected by walls and fences. About four million of these lived in communities where access was controlled by gates, entry codes, key cards or security guards (El Nasser 2002). The prototype is the medieval walled city. The agenda is still to keep out those who do not belong while insuring passive and permanent security for those who do, and the means are almost identical: perimeter barricades punctuated with gates, guard posts, and sophisticated systems of continuous surveillance. Because gated communities often appear outside urban areas previously abandoned by the professional middle class, they reflect a reversal of the medieval pattern of segregation: those of the city are excluded, while urban refugees retreat to fortified hinterland enclaves.

Hardening and Physical Partition

The observations above suggest that strategies of systematic exclusion developed in conjunction with cities since their earliest appearance in the western tradition continued through the twentieth century, and were frequently predicated on paranoid, defensive, and chauvinistic impulses.

Most urban partitions are conceived or constructed as temporary structures. The early perimeter walls of the pre-urban citadel, for instance, were permanent structures but intended for only occasional use. It is probable that during the same period even remote villages constructed crude moats or makeshift wooden palisade barriers in anticipation of specific episodes of hostility. Similar structures were still being used this way in the late twentieth century, when police barricades routinely appeared along ethnic boundaries in Los Angeles and Cincinnati as an initial response to local, episodic outbreaks of violence, and in the early twenty-first century, when foreign operatives in Baghdad's "Green Zone" surrounded themselves with cement barricades.

Like their precursors, these impermanent partitions have proven to be a highly flexible tool for containing urban violence. Unlike their precursors, internal walls are designed to protect a group of urban residents from potentially hostile neighbors rather than from external, unnamed invaders. This shift reflects the evolution of "insider" and "outsider" status in the urban lexicon.

Whatever their origins, there is a historic tendency for temporary urban partitions to become permanent. Laws are more rigidly enforced; gates close and do not reopen; segregated public institutions multiply. With the hardening of habit, law, and popular prejudice, this downward progression accelerates. When episodes of violence recur frequently along the same interfaces—often the boundaries separating groups distinguished by ethnicity or wealth—the efficacy of temporary measures diminishes. What follows is often hasty land expropriation, the building of major traffic arteries along hostile internal borders, or construction of linear industrial development to act as a threshold buffer. In Beirut, Solidere acquired large sections of the former Green Line in a mandatory buyout of prewar property owners; in Jerusalem Highway One—also known as Engineering Corps Street, as it crosses through the Mamilla neighborhood—replaced the confrontation line; and in Belfast small factory complexes are inserted into no man's lands between adjacent ethnic enclaves. One step beyond these remedies is the erection of a permanent physical partition.

The following chapters explore narratives of partition in the five cities under examination here. The objective is to provide sufficient background to illustrate an important common denominator among divided cities—a long, incremental, and avoidable process of physical partition.

Chapter 3
Beirut

Introduction

A Shi'ite sniper named Taha spent fourteen years on the top floor of the high-rise Shmona Building in West Beirut, firing Russian B107 artillery shells at nearby targets as part of an ongoing campaign to kill Phalangist militiamen. During the Israeli invasion of Beirut, Taha suffered severe injuries to his hands—the most vulnerable part of a sniper nested in a heavily fortified position. Though his brother was killed during the seventeen-year civil war, Taha seems to bear no grudge against his former rivals in Lebanon. He assigns blame for the violence to the unwelcome intervention of outside forces like the Syrian and Israeli armies.

He moves freely between formerly separated sectors of the city. He claims that Beirut is no longer physically or psychologically divided, and that former enemies now live their lives in a forgiving manner with an air of good sportsmanship.

Another Muslim Beiruti citizen named Salma lives not far from the Shmona Building where Taha was employed. She remains angry, confused, and resentful about the war. Her home is located just behind the former Green Line, and since she was unable to leave her house and children during the hostilities she was forced to experience the battles at close range. She witnessed rival militias fighting across the demarcation line and lost a young daughter in the process from sniper fire. Her family often went without electricity, water, and food. She has no explanation for the war. In her estimation it was fought for nothing and settled nothing. She said that during the war it became impossible to differentiate between friends and enemies. She laments that her youth was stolen and that the time lost spoiled her future. She believes that as long as there are militias tied to specific religions, the war will continue and the city will remain divided. The shells have stopped falling but the war goes on. Salma is convinced that, even after

TABLE 3.1. BASIC FACTS REGARDING THE PHYSICAL PARTITION OF BEIRUT

Antagonisms	Christian v. Muslim paramilitaries; Lebanese Front v. Lebanese National Movement; Nationalist v. Pan-Arab factions; pro-Government v. rebel factions
Names	Green Line, Damascus Road
Location	The Green Line corresponded roughly to Beirut's main north-south traffic corridor, splitting major roads and public spaces starting at the historic harbor and Martyrs' Square, then following the Damascus Road southward beyond the suburbs. In addition, numerous minor boundaries fragmented the East and West sectors created by the Green Line in accordance with ever-shifting territorial acquisitions of assorted paramilitary groups active within the city.
Context	The primary partition constituted a near perfect cross-section of the city, cutting through its historic core and the Phoenician archaeological ruins before passing through prominent commercial and residential zones and continuing through refugee camps like Shatila and semi-autonomous suburbs like Chiyah and Ghobeire.
Size	The Green Line was a fortified path approximately 9 km long and 18–90 m wide, protected on either side by solid barricades of various dimensions. Throughout the city, enclaves were likewise defined and protected by semi-permanent walls usually less than 3 m high and 1.5 m wide used to block important roads fully or partially; in addition, snipers' view sheds projected invisible 'target cones' onto the city, thus creating very effective physical obstacles to civilian movement.
Porosity	Passage of pedestrians and vehicles across the Green Line was hindered by several elements: physical barricades, checkpoints, gates, exposure to sniper fire, mines, debris, and intimidation. Three "official" crossings existed throughout the duration of the war: the Port Crossing near the old harbor and Parliament building, the Museum Crossing next to the Hippodrome and National Museum, and the Gallery Crossing nearest to the Beirut River and airport. Since paramilitary guards interested in the ethnicity of travelers controlled them, these were used mainly by paramilitary commanders, diplomats, and foreigners.
Materials	Partitions were constructed in a spontaneous manner using barbed wire, sandbags, abandoned vehicles, cement block, and nearby debris.

Status	All barricades have been dismantled along with structures associated with paramilitary activity and military occupation. The central business district is fully rehabilitated and several outlying sectors significantly reconstructed. Large sections of urban fabric remain abandoned and decrepit along with hundreds of buildings damaged or destroyed during the war that still await repair.
Actors	Paramilitary combatants were the primary builders of Beirut's partitions; based on the vicissitudes of their operations, the boundaries between ethnic enclaves were determined and fortified according to need and importance. All available materials were used with no indication of prior planning.

the city is physically reconstructed, it will not belong to the Lebanese who lived in it prior to 1975.

Background

Since the eighteenth century, Beirut's Christian residents settled mostly on the eastern side of the city and Muslim sects in the southern and western sections. One Lebanese historian observed that these clusters have shaped historic events in the city for many generations: "There was always a certain polarization of confessions and this polarization of confessional private areas would lead to a demarcation line, whenever a political problem appeared" (Salaam 2000). With the outbreak of full-scale civil war in 1975, these traditional demographic patterns shaped the conflict (Khouri 2000) and new patterns emerged.

Mixed districts also existed throughout the city's history, especially near central commercial zones such as Ain Mraisse, Hamra, and Ras-Beirut. Even among residents of these mixed areas, sectarian consciousness was strong, though such loyalties were subordinated by personal affinities or socioeconomic cleavages in many cases.

Beirut has traditionally functioned as a pluralistic but ethnically segregated city. Many of the spatial divisions that would later become physical partitions in Beirut were etched in the urban fabric by its nineteenth-century fortification walls. The eastern wall of the citadel was an urban threshold that shaped all subsequent phases of the city's growth; it defined the

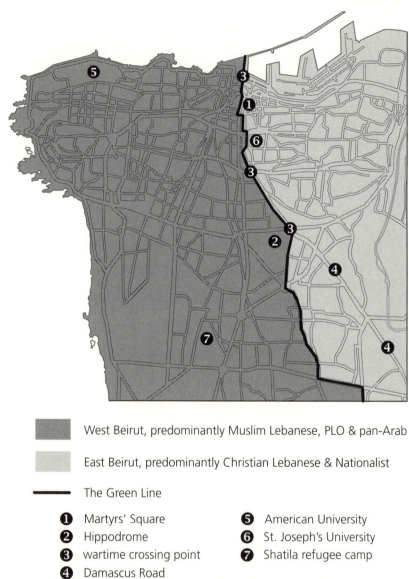

0   1 km

BEIRUT

West Beirut, predominantly Muslim Lebanese, PLO & pan-Arab

East Beirut, predominantly Christian Lebanese & Nationalist

The Green Line

❶ Martyrs' Square
❷ Hippodrome
❸ wartime crossing point
❹ Damascus Road

❺ American University
❻ St. Joseph's University
❼ Shatila refugee camp

Figure 3.1. Map of Beirut's partition, 1974–1990. Beirut is located at 3353′N and 3530′E, halfway along the western coastline in central Lebanon, which lies west of Syria and north of Israel. Byblos and Tripoli are to the North, and Sidon and Tyre are to the South. Beirut lies 585 km northeast of Cairo and 1296 km west of Baghdad. Authors.

Place des Canons, later named Martyrs' Square, and established the city's north-south axis. During that period the city's population was dominated by Sunni Muslims while the Greek Orthodox community, totaling about 25 percent of the urban population, lived and worked in a well-defined quarter (Davie 1994: 36). Land remained relatively plentiful, and there appeared to be room for the members of each ethnic group to pursue their livelihoods without threatening the prosperity of rival groups.

Early internal urban divisions in Beirut separated Muslim and Christian residents while the city walls separated urban dwellers from the nonurban. Other distinctions were etched into the physical fabric of the city as it grew: residential and commercial sectors, rich and poor neighborhoods, old and new enclaves, and civilian and military zones. Due to the small size of the walled city and the central role played by the port, such thresholds remained permeable for the sake of economic efficiency, if not good will. One observer notes, "through the souks, the city functioned as a complex urban entity, each sector depending on the other, independent of religion" (Davie 1994: 37).

Cycles of rapid urbanization reinforced many of these traditional ethnic boundaries and introduced unprecedented pressures on the city as a whole. One example is the influx, beginning in 1870, of Maronite peasants from mountainous rural areas, forced by poverty and overpopulation to seek jobs in Beirut. The Maronites are a Christian Arab group claiming Phoenician heritage. Most Christian newcomers chose to live outside the city in order to avoid Ottoman regulation and military requirements, and this tendency accelerated the emergence of a relatively homogeneous Christian enclave in the eastern suburbs of the capital.

By 1920, the Maronites had assimilated the social life in Beirut, gradually settling closer to the city center. Sympathies of the French mandate government allowed them to assume a prominent position in the national government. At that time, an Armenian immigrant population appeared in Beirut, fleeing violence in Turkey, and took up residence with fellow Christians in Bourj Hammoud on the eastern side of the city. On the western flanks of Beirut, Shi'ite and Sunni Lebanese from the countryside continued to settle in the city in the hope of reliable employment and improved living conditions. Though religious affiliation remained an important organizing force, distinctions between clans, classes, and native or non-native Beirutis remained powerful distinctions within the larger ethnic categories. As before, Beirut's central district and its souks remained thoroughly heterogeneous in character.

With the unwritten National Pact of 1943, Lebanon had gained independence under the leadership of Maronite archbishop Mubarak, who envisioned a Christian stronghold state in the Middle East acting as a counterweight to the impending Jewish state in Palestine. At that time Christian and non-Christian populations in Lebanon coexisted in a demographic ratio of approximately six to five, and these proportions were formally adopted as the basis for a quota system in the government from that point forward. This resulted in an ethnically representative national government in which the president was always to be a Maronite Christian, the prime minister a Sunni Muslim, and the speaker of the Chamber of Deputies a Shiʻite Muslim. From its inception, then, the Lebanese government reflected and reinforced traditional ethnic identities rather than supplanting them with political parties emphasizing ideological interests. This arrangement, similar to those in Cyprus and Bosnia during crucial moments of political transition, would severely limit the Lebanese government's capacity to initiate progressive social reforms sought later by disadvantaged minority groups.

Mubarak and his Christian allies in Lebanon were eager to protect the influence and privileges that accompanied majority status. Their vision of Lebanon as a permanent haven for Christian values in a region dominated by Muslim nations was put to a series of tests in the late 1940s, as Lebanon's demography shifted toward a Muslim majority with the influx of Palestinian refugees fleeing violence in Israel. The Palestinians were offered refuge but not full citizenship as they settled into camps on the southern flanks of Beirut. Beirut's economy was strengthened by the civil war in Israel, emerging as a liberal banking alternative to Haifa. Meanwhile, revenues from newly discovered oil in the Persian Gulf generated private wealth in Lebanon at unprecedented rates. Tensions resulted as traditional political and social systems were stretched to accommodate rapid expansion.

These were most obvious in the economic realm, where distribution of wealth and privilege conformed to traditional hierarchies and hereditary systems of clientelism. Newly arrived, poorly assimilated, and without political patronage, Palestinian communities in Lebanon struggled in response to perceived injustices in Palestine and perceived inequities in Lebanon. These grievances were not acknowledged or addressed in a strategic fashion by Lebanese leaders. Attempts to satisfy these grievances outside official channels were a driving force behind the Lebanese civil war and remain a major destabilizing factor in Middle Eastern politics.

Throughout the 1950s, migration of rural communities to the suburbs of Beirut intensified. Lebanon's government did not as a rule reply to rapid urbanization with balanced and progressive public policies. During this decade deepening social tensions were compounded by general unrest stemming from the Suez crisis in 1956 and the merging of Egypt with Syria to form the United Arab Republic in 1958. This short-lived union was heralded by many in the region as a victory for the pan-Arab cause and a model for other Arab nations to follow. It also gave the Lebanese Christian authorities another reason to feel uneasy.

Unease turned to crisis for Camille Chamoun's government in 1958, when his alliance with anti-Nasser western powers brought him into direct conflict with Sunni Muslim prime minister Rashid Karami and various constituents eager to see Lebanon support Arab nationalism. Insurrections, protests, and a general strike followed; the Lebanese Army was not mobilized for fear that engagement would split its troops along ethnic lines. American forces sent by Eisenhower in July to execute "Operation Blue Bat" saved Chamoun's administration from likely dissolution. A reconciliation government led by Karami followed the close of Chamoun's regular term.

The key events of these years established the outlines of a broader conflict in Lebanon. Part of this conflict was related to reconciling traditional ethnic loyalties within the framework of a secular national identity. Attempting to resolve the issue by forming a religious state, as was done with Israel, promised to aggravate regional hostilities and radicalize minority ethnic groups. Creating a heterogeneous secular state would lead to power struggles between majority and minority factions, weakening the authority of the central Lebanese government in the eyes of its neighbors. Lebanon chose a domestic struggle that ultimately spilled over in the international domain.

The narrow but conclusive defeat of pan-Arab factions during the 1958 crisis paved the way for a decade of relative calm and prosperity, while the population of Beirut continued to increase with rural immigrants and Palestinian refugees. Their numbers peaked following the West Bank expulsions caused by the 1967 Six-Day War. These changes conformed to earlier patterns of urban expansion in Beirut, in which suburban enclaves filled with restive and disadvantaged members of the Shi'ite minority, but Lebanese politicians failed to exploit the lessons gathered from previous episodes of social turmoil. They did not provide sufficient incentives for the assimilation of Palestinian refugees, who continued to crowd into suburban camps and chafe against curtailed legal privilege. Tolerated but not supported, Palestinian refugees in Lebanon became a major catalyst for ongoing political polarization along ethnic lines in Lebanese society as a whole. As before, a mixture of insecurity and desperation made recruitment by the Palestine Liberation Organization (PLO) in these camps easy. This politicizing process left Lebanese politicians with few ways to avoid a confrontation with Israel that would place Beirut at its epicenter.

Sequence

The ethnic violence that overtook Lebanon in 1975 is difficult to understand due to the large, complex array of sectarian groups in the country, most of which correspond historically to affiliations like clan or political party. Though the composition of these groups remained fairly consistent over many generations, the outbreak of civil war brought frequent, sometimes unpredictable adjustments to traditional alliances.

During the 1980s there were as many as ninety individual armed groups whose ideological and territorial rivalries contributed to violence in Beirut. Most were affiliated with Lebanese political parties that predated the war, though some had splintered away from these or were tied to foreign organizations in Palestine, Syria, and other neighboring countries.

Among the prominent Muslim sects active in Lebanese politics in the decades preceding civil war were the Sunni and Shi'ite factions, the Ismaili faction, the Alawis faction, and the Druze. The participating Christian sects included the Maronites, Greek Orthodox, Roman Catholics, Armenian Orthodox, and Phalangists. Numerous scholars of Lebanese political life (Salibi 1976; Khalaf 1993) have examined the intricate anatomy of these social and political factions, noting distinct tensions between bourgeois and populist agendas, and between militant and nonmilitant voices. Between the founding of the Lebanese state in 1943 and the onset of intercommunal violence in 1975, Lebanon was remarkable in the region for the relative success of its power-sharing arrangements among diverse sects, a political mosaic that supported a liberal, free market democracy (Seaver 2000: 254).

This success owed much to traditional group leaders called *zuama*. A Lebanese *zaim* wields hereditary patronage and provides members of his clan with access to services and resources in return for material support and unwavering loyalty, especially during elections. This system developed in rural areas as an outgrowth of the feudal land-tenancy system, but came to dominate urban political culture as well as many neighborhoods kept strong ties to villages.

On the eve of civil war, several *zuama* rose to become the leaders of political factions and played central roles in the escalation of violence. These include Bashir Gemayel of the Phalange Party, Camille Chamoun of the National Liberation Party, and Kamal Jumblatt of the Progressive Socialist Party, all of whom inherited their political authority and used it to maintain a loyal following throughout multiple cycles of upheaval. It has been noted that the *zaim* system "became progressively unadapted to solving the social problems of an ever-increasing population" (Davie 1994: 43). The viciousness and duration of the civil war can in part be attributed to the difficulty of adapting a traditional political system to conditions it was not designed to accommodate.

Escalation

In the early 1970s, two major events pushed the fragile situation in Lebanon to a breaking point. The first was the Jordanian government's vigorous reprisals in September 1970 against PLO activities inside its borders. The severity and effectiveness of the "Black September" campaign made Lebanon the last remaining prospect for PLO operational outposts adjacent to Israel and the West Bank. As a result, the PLO presence in Lebanon grew, especially among sympathetic Shi'ite communities in the south and the residents of Palestinian refugee camps on the periphery of Beirut.

These developments intensified pressure on the national government from two directions. From Western allies and Israel, there was pressure to renounce its blind-eye policies and take a firmer stand against radical Palestinian paramilitaries, or suffer the consequences. From the Shi'ite Muslim community and groups sympathetic to the pan-Arab cause, there was pressure to shield or even support the Palestinian cause. In that political climate, although the Lebanese government regretted the presence of its uninvited Palestinian tenants, an expulsion campaign similar to that of Jordan's King Hussein would have ensured political ruin for the Maronite president who proposed it. Adhering to its traditional ambivalence regarding the Palestinians, Lebanon's Maronite leadership attempted to buy time in hopes that the efforts of international negotiators to forge an Israeli-Arab settlement would rescue them from the need to make large-scale political commitments.

While the Lebanese government watched and waited, Israel acted. The second major event to propel the events in Lebanon forward was a secret commando raid by Israeli special forces against PLO targets in Beirut on 10 April 1973. A handful of Israeli soldiers approached by sea and landed on the beaches of Beirut in the early morning, fanning out silently in search of key Palestinian paramilitary leaders. By the time the Lebanese army was aware of their arrival, the attackers had killed four of their PLO targets and were already on their way back to Haifa. Besides demonstrating the vulnerability of Lebanese defenses to rapid infiltration and Israeli military intelligence, this event indicated that Palestinians in Lebanon could not rely on the Lebanese army for protection. It became clear that Israel was willing to take previously unimaginable liberties to curb Palestinian incursions from the south of Lebanon. In addition to the humiliation felt in the aftermath of the Israeli raid, the noncommittal Lebanese government was treated as an accomplice of resident PLO paramilitaries in this process. Neutral ground was disappearing quickly.

Thus the Israeli raid was a watershed for internal Palestinian-Lebanese relations and a catalyst for the escalation of paramilitary recruitment and training on both sides of the sectarian divide. It proved to Palestinians in Lebanon that they could not rely on military protection from hostile enemies. In May 1973, Palestinians organized public protests against the poor security conditions in Beirut, and the Lebanese army took up permanent positions on the perimeter of suburban Palestinian camps.

Though domestic and regional politics shaped the events leading toward civil war, less extraordinary and dramatic factors also contributed to the escalation of the crisis. Beirut had experienced a period of unprecedented expansion in the decades preceding the outbreak of civil unrest in 1975. This unplanned and poorly coordinated urban growth taxed the city severely, without proportional increases in economic productivity. The nature and rate of demographic change in the city tended to expose the inadequacies of a political system grounded in fraternal and ethnic allegiances.

The challenge to accommodate so many new urban residents paralyzed Lebanon's public institutions. The results in Beirut were shortages of food and water, rampant unemployment among first- and second-generation urban residents, irregular supplies of electricity and telephone services, poor or nonexistent infrastructure in squalid suburban residential zones, and unmet demands for decent housing. All these problems prompted social unrest even before ethnic rivalry and feelings of personal insecurity were added to the equation. While rapid, unanticipated growth presents challenges to even the healthiest city, in Beirut it aggravated deep and long-standing weaknesses in Lebanese society as a whole.

Negotiations

On the eve of civil war, the central government could no longer keep a lid on social problems neglected for decades. Widespread violence was ignited by circumstances largely outside the control of the Maronite leadership, taxed beyond its capacity to respond in a constructive way. Lebanon's leaders placed great trust in their alliances with powerful Christian leaders in Europe, a trust that in hindsight appears excessive. These allies made few, if any, documented attempts to negotiate or reach a settlement on behalf of the Lebanese government.

With respect to Beirut, which became the stage and the emblem of the of conflict as a whole, the traditional urban contract was breached by leaders unwilling to question or adapt systems of urban management and resource allocation that had become obsolete long before uncontrollable violence erupted.

Perhaps the last chance for peaceful negotiation between rival groups in Lebanon came on 26 February 1975 with a labor protest in Sidon—an event that was quite unrelated to the paramilitary struggles in the capital but proved to be incendiary nonetheless. On that day the fishermen's unions of Sidon, Tyre, and Tripoli staged a public protest against the creation of the Protein Company, owned in part by former Lebanese president Camille Chamoun, which promised to mechanize the industry (Seaver 2000: 256). The protesters expressed their concern about this threat to their livelihood, and they were joined by representatives of various leftist parties, including the Communists.

When the demonstration turned violent, both demonstrators and army personnel were killed and wounded. Most notably, the Sunni Muslim leader of the Popular Nasserist Organization of Sidon, Ma'ruf Sa'ad, was killed by the Lebanese army. Two days later the same groups organized a second demonstration in Beirut to protest against the Sidon incident, resulting in roadblocks and burned cars. From this point forward, violence swelled in an unremitting fashion among militant factions in Beirut. While the extent to which these incidents were planned in advance is unclear, they served as a signal for all paramilitary groups to enter the fray.

During this early phase of national unrest, several complaints were raised against the Lebanese government. Communists accused the central government of collusion with wealthy Arab business interests, and the conservative Muslim establishment accused the government of suppressing democratic liberties by quashing public demonstrations. Because the government was unable to formulate a coherent and convincing response to these criticisms, no adequate brake was applied to the accelerating violence.

A gap widened rapidly between "progressive" factions, generally called the Lebanese National Movement, and "conservative" factions, generally called the Lebanese Front. Muslims and Christians respectively constituted majorities in the two camps. The Lebanese Front demonstrated in support of the army, the government, and the status quo, placing blame for the discord on the shoulders of Beirut's radical Palestinian groups. Without effective army intervention, the threat of violence grew unabated. These activities reinforced a popular—though flawed—notion at the time that the interests of Christian and non-Christian Lebanese were somehow fundamentally incompatible, and that equitable treatment of Muslim Lebanese could not be achieved within the existing system of governance.

Remaining confident in moral and material support available from its western allies, the Lebanese government refused to pass substantial reforms. Middle-class Muslim citizens, too, were eager to downplay the intensity of the crisis and resist concessions that might have led to fundamental change. At this juncture, the government interpreted the popular violence in Sidon and Beirut as a serious but passing problem, to be contained by steady and forceful resolve. Having underestimated the size, resources, and determination of its detractors, the central government's strategy led to an expansion of violence between rival ethnic groups that had been at the brink of open hostilities for the better part of 1975.

Emergence

During the hostilities of 1956–58, a physical demarcation line in central Beirut had been established by armed opponents of President Chamoun, who "barricaded themselves in the Sunni quarter of al-Basta, turning it into a 'forbidden zone' for the internal security forces . . . throwing grenades at public buildings and utilities, and planting bombs in front of stores that defied the [United National Front general] strike" (Baroudi 2006: 20). This development, while temporary, confirmed that the two parts of Beirut had opted for two different political choices. The "Christians" to the east had sided with the Maronite nationalistic political line, while the "Muslims" followed the Sunni pan-Arab line, with of course many individual exceptions. . . . Barricades were constructed across main roads to block enemy infiltrations from "the other side." (Davie 1994: 41)

This line remained an active threshold between rival groups until the election of former commander of the Lebanese army, Fu'ad Shihab, as president in the late summer of 1958. He promptly dismantled the barricades as a public gesture of reconciliation and amnesty. They were reactivated in modified form when civil unrest again led to violence in 1975.

By then, a demographic pattern had been established in which the political groups loyal to the Maronite nationalistic platform were concentrated in the eastern side of the city, and those in favor of the predominantly Sunni, pan-Arab platform in the west. Though the two groups can roughly be characterized as "Christian" and "Muslim," their ranks were always mixed. Intergroup allegiances shifted frequently, and exceptions to the general pattern abound; an early and emblematic example is the enmity between Maronite President Chamoun and Maronite Patriarch Paul Meouchi throughout the 1958 conflict.

Full-scale warfare entered the streets of Beirut shortly after the demonstrations related to the Sidon Protein Company protest subsided. On 13 April 1975 paramilitary gunmen murdered four Phalangists during an assassination attempt on Kata'ib Party leader Pierre Gemayel, who was attending a church dedication ceremony in East Beirut. Assuming that their attackers were Palestinian radicals, the Phalangists quickly sought revenge by attacking a bus carrying Palestinian passengers through the Christian neighborhood of Ayn al-Rummana on their way back to the Tall al-Za'tar refugee camp. Approximately twenty-seven passengers were killed and twenty wounded. When this news spread through the city, general violence erupted in almost every quarter.

In the days immediately following, steady fighting broke out between Phalangist and Palestinian paramilitaries operating from increasingly well-defined and ethnically homogeneous enclaves spread in a patchwork across the city. One observer noted the role of the fortified urban threshold in Beirut during this period:

It has conditioned all aspects of life in the city; it has divided populations and given the excuse for massacres, deportations, and destruction; it was the main cause for the disappearance of multi-confessional quarters and their replacement by homogeneous ones. (Davie 1994: 36)

This patchwork demographic allowed snipers and others to attack with decreasing discrimination in enemy territory, thanks to the growing likelihood that even randomly chosen civilian victims would be members of a target group. Random violence, in turn, encouraged further territorial homogeneity.

During this initial period of violence, most civilians in Beirut suspended their normal activities and remained in their homes. It was commonly assumed that the crisis was limited to rivalries between fringe paramilitary groups and would be swiftly extinguished by the Lebanese army or by simple attrition. But conditions worsened week by week, leading to the establishment of a military cabinet toward the end of May 1975. Alarmed by developments they viewed as a prelude to the imposition of martial law, Palestinian paramilitary groups fortified their positions in the city and intensified their actions against all real or potential enemy targets.

Barricades and roadblocks multiplied in Beirut following the announcement of a military cabinet, dividing the city into eastern and western sectors with increasing deliberateness. Noting that his actions had backfired and hoping to ease tensions in the Muslim community in particular, President Franjiyah dissolved the cabinet. His efforts were in vain, the escalation of paramilitary activities continued, and increasing numbers of civilians were drawn into the violence as accidental victims or combatants.

By the second half of October 1975, heavy fighting had transformed downtown Beirut into a battleground devoid of commercial and residential activity. What had been the city's most thoroughly and consistently mixed sector became uninhabited and divided. The north-south boundary line, called the "Green Line" after its precursor in Jerusalem, began at the old harbor and Martyrs' Square and continued southward along the Damascus Road and into the suburbs. On either side, permanent paramilitary positions had been established that were nearly impassable. A no man's land lay in between, filled with rubble, garbage, and burnt machinery that made any attempted passage additionally precarious. One Lebanese observer affirmed that despite its improvisational and unplanned origins, the Green Line during that period of the war appeared "very clear on the ground: symmetrically ruined buildings; rubble on the streets; up-ended, mined or booby-trapped containers blocking every side road; sandbags at each window" (quoted in Davie 1994: 51).

Figure 3.2. Fortified sniper and surveillance positions along Beirut's Green Line, with markings used to identify their tenants, were commonplace during the years of violence. Authors.

Figure 3.3. In the mid-1970s, Beirut was punctuated by fortified checkpoints maintained by the assorted military and paramilitary combatants. These, in conjunction with sniper fire from elevated positions throughout the city, carved Beirut into a jigsaw puzzle of ethnic enclaves and no-man's-lands littered with rubble, vehicles, and wire. *An-Nahar* newspaper archive, used by permission.

Though pedestrian and vehicular crossings did exist along the Green Line near the old harbor, the Parliament building, the hippodrome, and the Palestinian camps in the south, these were used mainly by travelers enjoying relative immunity from paramilitary attack: military personnel, diplomats, and foreigners. All transverse roads except for the sanctioned crossings were blocked by large piles of debris. For most Beirutis, movement was limited to destinations in the ethnic enclave to which they belonged, with few incentives powerful enough to venture out of it. Businesses and apartment buildings barred their entrances, schools closed, regular commerce evaporated, and formerly up-market commercial districts were quickly transformed into open-air meat and fruit markets that operated during the gaps between the fighting. In these early months of the civil war, many Beirutis left the city to join their relatives in the countryside, as paramilitary combatants habituated themselves to a steady rhythm of feints, attacks, reprisals, and waiting.

Figure 3.4. View from a sniper's nest in Beirut c. 1974, defining a potentially lethal cone of vision which residents were obliged to move under and around. Credit: *An-Nahar* newspaper archive, used by permission.

Duration

For those who stayed, normal life had ended in Beirut. Public and private institutions not directly related to basic survival ceased to function. Essential visits and errands were timed in relation to the fighting, and movement between ethnic enclaves encouraged sniper fire when pedestrians intersected with the sightlines of enemy gunners. These pathways through the city formed a sort of unsteady labyrinth. Assorted markers helped civilians determine their location within it:

uniforms, vehicles or armaments, the newspapers read or available, the relationships between the civilian population and the militiamen, and key-words in conversations all combined to differentiate areas; one could "feel" a boundary, although it was completely invisible. (Davie 1994: 48)

As spatial patterns established themselves and became routine, Lebanese citizens found it increasingly difficult to envision the end of a war that had overtaken them without warning or explanation. The government, without full confidence in its military resources, could not produce an effective strategy for stemming the violence. Foreign governments and external media looked on with incredulity, but assumed that the violence was an outgrowth of Israeli-Palestinian affairs that were for the most part too opaque and remote to approach in a constructive way.

Meanwhile the cycles of attack and reprisal between rival paramilitaries continued unabated, gathering strength and frequency. An early crescendo was reached on 6 December 1975, when a Phalangist paramilitary group set up new roadblocks in Beirut and captured an estimated 350 Muslim civilians, all of whom were murdered on what was later referred to as Black Saturday. The Christian paramilitary forces responsible for these murders were aided by the fact that Lebanese identity cards, routinely examined at roadblocks by both Muslim and Christian paramilitaries since the start of the war, indicated the ethnicity of their bearer.

This incident, the first major civilian massacre in the civil war, introduced a new phase of hostilities in which noncombatants were used as leverage in the larger conflict. Black Saturday demonstrated several of the most lethal aspects of civil war in a segregated urban environment: the relative ease of inflicting civilian casualties in a patchwork of homogeneous ethnic enclaves, the close relationship between control of the major traffic arteries and prejudicial murder, and the tendency of retaliatory killing to spiral upward in scale and arbitrariness.

An episode with even more drastic consequences occurred about a month later, when Christian forces conquered the strategically vital Karantina slum and murdered up to 1,000 civilians living there. Those killed were mostly low-income Kurdish and Armenian families formerly protected by a small PLO detachment that had been routed. Two days later, on 25 January 1976, Palestinian paramilitary forces seeking revenge for the Karantina killings attacked the predominantly Christian city of Ad Damur, located about 20 km south of Beirut. Between 200 and 500 Christian residents of the city were reported to have been killed.

These events compelled many Beirutis living in mixed areas as members of a minority ethnic group to move to an ethnically homogeneous enclave that seemed to promise greater security. At this crucial juncture, about a year after violence first erupted in the city, large-scale coordinated population transfers began in the capital and throughout Lebanon, wherever the security of ethnic minorities was compromised. The disappearance of mixed residential areas, which were commonplace before the outbreak of hostilities, reduced the chances of reconciliation and accelerated the ethnic polarization of the city.

The Lebanese central government proved itself quite incapable of restraining the groups bringing ruin to the country. The underlying message sent to ordinary Lebanese citizens and paramilitary commanders was clear: no solution would be forthcoming from the central government and, barring any major intervention from abroad, combatants and noncombatants alike would have to fend for themselves as the conflict was allowed to run its course. Seizing upon this, Palestinian paramilitaries and their allies intensified assaults on official and unofficial rivals, pressing Christian forces further into East Beirut and compelling them to construct increasingly elaborate barricades along the perimeters of their positions.

In May 1976, circumstances had become worse for the Christian paramilitaries in possession of the port district who were attempting to block repeated Muslim assaults along the fortified barricades at Allenby Street. At that moment, when their success appeared especially uncertain, the civil war took another decisive turn as the rump Lebanese army finally entered the struggle on their behalf.

Up to that point, the Lebanese government and military had refused to take any formal position with respect to the activities of Christian and Palestinian paramilitaries. Their inaction was grounded two assumptions: engagement would splinter the army and neutrality would preserve their broker's role in the aftermath of hostilities. But in March of 1976 dissident Muslim troops in the Lebanese army broke ranks, as had been long feared. Under the leadership of Lieutenant Ahmad Khatib they formed the Lebanese Arab Army and lent their strength to the Lebanese National Movement, changing the balance of power in Beirut.

The remainder of the Lebanese Army then abandoned its neutrality and came to the aid of Christian paramilitaries. Its assistance was intended to avoid a total victory for the Palestinian forces and their allies that would have brought a cataclysmic shift in national politics. The army succeeded in defending the port district and repelling the Muslim paramilitaries, consolidating the Allenby Street frontier with a no man's land in the process. From that point forward, the Green Line was stable. No major military campaign seeking to gain or regain territory on the opposite side was subsequently attempted.

Tensions rose, culminating in a series of violent clashes between Phalangist and PLO paramilitary units in the suburban Palestinian camp of Tall al-Za'tar and elsewhere in July 1976. By August, riots and police checkpoints had become commonplace, paramilitary recruitment flourished and territorial consolidation by rival factions in Beirut began in earnest. Control over these circumstances eluded Lebanese politicians, giving way to a general breakdown of civil order. Routine bloodletting without police reprisal dissipated what little hope remained in Lebanese society for a quick and peaceful resolution of long-simmering antagonisms.

These developments sent an alarm signal to neighboring countries and the international community. Previously, external observers could continue to believe that the disturbances in Lebanon were peripheral to national politics and that the central government would weather the storm by simply allowing radical paramilitary groups to exhaust one another in battle. Once the Lebanese army became directly involved in the violence, this interpretation could no longer be supported. A month after the successful defense of Christian paramilitary positions in the port district, Syrian troops entered Lebanon. This dramatic intervention succeeded in quelling the worst of the violence, although it confirmed the impotence of the Lebanese government in resolving its own domestic crises, and left Syria with an extraordinary degree of influence over the internal affairs of its neighbor.

Seizing this opportunity, the Lebanese government called a peace conference in October 1976 in Riyadh, Saudi Arabia, where a formal ceasefire agreement was accepted. Eager to capitalize on a period of relative stability in Lebanon, the United Nations Security Council passed Resolution 425 on 19 March 1978, establishing a United Nations Interim Force in Lebanon designed to assist the Lebanese government in the difficult process of reasserting its authority in the area.

While these and other diplomatic developments resulted in significant stabilization in Beirut, they did not address the core complaints and conflicts that led to civil war in Lebanon. As a result, many Palestinian paramilitary factions shifted their emphasis from the capital to southern Lebanon, where they continued to organize raids on Israeli settlements near the Lebanese border. In this way, the hostilities in Lebanon shifted from one set of targets to another, further antagonizing an Israeli government already willing to assume that the PLO and the Lebanese government were collaborating to the detriment of Jewish interests in the region.

The civil war entered a new period of hostilities in May 1982, when Lebanon was invaded by Israeli forces in a full-scale attack designed to eradicate Palestinian paramilitary organizations in a single forceful sweep. Israeli forces surrounded West Beirut and a handful of other PLO strongholds after a series of full-scale attacks. Overwhelmed by the strength and organization of the Israeli army, Palestinian forces negotiated their capitulation quickly and agreed to evacuate the capital.

Their departure created an important vacuum among the Muslim and Christian paramilitary rivals left to fight amongst themselves for the territory and communal loyalties that were de-coupled from the Palestinian cause. New waves of violence and near total anarchy washed over Beirut—by then nearly unrecognizable as the prosperous city it had been ten years earlier. The Israeli invasion exacerbated old wounds and confirmed that Lebanon possessed very few resources in reserve with which to stem the ongoing crisis.

When President-elect Bashir Gemayel was assassinated on 14 September 1982, public outcry was momentous. The Israeli army chose to occupy West Beirut to prevent a descent into further discord that might have given additional advantages to their Palestinian counterparts. Exploiting the presence of the Israeli forces in their turn, Phalangist paramilitary units launched fresh attacks on the Sabra and Shatila Palestinian refugee camps in West Beirut. Once again, oscillations between indiscriminate civilian killings and in-kind retribution brought further misery to the city's residents. For the next six years, Beirut remained the epicenter of routine violence between paramilitary forces that used civilians as targets, with no significant resistance offered by the Lebanese government.

When the last remnants of a democratic system in Lebanon finally ceased functioning in 1988, the outgoing President, Amin Gemayel, appointed an ethnically balanced, six-member interim military government. However, the Muslim appointees refused to serve, and Lebanon's second war cabinet since 1975 was stillborn. With this fatal blow to the last vestiges of representative government in Lebanon, the shift from formal to informal government was complete. From that point onward, Lebanon was governed by self-appointed paramilitary leaders, one or more wielding control over the mainly Muslim West Beirut and others exercising authority over the mainly Christian sectors of East Beirut.

Dismantling

At last ready to accept major power-sharing concessions in order to insure its own survival in some form, the Lebanese government eventually sought to establish more equitable political representation at the national level. This capitulation was formalized in October 1989, when the Lebanese National Assembly convened in Ta'if, Saudi Arabia, to draft and approve the Charter of National Reconciliation. This Charter transferred significant executive powers from the presidency to the Cabinet, assuaging the concerns of many critics that a Christian president would always exercise the power of veto over initiatives that were of vital interest to the Muslim community, and gave Christian and Muslim representatives an equal number of seats in the National Assembly for the first time.

While these reforms were essential, they did not immediately neutralize the popular prestige and authority that had been cultivated by major paramilitary leaders over decades of relatively free rein in Beirut. This process still required military intervention, which came when Syrian and Lebanese Army units cooperated to eject the Maronite commander-in-chief, General Michel Aoun, from power on 13 October 1990. With Aoun's removal and constitutional reforms in place, the civil war in Lebanon finally came to an end and the Green Line dividing Beirut was dismantled.

Within the National Assembly's first year of activity, amnesty was formally granted for all crimes committed during the civil war between years 1975 and 1990. Since that time, the country has demonstrated astonishing resourcefulness and resilience in the long process of post-conflict revitalization, despite ongoing tensions with Israel and widespread instability in the Middle East. Meanwhile, many tensions between traditional rivals ethnic persist. One resident of Beirut observed that

it is still divided by Muslims from there and Christians from here and let's say people who belong to a certain party go to these institutions while others who belong to other parties go to other institutions. (Nora H., 2000)

A Christian bus driver in Beirut noted that divisions continue due to lingering distrust: "We would like to communicate with them [Muslims] and I'm sure they'd like to do the same, but we're both scared" (Nohra 2002). New crises and episodes of violence have interrupted life in Beirut since the Ta'if Accord, and many observers agree that "political unification has not erased psychological demarcation lines: many Beirutis, especially those who grew up in the war, still refuse to cross over 'to the other side'" (Davie 1994: 53). Ethnic partition in Beirut left an enduring legacy of distrust and instability that is fading slowly.

Impacts

Of a prewar population estimated at around four million, it is possible that Lebanon lost as many as one hundred and twenty thousand of its citizens

Figure 3.5. Ruined building in Beirut, c. 2002, near the former Green Line, showing the crippling effects of physical destruction and the slow pace of rehabilitation since the end of hostilities in 1990. Authors.

over sixteen years of civil war, about 4.5 percent of is prewar population. Up to 300,000 may have been wounded during the same period, about 11.5 percent of Lebanon's prewar population.

Since the number of paramilitary combatants never exceeded a few tens of thousands, civilian noncombatants bore the brunt of the violence. In addition to the casualties directly associated with the interethnic violence, some estimates suggest that as many as 700,000 Lebanese were displaced due to intimidation, loss of property, and shifting territorial acquisitions between rival ethnic groups, leaving the postwar population in 1993 at 2.7 million—less than three-quarters the prewar level (Nasr 1993).

It can be assumed that the material costs of the war were overwhelmingly large, since the city was more ruined than standing by the time the last wave of violence passed over its residents in the late 1980s.

If the overall productivity of the city is estimated at about 25 percent of national levels throughout the period from 1975 to 1990, then a rough estimate of combined material and opportunity losses can be derived from annual growth rate figures for gross domestic product before, during and after the civil war. Before the war Beirut was enjoying a relatively prosperous period from an economic standpoint, with growth rates of 4.7 percent in 1973 and 3.4 percent in 1974 on the eve of open hostilities. This rate dropped to −19 percent in 1975 and −57 percent in 1976.

Since the actual gross domestic product at this time was around $8 billion per year, initial economic losses totaled several billion dollars in official industrial productivity alone. The growth rate climbed back to 9.4 percent by 1979, as tensions eased somewhat in Lebanon, but fell back to −21 percent after the Israeli invasion in 1982. Growth fluctuated throughout the 1980s and again fell to negative numbers by 1990, just prior to full political settlement. Immediately after the Ta'if Accords were signed, the national growth rate jumped to 38 percent. A rough tally of net losses across the sixteen-year period of civil war based on these statistics points to figures in the neighborhood of $118 billion.

The psychological impacts of the war and of urban partition cannot be even roughly estimated, since there are limited clinical and sociological data available. The personal interviews conducted for this book confirmed that anxiety and resentment still lingered strongly in Beirut at the time of writing, especially among its least privileged residents who experienced almost constant anxiety during the lengthy periods of violence and received little compensation for their losses afterward. Political settlement has not been the capstone of a larger edifice of social reconciliation and recovery; at most, it may be considered a prerequisite for one.

Many Beirutis whose fears still exert a strong influence on their daily habits voluntarily limit their movements across the former Green Line. One observer notes that the ghost of the Green Line remains active:

It is still a barrier for the inhabitants of West Beirut looking for a change, while those from East Beirut will not easily cross over for superior restaurants or cultural life. Ethnic, political, linguistic, psychological, cultural de facto boundaries are still in place; their importance is now minimized, though not yet erased. (Davie 1994: 53)

Beirut's experience shows that the burdens of urban partition affect residents long after the violence and barricades have been officially removed.

Chapter 4
Belfast

Introduction

Paul M. lives with his family on Madrid Street in the isolated Catholic enclave of Short Strand. Madrid Street runs perpendicular to the local interface separating Catholic and Protestant communities in the neighborhood, and due to its proximity to both it has become an informal battleground, like those straddling many similar thresholds in Belfast. Though he admits that life in the Short Strand is difficult and he is anxious to the point of appearing "pathetic," he expresses no desire to leave since his life, relatives, and lifelong associations are there.

He believes that the peaceline is the only reliable form of protection his community can expect, since the police are not dependable. While some of his neighbors complain that the Short Strand has come to resemble the Alamo, Paul thinks that the situation is not as bad as it sounds, because his community is protected by walls that make the transition from Catholic to Protestant territory unmistakable.

Paul places special emphasis on the terrors associated with Protestant Orange Order marches every summer on 12 July, which he refers to simply as "the Twelfth." His concerns confirm that the calendar is a highly reliable predictor of violence in Belfast—a condition found in none of the other divided cities examined in this book, although violent episodes have occurred in Belfast throughout the year since the Troubles began in the late 1960s. When researchers (Murtagh 1995; Boal 1995; Murray 1991) compiled statistics for monthly fatalities for the years 1969–1998, the measurable increase in deaths related to sectarian violence was seen to have taken place in late summer. This pattern is linked to the marching schedule of Protestant fraternal organizations such as the Ancient Order of Hibernians, Apprentice Boys of Derry, Independent Orange Order, Loyal Orange Institution, and Royal Black Institution. These marches are part of the Irish Protestant cultural heritage, with no equivalent among Catholics. Approximately

TABLE 4.1. BASIC FACTS REGARDING THE PHYSICAL PARTITION OF BELFAST

Antagonisms	Catholics v. Protestants, Republicans v. Loyalists, Nationalists v. Unionists
Name	Peacelines
Location	The first peacelines were constructed spontaneously in the vicinity of Leeson, Cupar, Bombay, and Brookfield Streets in northwest Belfast. Many were subsequently constructed as sectarian violence migrated away from these places and erupted at other sensitive interfaces. No overarching logic guides their placement with respect to the city as a whole; rather, the walls are built in direct response to specific and chronic episodes of local violence. They all correspond to segments of interfaces where residential areas occupied by rival communities meet.
Context	Peacelines occur almost exclusively in the less affluent parts of the city, specifically the western and northern sectors. They generally follow streets that function as traditional boundaries between residential enclaves, though they sometimes split residential streets along alleys or backlots. Some block streets running perpendicular to the interfaces in order to block or regulate traffic between enclaves.
Size	The largest peacelines are more than 12 m high and in excess of 1.6 km in length, forming a defensive perimeter wall. The smallest are 3 m high and 30 m wide, forming a blockade or gate. Most span several residential city blocks where proximity between rival communities is closest and are designed to prevent the passage of thrown projectiles.
Porosity	Peacelines are built to prevent pedestrian incursion, and so most are impermeable throughout their length. These lengths are almost always open-ended, however, and do not form a complete seal around residential enclaves. These configurations allow for near total control at vulnerable locations and relatively unobstructed movement across interfaces elsewhere along an enclave perimeter. Gates in peacelines can be operated at the discretion of police and/or monitoring residents. During marching season, for example, many openings are shut and locked to reduce the likelihood of spontaneous riots. Many peacelines provide visual transparency while preventing penetration of people, projectiles, or vehicles.
Materials	The construction of peacelines reflects the needs, taste, and resources of the communities that commission them. Typical

	materials are brick, concrete, iron railing, corrugated steel, barbed wire, and open wire mesh.
Status	In 2002 there were 14 major peacelines partially separating Protestant from Catholic neighborhoods in Belfast.
Actors	Though many peacelines were first constructed as spontaneous and unplanned responses to rioting, none of these structures remain. Many have disappeared altogether, and some have been replaced by more carefully constructed partitions built and paid for by the municipal government. This process is initiated by beleaguered community representatives who report episodes of violence to a Member of Parliament and build a case for the erection or extension of a peaceline. If accepted, a construction contract is let according to a standard bidding process, and the work is undertaken according to normal building codes and practices.

twenty traditional marching dates are observed annually in Belfast by one or more of these groups, many in July and August to commemorate key historic events such as the Battle of the Boyne, the fall of Irish Protestant soldiers at the Battle of the Somme, and the Relief of Derry. Because these commemorations so often bring strong emotions and painful memories to the foreground of community consciousness, they have routinely provoked sectarian strife in Northern Ireland and Belfast in particular.

The days leading up to 12 July have always brought feelings of insecurity and dread to residents of the Short Strand, since Protestant marchers skirt the southern boundary of the enclave, following the Albert Bridge Road toward the Lagan River. Paul's daughter automatically recognizes the music of the marches that are almost invariably associated with violence and social upheaval in the city: "My wee one is terrified when she hears the bands because she knows it means trouble." The summer of 2002 was the first in ten years that Paul allowed his family to stay in their home during the marching season, but even then no one slept soundly. Paul remained awake throughout the night and kept his clothes on, prepared to defend his house in the event of trouble. He admitted that there was something perverse about waiting for your windows to be broken with bricks, but he remains unwilling to abandon the neighborhood where he grew up.

Paul emphasized repeatedly the central role of children in the maintenance of social tensions. Because children in isolated enclaves like Short

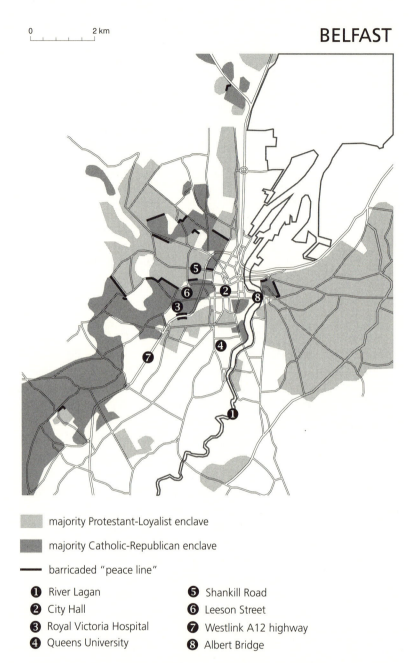

0   2 km

BELFAST

majority Protestant-Loyalist enclave

majority Catholic-Republican enclave

barricaded "peace line"

1 River Lagan
2 City Hall
3 Royal Victoria Hospital
4 Queens University

5 Shankill Road
6 Leeson Street
7 Westlink A12 highway
8 Albert Bridge

Figure 4.1. Map of Belfast's partition, 1974–2008. Belfast is located at 54° 36′ N, 5° 57′ W at the extreme northeast of Ireland on the western end of Belfast Lough and at the mouth of the River Lagan. Belfast lies 140 km north of Dublin and 517 km northwest of London. Authors.

Strand are frequently bored, have few interesting diversions, and are unable to leave the area out of fear for their safety, they sometimes break the monotony by arguing and fighting with members of a rival community across the interface. When these small scuffles draw in older relatives, the violence can escalate quickly. Unwilling to rely on police to ensure their security, residents on either side of an interface like the one surrounding the Short Strand often mobilize to create or buttress physical partitions. Paul agrees that the prospect of a more harmonious future depends on the young generations overcoming the hatreds of their parents, but he stops short of encouraging his children to mix freely with Protestants in his neighborhood. "I don't want it to be my children. You know what I mean? I know that's passing the buck, but that's the way it has to be."

Background

Social dynamics between Protestant and Catholic citizens in Northern Ireland have been marked for centuries by violent unrest and discrimination. In 1649 Oliver Cromwell suppressed the Ulster Rebellion, killing more than 4,000 Catholic civilians associated with a demand for popular sovereignty. The roots of "the Troubles" can be traced back to this period, when Protestants were given ownership of land cultivated by native Catholic farmers in one of Ireland's most fertile sectors. Escalation of tensions between Catholic farmers and Protestant landowners culminated in the Battle of the Boyne in 1690, leading to the defeat of Catholic King James II by English forces led by William of Orange.

To secure their victory and preclude future Catholic rebellions, the Protestant governors of Ulster instituted the 1697 Penal Laws barring Catholics in Northern Ireland from secondary education and the professions, among other things. These policies formalized the legal disenfranchisement that would persist for about 250 years. Superior in numbers but weak with respect to the Protestant establishment, the Catholics pushed back with increasingly well organized armed resistance throughout the eighteenth century. Protestants with large investments in Northern Ireland attempted to counteract growing Catholic militancy by strengthening the Orange Order in the early 1790s, having recognized its "antirevolutionary potential." The Orange Order was dedicated to the defense of Northern Ireland against assertions of Catholic sovereignty, and "the members of the gentry took over, armed the membership, and persuaded the government that no-popery was an effective tool of law and order" (Hachey 1972: 7).

Though disputes between Catholics and Protestants occurred in both rural and urban areas of Northern Ireland, paramilitary activities focused increasingly on large cities like Derry/Londonderry and Belfast. Voluntary segregation between Catholics and Protestants in Belfast continued throughout the nineteenth century. By the time the first interface riots occurred in the second half of the nineteenth century—most notably in 1857, 1864, and 1872—the demographic character of Belfast mirrored the problematic relationships between Catholics and Protestants in Northern Ireland as a whole. Catholics were relatively poor but more numerous than Protestants. Industries like shipbuilding and linen manufacture were segregated by religious group, with managerial jobs reserved for Protestants. Residential neighborhoods were becoming increasingly homogeneous.

On 4 June 1886, riots began in the shipyards of Belfast in anticipation of the Home Rule Bill and spilled over into the city after the bill was defeated by thirty votes in Westminster on 8 June. Bloody fighting took place along Donegall Street, pitting Catholic residents against their Protestant neighbors and both groups against the police—who were predominantly Protestant but generally not Belfast natives. A series of attacks and reprisals—mostly centered in the Shankill and Springfield areas of working-class West Belfast—kept the city in an anxious state throughout September, by which time 50 citizens had been killed, 370 police officers injured, 190 Catholics expelled from their jobs at the shipyards, and 31 public houses looted (Bardon and Bell 1982: 185). These riots established a precedent for sectarian violence stemming from the failure of political processes to create an independent Irish state. Belfast became a pivotal point of resistance in the struggle for sovereignty and territory in Northern Ireland.

During the early twentieth century, tensions in the city continued to rise and paramilitary recruitment on both sides of the ethnic divide was brisk. By 1905 many Catholics in Northern Ireland had lost faith in the possibility of support from more powerful Catholic nations, leading to the establishment of a radical reform party by Arthur Griffith called Sinn Fein—Gaelic for "we ourselves." Sinn Fein pressed forward with a political agenda favoring Irish Catholic sovereignty without the expectation of any foreign assistance.

Alarmed by the increasingly militant and effective rhetoric emerging from the Catholic political apparatus, Protestants again strengthened their own paramilitary networks and sought support from Britain in the event of civil war. An implosion of the Catholic-Protestant dispute seemed imminent by 1914, but the dispute was overshadowed by even more cataclysmic events in Europe and the entrance of Britain into World War I.

Protestants in Northern Ireland were obliged to muster Irish conscripts as German forces moved steadily across France. Simultaneously, increasingly effective Republican paramilitary attacks made their presence at home vital. Under increasing pressure from London, the Protestant leadership in Northern Ireland contributed a large portion of the Ulster Volunteer Force (UVF) to the ranks of the British army, handing a major advantage to its domestic adversaries. At dawn on 1 July 1916, the anniversary of the Battle of the Boyne, the Thirty-Sixth Ulster Division of the British Army—comprised mostly of Ulster Defence Force members—suffered a heavy defeat during the Battle of the Somme when it was ordered to attack and occupy the German Schwaben Redoubt. The ill-planned attack and subsequent capitulation cost more than 5,000 Irish lives in addition to 60,000 British ones.

Despite the failed Easter Rising of 1916 and admiration for Loyalist sacrifices in France, the end of the war brought a surprise victory in 1918 for the revolutionary nationalists and Sinn Fein in Dublin. This episode led to the bitterly fought War of Independence of 1919–21. When the war concluded with the Anglo-Irish Treaty, political arrangements were put in motion for the creation of an autonomous Irish state. Exclusion of Northern Ireland from the new Irish Free State was a concession during the final stages of negotiation with British Prime Minister David Lloyd George, who crafted the partition plan to preserve Dominion status in Ireland and echo the abortive Government of Ireland Act of 1920 (Fraser 2000: 2). Carefully constructed to be as large as possible while retaining an absolute majority of Protestant citizens, the six Ulster counties of Northern Ireland were the last colonial stronghold for Great Britain in the northern hemisphere and one of the most ambitious acts of ethnic gerrymandering in recent history.

While the rest of Ireland celebrated its long-awaited independence, the Catholics of Northern Ireland continued to wait. Their isolation deepened in the years that followed as hope for nonviolent solutions faded. Violent episodes became increasingly common in the working-class neighborhoods of Belfast. The heaviest losses fell on isolated residents, who were especially vulnerable as "intimidation, house-burning, rioting and assassination drew the lines between the two religions in the city more tautly than ever" (Bardon 1982: 200). Discord became especially intense in 1922 and 1923, when more than 450 citizens lost their lives during inter-ethnic rioting.

Meanwhile union organizers in Belfast attempted to convince working-class Catholics and Protestants that their shared interest was to organize effectively together against the gentry who kept their living conditions unsatisfactory. These efforts, emphasizing common economic interests rather than sectarian differences, met with considerable success in Belfast. Had the labor organization managed to trump sectarian paranoia there, the course of politics in Northern Ireland might have been different. It did not, largely due to the intervention of industrialists determined to protect their large-scale investments by avoiding class-based conflict.

Their strategy was to enlarge their support for the Orange Order fraternal lodges, then to stand back and let sectarian struggle in the working class take its course. This approach absorbed some of the energy that might have been spent developing a unified front against the inequitable labor practices that remained in full effect throughout the Troubles. This approach allowed the Tory elite "to preserve its prerogatives by fostering sectarian strife among its opponents" while "Protestant workers ignored their real economic interests and gave their support to the Unionist party" as had happened many times before (Henderson, Lebow, and Stoessinger 1974: 209). The resulting chain reaction of inter-ethnic violence worsened conditions for the working poor of Belfast.

Escalation

Between the 1920s and 1970s, continuing conflict and religious division brought changes to Northern Ireland that compounded its existing problems. Migration to the cities began in the mid-1920s and intensified throughout World War II, leading to such rapid and unprecedented densification in Belfast that urban planners struggled to provide even the most basic services for the city's new residents. Numerous attempts were made to slow down this growth and force vertical development instead of peripheral sprawl, but most of these were unsuccessful due to the strong traditions of low-rise terraced housing in the working-class areas of the city. Competition for scarce housing and jobs did much to intensify feelings of sectarian prejudice in Belfast during this period.

Further distress came with the Irish potato famine of the mid-1940s, which left many citizens desperate. In response to pressures for reform, the British government passed the Education Act in 1947. This gave Irish Catholics in Northern Ireland equal access to secondary public education for the first time. Although most Catholic students continued to attend church-run schools, the legislation was a watershed in Northern Irish politics and paved the way for a new generation of informed social activists who would shape the civil rights movement during the late 1960s and 1970s.

Other broad reforms were pursued by the British administration, resulting in the first Northern Irish government with genuinely liberal and progressive attitudes regarding discrimination against Catholics, led by Ulster Unionist leader Terence O'Neill. Promising sweeping reforms and opportunities in the political sphere, O'Neill's agenda was met with guarded optimism by moderate Catholics hoping to achieve their political goals without violence. By the mid-1960s many of these hopes were already fading. O'Neill's promised reforms were slow to materialize due to his obstructionist opponents and the steady decline of Belfast's major industries—linen, shipbuilding, and heavy engineering. As faith in political reform and economic revitalization dwindled, Catholics in Northern Ireland again began to contemplate reform on their own terms.

Throughout the 1960s the civil rights movement was gaining strength among liberal, educated Catholics in Northern Ireland. Inspired by the strength and success of similar efforts in the United States and France, many believed that well-orchestrated street demonstrations could be more effective than diplomacy because they would attract international journalists, and with them the sympathies of liberal western governments in North America and Europe. These ideas were tested in 1966 on the fiftieth anniversary of both the Easter Rising and the decimation of Ulster Defence Force members at the Somme.

In February 1966 a bomb was detonated at the Unionist headquarters in Belfast, followed two days later with the bombing of a Catholic school nearby. As tensions rose, the Rev. Ian Paisley staged a march through Cromac Square, an interface area of working-class Belfast, followed immediately by numerous local riots. By 1967 Catholic organizers had created the Northern Ireland Civil Rights Association to conduct protest marches in support of political reform. In July that year, a brick hit the hood of Queen Elizabeth's car as her entourage drove down Belfast's Great Victoria Street during the first royal visit to Northern Ireland in decades. This ominous episode brought to a close Belfast's last period of relative quiet before the official onset of "the Troubles."

Negotiations

Tensions throughout Northern Ireland rose steadily in the late 1960s, but the government still pursued a policy of gradual reform. By the end of 1968, it was clear that O'Neill's liberal agenda had backfired. The reforms not waylaid by political infighting were generally perceived as inadequate by Catholics, while a significant proportion of Protestants felt betrayed by his attempts to appease Catholic concerns on any level.

As the grassroots Catholic civil-rights movement grew in popularity and sophistication, feelings of insecurity mounted among Protestants who rallied in greater and greater numbers around reactionary figures like Ian Paisley. Throughout this sequence of events one pattern was increasingly clear: both parties to the sectarian conflict in Northern Ireland were reinforcing means and mechanisms with which to confront their rivals, and demonstrating increasing skepticism of the government's capacity to intervene effectively.

Belligerent Protestant groups organized Loyalist marches passing through or near sensitive Catholic enclaves in cities like Derry/Londonderry, Armagh, and Belfast during the 1960s. These marches intensified sectarian violence by emphasizing issues of territorial sovereignty in cities where competition for housing and public space between Protestant and Catholic working-class communities was intense. Protestant marches consciously exploited the sensitivity of these interface areas and resurrected painful memories of the Battle of the Boyne, the Easter Rising, and World War I. Perceived incursions sometimes provoked inflammatory results. The parades called for heavy police supervision in exactly the areas of the major cities where Catholic distrust of the predominately Protestant police force was most acute. The provocative potential of the marches was enhanced by the fact that neighborhood homogeneity had been increasing steadily for decades on both sides of the sectarian divide. As more Catholics and Protestants families moved closer to members of their own ethnic group, the boundaries between residential enclaves became more pronounced, more arbitrary, and more symbolically significant.

As security concerns grew more pervasive, the need to defend and regulate these boundaries intensified. While in 1911 only 41 percent of Catholics and 62 percent of Protestants in Belfast lived in segregated neighborhoods, by 1967 the territorial division of working-class Belfast between Catholic and Protestant groups was almost total (Murtagh 1995: 211). Riots frequently took place along the interface areas, and "the overwhelming impression on both sides of the [Belfast] battlefield was one of dull, unbroken, depressed gloom" (Hastings 1970: 141).

In August 1969 rioting broke out along Shankill, Divis, and Crumlin Roads, partly in response to violent exchanges between Catholics and police in Derry/Londonderry during the "Battle of the Bogside." The police were forced to intervene against Protestant rioters in Loyalist communities, earning the resentment of both Protestant and Catholic groups in Belfast and opening a third front in the urban battle. Hostilities had developed to a point where the police could no longer guarantee the safety of regular citizens caught in the crossfire.

Emergence

On the night of 14 August 1969 fighting began along the Falls Road in West Belfast and quickly led to a sequence of reprisals. Violence broke out between Catholics and Protestants in the Ardoyne neighborhood near a major interface, and when police intervened they returned fire with Browning machine guns mounted on armored vehicles, killing several rioters. Catholic houses were burned in the Bombay Street area, provoking "a retreat into their own areas by outlying members of the two communities, for the sake of security" toward more homogeneous enclaves like Andersonstown and Ballymurphy (Scarman 1972: section 1.17).

Physical barricades constructed by anxious residents appeared along the perimeters of several Catholic enclaves in the area, hastily assembled from telegraph poles, hijacked bakery vans, municipal buses, upturned cars, scaffolding, and paving stones. Mountainous obstacles designed to slow or prohibit mob violence appeared at key intersections, guarded by Protestant and Catholic residents unwilling to leave the area.

By the afternoon of 15 August the police commissioner and deputy commissioner concluded that their officers were "unable any longer to control serious disturbances in the City of Belfast" (Scarman 1972: section 1.18). They turned the city over to British army units sent to secure the Falls Road area and other volatile areas. The British soldiers were initially welcomed by many Catholic enclave residents who felt trapped and besieged. This unprecedented military presence was not, however, enough to prevent the outbreak of further violence. Almost all the houses on Bombay and Brookfield Streets, those closest to Protestant neighborhoods across the Falls Road, were burned in ensuing riots. These brutal events prompted a special

Figure 4.2. Impromptu and temporary barricades along Leeson Street in Belfast during the riots of August 1969 were the first physical divisions erected in the city, later to evolve into semi-permanent "peacelines." Henry Bell, used by permission.

inquiry by the Scarman Tribunal, which concluded in its 1972 report that of the 1,820 families who had fled their homes during the short period of rioting, 1,505 were Catholic, a number comprising more than 3 percent of all Catholic households in the city at that time (Scarman 1972: ch. 31).

Recognizing their vulnerability in unfamiliar terrain, the British forces in Belfast dug in, adding new partitions to the labyrinth of residential barricades. These were intended to obstruct pedestrian movement along neighborhood interfaces where sectarian violence was concentrated. The first partitions were built hastily with prefabricated "knife rests"—sturdy iron frames interlaced with concertina wire, running parallel to the interface roads (Bardon and Bell 1982: 283).

These modular constructions were quickly replaced with more permanent walls of corrugated iron and barbed wire. Embattled residents typically followed suit, reinforcing and improving makeshift walls. Many threatened resident groups formed "defense committees" and fortified their enclaves while the army attempted to discourage violence, monitoring the no-man's-lands between enclaves and defending itself against attack. These were the first physical partitions of the twentieth century in Belfast. Though some were removed with the dissipation of violence in September 1969, many evolved into the peacelines that remain in highly modified forms throughout the city.

Duration

The social and political struggles that led to this partitioning were not quickly resolved. In August 1971 laws permitting internment without trial for political prisoners in Northern Ireland were passed in response to the growing scope of Catholic paramilitary operations. The outcome of Derry/ Londonderry's nonviolent political protest in January 1972, later called "Bloody Sunday," marked the low point of another cycle of sectarian violence, punctuated by imposition of direct rule from Westminster in March the same year. By 1975, self-government had not been restored and the toll from the Troubles was high and climbing. Hundreds of civilians were dead, thousands wounded and displaced, and more than 9,000 homes in Belfast alone were irreparably damaged or bricked up despite the ongoing housing shortage.

Much progress was made on the political front throughout the 1990s, culminating in the Good Friday Agreement of April 1998 and subsequent reforms that contributed significantly to social reconciliation. Violent interaction between Protestants and Catholics has not ceased, but the inclusion of Sinn Fein representatives and other previously marginalized political groups in the broader political dialogue improved the prospects for peaceful negotiation and settlement.

Along with the rest of Northern Ireland, Belfast continues to distance itself from the violent struggles of its recent past. Along the way, however, the city and its working-class residents remain hampered by the weight of their previous struggles. Belfast's working-class enclaves are significantly more homogeneous in 2007 than they were in 1960 (Jones 1960). A member of the Legislative Assembly in Belfast noted:

It involves everyone, and it divides everything; it divides sport, education . . . just divides everything. It divides us as people living together, right? Because we largely live separately, you know? It's hard to give a percentage, but you could talk in terms of about 90 percent of people actually living in separate neighborhoods. And that's not just North Belfast, it's right across Northern Ireland . . . on a sectarian basis.

That's the reality of the situation. We just haven't tackled that in any serious way. (Maginness 2001)

More than thirty interface partitions, called peacelines, still exist in the city, and plans to construct new ones are continuously being developed by government agencies responding to popular petitions. These active ethnic partitions have been documented by several researchers with great care (see especially Boal, Clarke, and Ober 1976; Boal, Doherty, and Pringle 1978; Boal, Douglas, and Orr 1982; Boal 1995).

   An urban planner in Belfast has described the three phases of peaceline development since 1968 as follows:

temporary ones were put up, then the temporarily permanent, and then the permanently temporary, and they were actually planned after that. The first ones went up at flashpoints, obviously, then the demarcation lines were planned, and then you had rebuilding and as that was continuing you had them actually built into the new structure. (Richard S. 2000)

Much energy and money have been invested in the creation and extension of Belfast's physical partitions. Though the bloodshed related to sectarian violence has diminished drastically in the last decade and the Northern Ireland Assembly was restored in May 2007, the less affluent areas of Belfast remain spatially and socially divided.

Impacts

In no other divided city investigated in this book have the losses associated with inter-ethnic partition been documented as thoroughly or carefully as in Belfast. Many reliable studies have been undertaken before, during, and after the major cycles of violence by both government and academic researchers. These findings are indispensable with regard to Belfast, and aid the analysis of other cities. Significantly more is known about the impact of sustained sectarian conflict in Belfast than about the other four cities put together. Most of this information was gathered through the "Cost of the Troubles" study of 1999 and analytical publication of the same year (see Fay, Morrissey, and Smyth 1999).

   This landmark report reveals patterns of violence, suffering, and insecurity that plagued Northern Ireland for about forty years. The factors most strongly correlated to sectarian violence were class and physical location.

Figure 4.3. Peacelines in Belfast's Unity Flats enclave near Shankill Road, 2002.
Authors.

Figure 4.4. Local residents regulate movement through a gated barricade in the Torrens enclave of Belfast near Oldpark Road, 2002. Authors.

The working-class neighborhoods of Belfast ranked highest in incidence of sectarian violence, and in these neighborhoods interface areas were the most sensitive and dangerous places. Because violent episodes tended to occur near these interfaces, they became the "high-intensity areas" in which the researchers focused their efforts. Not surprisingly, their research showed that human costs were highest in high-intensity areas, and that these negative impacts fostered lasting anxiety, insecurity, and resentment. These conditions led to acts of intimidation and reprisal, which accelerated the homogenization of the city's ethnic enclaves, multiplying and strengthening the interfaces between rival communities.

The fact that proximity to sectarian interfaces was found to be the most reliable index for predicting the likelihood of violence in Belfast is of special importance. It suggests that antagonisms in Belfast, regardless of their origins, contribute to predictable and self-perpetuating cycles of discrimination. Simply by living or working near the interface areas, working-class enclave communities were exposed to disproportionately high levels

Figure 4.5. Structually sound row houses too close to an interface area of Belfast are often abandoned and incorporated into the barricade through attrition, 2002. Authors.

of anxiety and insecurity that triggered a lengthy and well-documented sequence of actions and reactions in the social sphere. The partitions affirm the prejudice and paranoia that made them appear to be necessary in the first place. Interfaces, and the partitions defining them, are not just expressions of conflict. In advanced stages, the conflict is incubated by these fortified enclaves, and its message confirmed in them. One observer of Belfast has thus noted that, while the interfaces are products of discernable social and political forces, they also "generated certain preconditions for the autonomous reproduction of violent reciprocity" (Feldman 1991: 35). Walls that decrease localized violence can simultaneously provide fertile conditions for the roots of the conflict to spread.

Within the high-intensity areas of Belfast, men between ages forty-five and sixty-four suffer the widest array of negative impacts as a result of the Troubles, including hardships related to mental health, employment, and routine violence, while those aged between five and nineteen years suffered the highest incidence of death and physical injury.

Though age and gender are statistically correlated with episodes of sectarian violence in Belfast, similar levels of injury and insecurity were not found among teenaged and middle-aged men in every neighborhood. Rather, Belfast's poorer Catholics in general suffered more as a group than its poorer Protestants, though suffering among Catholic and Protestant residents of working-class neighborhoods was far greater than that among the residents of middle-class neighborhoods, regardless of their ethnic makeup or the proximity of a rival community.

The most prominent impacts of partition in every divided city are loss of life and physical injury. Of approximately 3,600 violent deaths directly associated with sectarian conflict in Northern Ireland between 1969 and 1998, about 1,220—almost exactly one third—took the lives of Belfast residents, the majority of whom lived in the traditional working-class sectors of the city in the north and west. These figures offer precious quantitative support for the intuitive conclusion that relative deprivation, economic hardship, and sectarian violence are intimately and routinely related. Most studies support the assumption that physical injuries outnumbered deaths in Northern Ireland during this period by about ten to one, and occur to the same kinds of victims in similar geographic locations. These rough estimates suggest that over 13,000 Belfast residents suffered injury or death as a direct result of sectarian violence, about 4.5 percent of the city's average population between 1987 and 2001.

The number of Belfast residents physically affected by the Troubles

Figure 4.6. This extended barricade in the Cliftonville enclave of Belfast is modest in comparison with more towering specimens engineered by the city, but all partitions help to define interface areas and perpetuate and widespread sense of distrust. Authors.

grows significantly if those afflicted by secondary health problems such as substance abuse, depression, and chronic anxiety are added to the rosters. The "Cost of the Troubles" researchers note that "the combination of deaths and injuries represents the primary human cost of the Troubles although these do not encompass the trauma of grief, imprisonment and intimidation" (Fay, Morrissey, and Smyth 1999: 138).

Indicators used by the Belfast researchers to measure indirect impacts include post-traumatic stress disorder, violent nightmares, involuntary recall of violent episodes that were experienced directly or indirectly, and a pervasive feeling of guilt related to surviving the events that had claimed the lives of others. The incidence of all these symptoms was greatest in areas of high-intensity violence, which had already been strongly correlated to interface areas of working-class North and West Belfast.

Other psychological impacts of less diagnosable nature can be assumed to conform to the same general patterns, including an overarching sense of helplessness, xenophobia, claustrophobia, and fatalism. Many Belfast residents interviewed by the authors said they were afraid to leave the enclaves of which they were members, and often felt trapped by the assumption that terrible things would happen if they ventured too far from these relatively safe havens. Because workplaces, too, were frequently segregated during the periods of worst violence, they rarely provided relief from the monotony of life in the sectarian enclaves.

Exposure to violence and associated trauma was also found to be highest among those with the lowest levels of wealth and productivity. Participants and victims alike tended to have relatively low income levels, along with high levels of public-housing occupancy, unemployment, and benefit dependency. These indications seem to have functioned as both prerequisites and byproducts of exposure to sectarian conflict in the city, since interface areas were the epicenters for violence, and these neighborhoods of last resort were inhabited by Belfast's least affluent citizens due to the low rents and high vulnerability of housing in these areas. Physical and psychological injury accompanying exposure to violence further undermined the capacity of the affected individuals to earn money or improve their upward mobility.

Such strains were often compounded by the negative effects of internal migration across sectarian lines in the city, as assorted forms of intimidation prompted threatened residents to relocate to neighborhoods where they were part of a local ethnic majority. Between 1969 and 1976, approximately 25,000 Belfast households were destroyed or damaged by explosions, forcing the inhabitants to relocate. These movements drove a process of homogenization that contributed greatly to the overall social destabilization of the city, intensified the emblematic significance of territorial boundaries, and reshaped Belfast in the decades following 1968. While the overall losses of income and productivity to both employers and individuals associated with these patterns has not been calculated, it can be assumed to be substantial and debilitating.

At the most superficial level of analysis, the partitions themselves are structures that are expensive to build and monitor. Figures published by the Belfast Development Office show the cost of individual peacelines commissioned and built by the city ranged from about $25,000 to more than half a million dollars (Springfield Inter-Community Development Project 1993). Taking these estimates as a guide, a conservative estimate of city government expenditure would suggest that more than $U.S.8 million has been used for the construction, maintenance, and extension of partition walls throughout the city.

Figures of this magnitude do not represent significant portions of the city's annual expenditures; to estimate the actual material cost of partition in terms of public revenue, direct costs must be combined with indirect ones, such as forfeited rents and lost taxes on vacant and destroyed properties, police surveillance, and bureaucracy. Though reliable and comprehensive estimates of administrative and maintenance costs are difficult to ascertain, it might be safely assumed that they reduce local budgetary allocations for social rehabilitation programs by a significant margin.

Chapter 5
Jerusalem

Introduction

In 2002 an Israeli scholar named Yehezkel Lein was on his way from his office in West Jerusalem to an appointment at the United Nations headquarters in East Jerusalem. The building is a ten-minute drive north from Damascus Gate along Nablus road, a major artery in that part of the city. But Mr. Lein had a problem: his taxi driver had never been there. The driver said that for fifteen years he had not visited "their place" (East Jerusalem), though no barricades or restrictions had existed during that time. He was hesitant to make the journey, but finally agreed when he was informed that the office was next to the Old City and just 100 m to the east of Road #1—the highway to Ramallah built along the boundary that had once divided East and West Jerusalem. Israeli politicians assert that Jerusalem has been unified since 1967 and that the severance of East Jerusalem from the whole is a fantasy, yet for this driver a trip across the former Green Line was a dangerous journey into foreign territory.

Mr. Lein says that this contradiction is normal. He says that if you ask most Israelis for directions to old, large Palestinian neighborhoods, the inquiry would constitute their first exposure to the names and, "of course they will not know how to get there." He offered his wife as an example. She is an Israeli and very familiar with West Jerusalem, but she had never heard of the main hospital serving Arabs in East Jerusalem, being unfamiliar with the name, the location, and its very existence. Likewise she was unaware of the location or name of large Palestinian enclaves in her own city where up to 15,000 Jerusalemites reside. This general lack of awareness at the most basic level, which Mr. Lein asserts is quite widespread, leads him to the conclusion that there is not one Jerusalem but "two metropolises: a Jewish and Arab metropolis, and they do not live together" (Lein 2003).

The lack of familiarity regarding urban terrain is not symmetrical. While many Israeli Jerusalemites choose not to look at or visit the Palestin-

TABLE 5.1. BASIC FACTS REGARDING THE PHYSICAL PARTITION OF JERUSALEM

Antagonisms	Israelis v. Palestinians, Jews v. Arabs, Israel v. Jordan
Names	Green Line, Dayan-al-Tal Line, Armistice Line
Location	The Green Line through Jerusalem was just one segment of a larger demarcation line separating the whole of Israel from the West Bank in 1948–67, which comprises all the territory west of the Jordan not claimed by the Israeli government. This boundary comprised two forward position lines—one Israeli, one Jordanian—separated by a no man's land. Starting from the north, the Line approached the city obliquely from the west until it reached the western spur of Mount Scopus, west of the main north road to Ramallah; from there it turned southward, skirting the American Colony until the Damascus Gate of the Old city; from there it traced roughly the outside of the city walls to the south and east until Jaffa Gate, where it dipped slightly to the south and continued parallel to the walls until the Zion Gate; from there it continued in a southerly direction toward the UN Government House and from there gradually eased off to the west again.
Context	The Green Line reached like a finger far into the West Bank in order to encompass the city, leaving Israeli-controlled West Jerusalem as an isolated colony at the end of a political and geographical cul-de-sac. By dividing Jerusalem, it automatically traced the geographic boundary formed by the ridge of the Judean Mountains separating "green" agricultural lands to the west from "gold" pastoral desert territory to the east. As it cut through the city, crossing and closing former thoroughfares, the Line engendered dereliction in all the neighborhoods adjacent to it, leaving ruined and impoverished areas in the center of the city after its unification in 1967: north of the city between Shmuel Hanavi and Shaykh Jarrah, in the center opposite the Damascus Gate between Nablus Road and the Musrara quarter, and in the southern central part of the city known as the Mamilla quarter opposite Jaffa Gate below Yemin Moshe.
Size	The Green Line in Jerusalem after 1962 constituted a physical barricade about 2.4 km long encompassing a no man's land including 150 structures. Defensive ramparts 5–12 m high and of equivalent width were constructed to block transverse roads from sniper fire.

Porosity	The Green Line formed an almost hermetic seal between eastern and western sectors, passable only by privileged persons at the crossing nicknamed the Mandelbaum Gate located about 0.8 km north of the Damascus Gate. Prior to 1962 the boundary was not fenced, but the frequency of hostile and accidental incursions led to the construction of barricades in that year.
Materials	Barbed wire, corrugated iron, concrete, steel, land mines.
Status	Physically dismantled following the Six Day War in 1967, leaving only scars and voids now filled by roads and new commercial development. The legal status of the Green Line remains nebulous, since the annexations of 1967 have never been recognized by the United Nations as legal, nor the boundaries they established as permanent. Many Palestinian representatives still advocate the creation of an international boundary along the former Green Line, effectively returning the territorial map to its 1948 configuration.
Actors	The Green Line was created in two steps: military actions during the 1948 civil war between Israeli and Jordanian forces established front-line positions that were largely unchanged as official government representatives approved a settlement in 1949. Since that time, military personnel maintained the border according to directives from their respective national governments.

ian side of the city, Palestinian residents of East Jerusalem and the West Bank can hardly afford to ignore their neighbors. They rely on Israeli institutions and bureaucrats in order to sustain the most fundamental components of their lives: jobs, free movement, travel visas, building permits, and so forth. They often travel the short distance to West Jerusalem in order to visit the governmental offices or to go to work. Taxi drivers from East Jerusalem generally navigate both halves of the city with confidence.

A Palestinian cab driver named Mustafa is one example. He grew up in and near East Jerusalem and crosses the former Green Line many times a day without noticeable hesitation. He would be unable to make a living if he refused to do so. Mustafa describes Jerusalem as a highly divided city in which one side is thriving while the other is just barely surviving. His job helps to support a part of his family living in the West Bank, where they sometimes do not have enough money to buy bread. "If you make me very hungry," Mustafa observed, "one week, two weeks, one month, two

0 km   1 km

JERUSALEM

Israeli West Jerusalem 1948-67, predominantly Jewish

Jordanian East Jerusalem 1948-67, predominantly Muslim

developed area

demilitarized zones

Green Line

no man's land

❶ Old City
❷ Mandelbaum Gate
❸ Government House
❹ Knesset

❺ Jaffa Road
❻ Mount of Olives
❼ Mamilla
❽ Silwan

Figure 5.1. Map of Jerusalem's partition, 1948–1967. Israel is bounded by Lebanon to the north, Syria to the northeast, Jordan to the east, and Egypt to the south. Jerusalem is located at 31°47′N, 35°13′E in the Judean Mountains, between the Mediterranean Sea and the northern tip of the Dead Sea. Jerusalem lies 60 km east of Tel Aviv, 69 km west of Amman, and 1171 km SE of Istanbul. Credit: authors.

months, there is a limit, you know? After that I will be very, very, very nervous, and I will do a lot of things to have food. True or not?"

He said that while the conditions for residents of East Jerusalem are quite bad, they are still many times better than those in the West Bank, which is why Palestinians still struggle to remain in the city and to cope with the limitations of the Israeli system. Mustafa believes that the Palestinians have adopted a militant posture out of desperation, and that they would not be political at all if they were able to live a normal life. Though his outlook is gloomy, he added, "I hope one day I can open my eyes and see the peace and people moving back and forth with no problem."

Background

Situated on a steep and rocky slope far from the nearest river, sea, and trade route, the siting of Jerusalem has little in common with other important cities in the region. According to scholarly interpretations of the Old Testament regarding Jerusalem's origins, King David founded his capital in this unlikely place to serve the interests of political integration and social reconciliation (Benvenisti 1996: 144). It straddled the border between rival southern and northern tribes of his period and belonged to neither. Despite the compromise rooted in the city's siting and origin, it was besieged and conquered more than thirty times during the 4,000 years that followed. It is among the world's most frequently disputed cities.

The demise of the Ottoman Empire in the early twentieth century led to colonial enterprises that brought lasting and generally unfavorable long-term repercussions to Jerusalem. One of the earliest was the Sykes-Picot Agreement of 1916, a concerted effort to address ethnic sovereignty in the former Ottoman Empire. Representatives of the major western European nations, anticipating victory in World War I and control over these territories, sketched the outlines of regional partition along ethnic lines.

Special attention was paid to the question of Jerusalem. The tentative operational framework for an international administration of the city provided by Sykes-Picot was viewed with suspicion by native and neighboring powers. In 1916 the political status of Palestine remained indeterminate while de facto sovereignty was given to Britain, whose other acquisitions in the agreement included the rich oilfields of Baghdad and Kirkuk.

Meanwhile, the proponents of Zionism had made significant political inroads in London. These culminated in a letter of November 1917 from

Lord Balfour to Lord Rothschild granting formal recognition of a Jewish home in Palestine by the great powers for the first time. The Balfour Declaration addressed the status of indigenous communities directly, stipulating that "nothing shall be done which may prejudice the civil and religious rights of existing non-Jewish communities in Palestine" in the course of the formulation of Eretz Yisrael. With this guarantee in hand, the leaders of the first Jewish state needed only to await the end of international hostilities to inaugurate their new political project in Palestine. They did not need to wait long, as Ottoman forces surrendered in Jerusalem to General Allenby during the second week of December 1917.

The three strands of political influence in Palestine that were braided together during the final years of World War I—joint international oversight of Palestine, direct local administration by Britain, and emblematic authority for Zionists—appeared compatible to most foreign observers. Yet the same strands ultimately became tangled and fostered ethnic rivalries lasting several generations. Rejection of these schemes by the group most conspicuously excluded from the process of formulating them—the Palestinians—quickly followed the publication of the Balfour Declaration. By the end of January 1918, it had been rejected by the first Palestinian National Congress, convened in Jerusalem to demand independence from Israel and to gather support from the international diplomatic community. Palestine had been released from Ottoman administration for less than two months before competing claims for sovereignty verged on violence. These disputes proved to be more than mere growing pains; many of them are still unresolved (Benvenisti 1982: 101).

Great Britain obtained a mandate from the League of Nations in 1922 to govern Palestine, and Jerusalem became the capital of its civil administration. During this period, the resentment of British authority among both Israelis and Palestinians was at least equal to the resentment they felt toward each other. A similar circumstance was evident in Cyprus through the mid-1950s. Though Palestinians were the less favored minority, Israeli frustrations were the first to spill over into violence. A disturbance at the Wailing Wall in 1922 sparked an intermittent series of hostile confrontations with the British authorities over the next five years. As the British presence became more familiar and its methods of governance more sophisticated, challenges to the central administration were replaced by growing interethnic competition for privilege, autonomy, and political leverage within the Mandate system. This shift of tensions from solidarity against the foreign administration to intercommunal rivalry was compounded by Britain's infamous "divide-and-rule" strategy in Palestine (Schaeffer 1990: 100). This policy was shaped by "considerations which have little to do with the needs or desires of the people who are to be divided" and in Jerusalem culminated in a "divide-and-quit" exit strategy (Kumar 1997: 6).

For the purpose of municipal governance, the British designated twelve wards according to religious majorities—six Jewish, four Muslim and two Christian—each gerrymandered to achieve maximum ethnic homogeneity. These were the first ethnic fault-lines to be formally inscribed in Jerusalem during the twentieth century (Benvenisti 1996: 56). This approach fostered constant intergroup competition in a system mediated by the British, deepening animosities between traditional rivals in Palestine.

Throughout the late 1920s and 1930s, Jewish immigration to Palestine increased dramatically. The growing Jewish presence in Palestine, which peaked around 1936, sparked a series of riots that were centered in Jerusalem and coincided roughly with major waves of immigration. These episodes involved Israelis, British soldiers, and Arabs, claiming several thousand lives (Gilbert 1996: 151). Sir Charles Tegart, an Irish expert in counterterrorism, was given command of approximately 28,000 British soldiers and policemen in order to improve security conditions in response to the Arab rebellion. This was accomplished through security fences, police fortresses, concrete guard posts, aggressive physical interrogation of Arab suspects, and the introduction of Doberman attack dogs from South Africa. The barbed wire fence constructed under his direction sealed the northern boundary of Palestine with Lebanon, cutting off a valuable trade link and provoking fresh acts of defiance by Arab Palestinians (Segev 2000: 415).

The rapid destabilization resulting from these violent episodes generated concern in the international community. By late 1938 the British Peel Commission recommended an annual ceiling on the influx of Jews to Palestine in order to appease the Arabs. The Peel Commission report also recommended the partition of Palestine along ethnic lines, while retaining control over Jerusalem in the hands of an international administration, echoing and amplifying the recommendations embedded in the Sykes-Picot Agreement twenty years before.

This seemingly cynical solution to Palestine's interethnic conflict was a precursor of the physical partition of the city that took place almost exactly ten years later. The chair of the Commission, Sir John Woodhead, noted that the primary concern to be anticipated from the proposed partition related to security along the boundary between rival populations, which were presumed to be homogeneous. His report recommended that the problem of breaches "would have to be solved by the construction along the boundary of a road with a railing down the middle" (Wasserstein 2001: 113ff). Woodhead's proposal reflects the British assumption that physical proximity was a root cause of ethnic conflict, rather than the tensions related to entitlement, sovereignty, and injustice.

Though prescient, the Peel Commission report was repugnant to many Israeli Jews and Arabs alike. Jews rejected any limitations imposed upon immigration, citing the moral imperative presented by increasingly hostile anti-Semitism in Europe and elsewhere. Arabs rejected the idea of an informal Jewish state implied by a permanent boundary, intensifying their defense of a mixed and communal state in Palestine. The report's recommendations were largely dismissed in Palestine and abroad (Gilbert 1996; Wasserstein 2001). Still, the insecurities it aroused accelerated the disintegration of Jewish-Arab relations. Meanwhile, the report planted the idea of partition as a legitimate settlement strategy in the minds, or least the imagination, of foreign diplomats to confront the conundrum of Palestine in subsequent decades.

Trapped in a diplomatic bind between Arabs and Jews in Palestine, the British mandate authorities finally endorsed legal limitations on Jewish immigration with their approval of the 1939 MacDonald White Paper. Jewish leaders complained that this new policy contradicted the Balfour Declaration. The more radical and militant political factions declared that the end of the British Mandate was their primary political aim. On the eve of World War II, Jewish paramilitaries intensified their engagement with their internal enemies on two fronts.

As violent exchanges multiplied, the shape and composition of Jerusalem changed. British administrators increasingly retreated into the fortified "Bevingrad" compound carved out of the central city, while the mixed residential suburbs of Jerusalem were spontaneously redrawn as a patchwork of largely homogeneous ethnic enclaves. These intensifying cycles of segregation and intercommunal violence would almost certainly have erupted into civil war had the larger international crisis not intervened to put the Palestinian question on hold until 1945 (Wasserstein 2001: 123).

Escalation

By the close of World War II, the political landscape in Palestine had undergone a massive alteration. Among the most immediate and important repercussions of the global upheaval was the gradual emergence of international support for an Israeli state, prompted by German atrocities against the Jews during the Holocaust, the dramatic increase in immigration to Palestine by European and Russian Jews, and the flagging enthusiasm for colonial projects felt by a British government crippled by the war.

Having lost its capacity and its appetite for the continued maintenance of an unpopular mandate administration and with security conditions eroding, Britain initiated its withdrawal from Palestine. Chief Justice Sir William Fitzgerald was commissioned to coordinate the transfer of the reins of municipal government to local actors in Jerusalem. His observations echoed those of the Peel Commission seven years before: "normal majoritarian democratic solutions" would not be effective, and "the only hope of a cure lies in a surgical operation" (quoted in Wasserstein 2001: 122). Partition was sanctioned by anxious and retreating foreign authorities as a solution of last resort for the containment of burgeoning ethnic antagonisms.

Low-intensity intercommunal tensions shaped social relations in Palestine since the 1920s. A gradual voluntary process of population displacement in Jerusalem had been underway for several decades prior to the end of the British mandate there. By the late 1940s, Arab and Jewish populations in Palestine in general tended to be separate and homogeneous, and this trend was clearly reflected in the shifting demographics of Jerusalem as well.

By 1947 Jerusalem was physically and functionally divided into Arab and Jewish zones in a patchwork configuration, not monolithic territories on either side of a dividing line. Polarization would come later, with the departure of the British and civil war, but in the meantime ethnic clusters of an increasingly homogeneous nature created informal social boundaries in the city. These were a precursor for Jerusalem's subsequent formal and physical partition.

Negotiations

As mutual suspicion between the two communities mounted through 1947, Britain hastened its departure from Palestine, leaving its domestic problems to be resolved by the United Nations. The prospect of the British pullout did little to assuage the insecurity of Jews and Arabs in Palestine. Despite their historic ambivalence, both groups had relied on the mitigating influence of the British, who acted as brokers and mediators through many treacherous diplomatic passages. Anticipation of a scramble for power and territory following the British pullout intensified intergroup antagonism.

Confronted with an alarming power vacuum and intercommunal tensions near a breaking point, the United Nations General Assembly passed Resolution 181 in late November 1947. It called for the internationalization of Jerusalem and a revised partition plan for Palestine. Intended to preempt civil war, the announcement of this partition plan prompted Palestinians to stage a three-day general strike while both sides prepared for war. Jerusalem became the center for many significant political events to follow. Situated deep within the West Bank territory that had been assigned to Arab control by the United Nations partition plan, Jerusalem was a cul-de-sac and a symbolic stronghold of Israeli-Jewish sovereignty in the region.

As popular fear mounted, the movement of civilians away from their homes in mixed areas toward friendly ethnic clusters increased. British administrators looked on with some disbelief as the capital city descended into chaos. Jewish forces set up roadblocks where even British army and police vehicles were occasionally stopped and searched when entering Jewish-held areas. The contours of the partition line reaching from the village of Beit Safafa in the south to the Batei Pagi neighborhood in the north by this time had been established with some firmness through spontaneous processes of internal migration and armed conflict. The informal division of Jerusalem was accomplished at this time, to be converted into a formal boundary almost exactly a year later with the signing of the armistice agreement between Israel and Jordan.

Emergence

Six months of siege and civil war cemented hostilities between the two rival factions, but military maneuvers during this period altered the partition line very little. Hostilities were formally ended with a ceasefire agreement negotiated by Israeli and Jordanian representatives on 30 November 1948. Their most pressing task was to specify and formalize the line of confrontation through the city, which had evolved in a relatively spontaneous manner up to that time. Its contours were drawn on a city map projected at a scale of 1:20,000. This map had been unfurled on the dirty floor of an abandoned house in the Musrara quarter of the city, itself located in neutral territory along the line of confrontation.

Israeli lieutenant colonel Moshe Dayan, Jerusalem's district com-

Figure 5.2. Citizens' spontaneous barricades preceded the construction of an official armistice line in Jerusalem, this one built in the Mamila neighborhood from dirt, stone, and refuse, November 1948. Israeli Government Press Office, used by permission.

mander, traced the Israeli line to the west with a green wax pencil while his Jordanian counterpart, Lieutenant-Colonel Abdullah al-Tal, commander of the Jordanian forces in Jerusalem, drew a roughly parallel boundary in red wax pencil to the east (Benvenisti 1996: 57). These freehand gestures constituted the genesis of the Green Line in Jerusalem.

This Line was comprised of two boundaries with a no man's land of approximately 3 square km in between, designed to discourage and prevent hostile incursions. This physical swath widened and narrowed in response to its context, passing through dense sections of the city and rendering worthless thousands of structures and large areas of private property. Though the Green Line was intended to be a temporary measure pending a full diplomatic settlement, for the next nineteen years it remained. Israeli Defense Force units and Arab Legion soldiers maintained a stable, if uneasy, truce across the gap. The wax pencil lines on the map themselves corresponded to strips of urban terrain about 60 meters wide, provoking serious accidents and misunderstandings later on regarding the exact military status of streets and properties falling within their cartographic shadow—including about 125 houses and large sections of the Old City walls.

On 3 April 1949, negotiations with the Jordanian government in Rhodes culminated in the signing of an Israeli-Jordanian General Armistice Agreement. Emphasizing the provisional nature of the boundaries recognized by the armistice, the Jordanian-Israeli agreement stated: "no provision of this Agreement shall in any way prejudice the rights, claims, and positions of either Party hereto in the peaceful settlement of the Palestine questions, the provisions of this Agreement being dictated exclusively by military considerations" (Art. II.2). Still, the Rhodes Agreement accepted the Dayan-al-Tal map as the sole binding document regarding the division of the city and, in the process, recognized only Jordanian and Israeli sovereignty as relevant to the question of the city's current and future status.

Jordanian recognition of the state of Israel was viewed by many Palestinians as an act of betrayal and capitulation. Their disappointment was compounded by the fact that the Green Line was approved by Jordanian officials who had only limited familiarity with the city and the value of the land lost or sacrificed in the process of formal partition. Jordanian negotiators had ceded productive land that had belonged to Palestinians for centuries, upon which the livelihood of whole Palestinian villages depended. The announcement of the armistice agreement in effect opened up a new front in the domestic war for sovereignty in Palestine, as native Palestinian communities refused to accept partition and felt increasingly alienated from Jordanian administrators.

Resentment intensified in subsequent decades as Jordanian investment in East Jerusalem diminished. Meanwhile West Jerusalem grew dramatically with steady rates of immigration. In sharp contrast to King Abdullah's neglect of Jerusalem, Ben-Gurion embraced the city as "an organic and inseparable part of the state . . . the very soul of our people" (Benvenisti 1976: 12). Development within the two halves of Jerusalem here sharply diverged.

Duration

From 1948 until 1967 the partition line could be legally traversed at only one crossing point known as the Mandelbaum Gate, less than a kilometer north of the Damascus Gate. Diplomats, Christian clergy, pilgrims, and privileged foreigners were allowed to pass between the Jewish and Arab sectors; Jewish and Palestinian residents were not. Along the Green Line in Jerusalem,

Figure 5.3. The partitions of Jerusalem around 1950, designed with staggered openings to limit the sniper's view where the Green Line skirted populated Israeli areas. Zev Radovan, used by permission.

thirty-one fortified surveillance positions were built: twenty-two by the Jordanian forces and nine by the Israeli Army (Kliot 1999: 204). In addition, high barricades were built in staggered layers where large streets ran perpendicular to the boundary in order to shield Israeli pedestrians from Jordanian snipers positioned above on the Old City walls.

During the fourteen years following its creation in 1948, the Dayan-al-Tal partition line as it passed through Jerusalem was neither fenced nor marked. With an increasing incidence of illegal crossings, violent confrontations and accidental incursions by civilians into the no man's land, the Israelis decided to fence the border in 1962, less than a year after the construction of the Berlin Wall began. Ten miles of barbed wire barricades and tens of thousands of landmines were then inserted into the no man's land, completing the physical partition of the city (Benvenisti 1996: 61).

The almost hermetic seal of the Green Line in Jerusalem was broken by a swift series of events beginning with the Jordanian army's attempt to capture Government House on 5 June 1967. They were a direct result of hostilities between Israeli and Egyptian forces in the Sinai Peninsula. This was the first attempt to secure territory by military means across the Green Line since 1948 and it resulted in a series of decisive military responses from the Israeli government, known subsequently as the Six-Day War. Before most politicians in the Middle East and beyond were fully aware of what was taking place, Israel had responded to the Jordanian assault with the successful capture of East Jerusalem and large portions of the West Bank from Jordan, the Golan Heights from Syria, and the Sinai peninsula from Egypt. The majority of these territorial acquisitions were forfeited by Israel during subsequent settlement negotiations, but East Jerusalem was retained despite its classification as "occupied Arab territory" by the United Nations. The weeks following Israel's surprise victory brought the unification of Jerusalem after nineteen years of division.

Dismantling

The poignancy of this moment can hardly be exaggerated. Lieutenant-General Moshe Dayan, then minister of defense, ordered the demolition of all barricades and partitions along the former Green Line immediately following the capitulation of the Jordanian government on 7 June 1967. This was Dayan's first command following the city's capture, and it was repeated several times in the days that followed. Dayan, a coauthor of the line in 1948, was eager to hasten the removal of "ugly walls that cut grotesquely across this city" (quoted in Wasserstein 2001: 208) and to unify the two alienated halves of Jerusalem.

By noon on 29 June all barriers had disappeared from the city and citizens from both sides were encouraged to cross over the scar of the Green Line. Several observers noted that "a heavy air of nostalgia" permeated this unexpected episode of "mutual invasion" (Benvenisti 1976: 127). This extraordinary moment in the history of the city was unmarked by hostilities. Thirty years later, the assessment of communal relations had grown much more somber: "Jerusalem is a city held together by force. Take away Israel's coercive powers, and the city splits on the ethnic fault line" (Benvenisti 1982: 199). This prophecy may have been fulfilled in 2002, when Israel began building a "security fence" throughout Jerusalem and the West Bank, in some cases making additional claims to disputed Palestinian properties by penetrating beyond the former Green Line in northward and eastward directions, a topic addressed in greater detail in the Epilogue.

Impacts

Quantitative estimates regarding the impact of partition on Jerusalem residents are rare, due perhaps to the continuing volatility of the political situation in Israel and the West Bank, the political sensitivity of all statistics relating to demographics and living conditions in the city, the difficulty of conducting social surveys among Palestinians whose legal status is ambiguous and who are frequently suspicious of scrutiny, and the limited access for researchers to government documents which have been withheld because their content is assumed to be politically inflammatory. Whatever the reasons, even the most basic evaluation of human and material impacts resulting from the partition of Jerusalem must rely on speculation.

Looking at the city a whole in the years that followed partition in 1948, it is clear that its physical division had a devastating effect on both Israeli and Palestinian residents. Most reliable sources estimate between 8,000 and 14,000 combatant and noncombatant deaths resulting from the Arab-Israeli civil war in 1948 (White 2003). These were the lives lost in the process of partitioning Israel from the West Bank. One hundred or more casualties occurred between 1948 and 1967 along the Green Line, despite the fact that it had been created in order to prevent further conflict and bloodshed. The number of persons wounded during the same time-span is assumed to be many times the number of dead. In the months leading up to the war, the interethnic boundary hardened and massive internal migration took place within Jerusalem to complete the demographic segregation of the city.

By late April 1948, more than 25,000 Palestinians living in West Jerusalem had left to find new homes in East Jerusalem, elsewhere in the West Bank, or outside the country. The majority of Jews living in the Jordanian-held sectors of the city resided in the Jewish quarter of the Old City, which was completely abandoned as more than 2,000 residents became refugees in western Jerusalem. Between 1946 and 1948, more than 30,000 Jews left Jerusalem altogether.

Those who stayed witnessed an extraordinary splitting exercise. The two halves of a city that had once been knitted together so tightly, firmly fastened by the religious and commercial activities of the Old City, bifurcated rapidly and were catapulted along two quite separate developmental paths. Each formed a new business and commercial center as former trade intersections were nullified by the Green Line. As with every other divided city, Jerusalem was obliged to duplicate itself in every conceivable way. It developed two road systems, two hospital systems, two municipalities, two school systems, two transportation networks, two identities, and two economies.

As the development of East and West Jerusalem proceeded in two very different directions, the standards of living on either side of the Green Line became increasingly disparate. While West Jerusalem shifted its commercial and business center away from the Old City walls to the west, north, and south, the population and prosperity of East Jerusalem shrank, dragging the living conditions of Palestinian residents down along with them.

The dereliction that infiltrated every neighborhood adjacent to the Green Line during the period of partition caused a strange reversal of traditional development patterns. In areas close to the center of the city, where real estate had once been most valuable, houses and businesses were either abandoned or occupied by the poorest citizens of Jerusalem, who could not afford to live elsewhere in the city. These frontier residents were often immigrants, refugees, or the destitute. Being so close to the border brought many hazards and anxieties not felt by residents living even a few blocks away.

In West Jerusalem, Jewish immigrants were installed along the Green Line in the largely ruined neighborhood of Musrara to provide visible evidence that every part of Jewish-held Jerusalem—including those that had previously been occupied by Arabs—was possessed by the state of Israel in an active and irreversible way. A Moroccan Jew living in this neighborhood described a life full of uncertainty and apprehension:

If I took a wrong step, I would be shot by an Arab sniper . . . stones were thrown and bullets fired through my window from the other side . . . because it was such a dangerous place to live, the authorities never required me to pay rent or to buy the house. (Tamari 1999: 123)

All these dangers, both real and imagined, took a heavy toll on those obliged to live and work near the partition between East and West Jerusalem.

While systematic studies are not available regarding the impacts of proximity on the psychological health of these residents, numerous anecdotes draw a fairly consistent picture of sublimated fears and routine denial. Because the city was completely bifurcated by the Green Line, most of its inhabitants became accustomed to life in one half or the other and by degrees learned to forget that another reality and another city continued to evolve nearby.

This amnesia probably came more easily to Jewish residents of West Jerusalem than to their counterparts in the East, since the net impacts of partition were for them less burdensome and less pronounced. The apathy and mutual avoidance forcibly imposed during the years of partition continued in large part afterward on a voluntary basis, prompting one scholar to observe that "Israel's conquest of Jerusalem [in 1967] and the reunification of the city did not change the components of the conflict, merely the character of the struggle" (Benvenisti 1982: 114).

Beginning with these massive and lopsided population shifts, living and working conditions for the average Palestinian declined further and more sharply than those affecting the average Israeli. Because the Jordanian government focused its development investments on Amman after the status of Jerusalem was temporarily stabilized, Palestinian professionals in Jerusalem were drawn away to the capital so that population growth in East Jerusalem lagged behind the rate of natural increase.

Palestinian residents of East Jerusalem had suffered a triple blow: they believed that their interests had been sorely compromised by the armistice agreement signed on their behalf by the Jordanian government; their economic prospects were worse than ever while the stress of refugee influxes placed unusual strains on the public coffers; and their political patrons decided against aggressive development schemes for their part of the city, appearing content to allow Jerusalem to languish in geographic and political isolation. These concerns were compounded by unreliable supplies of electricity and water, lost access to Jerusalem's central business district and surrounding towns, and the rapid hemorrhaging of white-collar jobs.

Determined to secure and expand their holdings in West Jerusalem, the Israeli government adopted a strategy quite distinct from that of the Jordanians. It encouraged immigration and relocated government ministries from Tel Aviv to Jerusalem in order to anchor the middle class and improve employment prospects. Physical infrastructure projects and housing construction flourished as politicians burnished poetic remarks regarding the importance of Jerusalem to the Israeli state and psyche. Though its development was strikingly swift and efficient in relation to the situation in East Jerusalem, West Jerusalem still suffered a steady decline between 1948 and 1967 in relation to more prosperous Israeli cities like Haifa and Tel Aviv.

The civil war left Jerusalem at the end of a cul-de-sac with traditional links to its northern and southern agricultural hinterlands severed, the commercial markets in the West Bank lost, and the religious and tourist destinations in the Old City now out of reach. The former commercial hub of the Mamilla declined due to its close proximity to the Green Line, and the flatlands around Talbiya that had been earmarked for industrial development were likewise overlooked for investment, due to their vulnerability to Jordanian artillery.

A stark disparity of social conditions and opportunity between Israeli and Palestinian residents of Jerusalem developed during the period of physical partition and did not disappear with the barricades. It quickly became obvious to all observers that the distrust and rivalry between ethnic groups in the city that had brought about violent conflict in 1948 were continuing to poison the well of urban coexistence nineteen years later. These resentments and prejudices were now projected onto a very different set of political relationships.

By 1967, Israel had evolved into an extraordinarily powerful, prosperous, stable country in which patriotic fervor had achieved mythical proportions and was deeply intertwined with the symbolism of Jerusalem. Meanwhile the Palestinians lacked sovereignty, a formal political apparatus, economic leverage, and influential allies. Their weakness in relation to their domestic rivals had never been more pronounced.

Residents of East Jerusalem in the aftermath of the Six-Day War found themselves the secondary citizens of a second and decidedly lesser Jerusalem. By the time Jerusalem was physically unified in 1967, its Palestinian residents accounted for 26 percent of its overall population but only 6 percent of the purchasing power in the city; 60 percent of East Jerusalem residents lacked running water and 30 percent lacked electricity, while all the residents of West Jerusalem enjoyed these basic amenities. Per capita income was four times higher in West than in East Jerusalem, where illiteracy was 2.5 times more common and the likelihood of meeting a university graduate five times lower.

Their systematic disenfranchisement by the Israeli government was commonly rationalized with reference to their refusal to participate in municipal government and an ambiguous legal status that deprived them of the basic human and communal rights automatically enjoyed by their Israeli counterparts. These inequities persist in Jerusalem and beyond, insuring that a reliable peace will be postponed until they are addressed in a fair and comprehensive manner.

Despite its physical disappearance in 1967, Jerusalem's Green Line lives on in ghostlike form and lingers in common parlance. Its contours are still etched in the minds of Palestinians in particular, many of whom still anticipate a settlement with Israel in which the Green Line is reactivated as an

Figures 5.4 and 5.5. The Green Line in Jerusalem's Mamilla quarter before and after 1967, less than a mile from the Damascus Gate. Zev Radovan, used by permission.

Figure 5.6. Former no-man's-land in central Jerusalem c. 2003, never quite reclaimed by the city and derelict in appearance. Authors.

international border, giving definition to a future sovereign territory of their own.

The Green Line is still the last legal and internationally recognized territorial boundary between Israeli and the disputed territories west of the Jordan River. It remains a fold in the mental map of all Jerusalemites, defining perceptions of vulnerability. Though gradually disappearing with new development, the no man's land can still be felt as derelict space in the heart of the city.

Citizens of Jerusalem from both sides of the city continue to treat the Line as an invisible border, on the other side of which things are different. Many of these perceived discrepancies are real. The rights, services and opportunities afforded by citizenship in Jerusalem diminish measurably east of the former Green Line, fostering ongoing conditions of relative deprivation due to an unbalanced allocation of resources. The Green Line remains a deeply etched landmark in the mental landscape of Jerusalem's residents.

Chapter 6
Mostar

Introduction

Lejla was fourteen when the first phase of interethnic conflict began in Mostar. Her family had been in the city for generations, and her relatives in Mostar resided on both the old and new sides of the town. When Serbian extremists took control of the Yugoslav national army in 1992 and used it to punish Mostar for following the secession of Bosnia-Herzegovina from the rump of Yugoslavia, Leila and her family were forced to move. They abandoned their apartment in East Mostar when Serbian forces occupied that side of the Neretva River, which formed a natural border between those massed to defend the city and those attempting to overwhelm it. At first she lived with relatives in the newer, western part of the city. Later her family retreated to the Dalmatian coast in order to avoid the escalating violence that claimed the lives of many civilians.

Lejla described a unified effort on the part of Mostar's Bosniak and Croatian residents at that time to defend their city against the hostile Serbian forces that planned to occupy Bosnian territory as far west as Mostar to form a Greater Serbia. When this effort failed, local forces expelled the Serbian army—what she called "its extreme parts." Lejla and her family returned from the coast to celebrate the liberation of Mostar and resume a normal life. What followed was the Second Battle of Mostar, and a period of violence that Lejla calls "even the worst part . . . maybe one's worst nightmares, you know, but it really happened . . . it really happened."

Around 9 May 1993, a highly organized program of ethnic cleansing was undertaken by Croatian paramilitary units against the Muslim residents of Mostar. Having acquired lists of occupants of the major apartment blocks in western Mostar, paramilitary soldiers went from door to door examining the names of the residents in order to identify and confirm the Muslims who were to be removed. Along with hundreds of others, Lejla and her family were wakened late at night by Croatian soldiers. They were

TABLE 6.1. BASIC FACTS REGARDING THE PHYSICAL PARTITION OF MOSTAR

Antagonisms	Croatians v. Bosniaks, Christians v. Muslims
Name	The Boulevard, or *Bulevar Narodne Revolucije*
Location	The partition line ran roughly north-south and parallel to the Neretva River as it passed through the dense sections of the city. It began its course through Mostar at the base of Hum Hill in the south and ran due north, coinciding with the width and length of the Boulevard before turning eastward on a side street just north of the Gymnasium and Spanish Square, then followed Santica Street northward for 30 m before slanting in a northeast direction and cutting through a complex of ruined apartments to arrive at the river bank, and from that point forward corresponds to the winding median of the river itself beyond the north military campus.
Context	The front line followed clear open spaces available within the constraints of combat, never touching the eastern bank of the river or interrupting the historic fabric in the city. Its placement represented a physical compromise between the practical advantages of a wide avenue in support of a prolonged urban stalemate and the military ambitions of the Croatian forces to press as far as possible toward the river. The most active and violent section of the front line falls along the Boulevard, which was hemmed in on both sides by two roughly symmetrical street walls made up of large, abandoned concrete buildings ranging 3–5 storys in height.
Size	The partition line for most of its course through Mostar was the width of the Boulevard: about 30 m. On both sides, combatants were ensconced in low, protected fortifications usually set into the basement story of the abandoned buildings along its length. When the line diverged from the Boulevard north of the Spanish Square, jogging eastward to merge with Santic Street, it narrowed and became noticeably more porous due to the looser configuration of surrounding buildings.
Porosity	During the first days following its establishment, in the second week of May 1993, limited pedestrian and vehicular movement across the partition line was allowed. For several months following the violent expulsion or voluntary departure of all Muslim citizens residing in the western section of the city, no further crossings were permitted. The entire length of the urban boundary was militarized for the remainder of the civil war. During calm periods a limited number of women could cross from east to west to visit

relatives or shop; eastward visits were very rare, given the crippled condition of the Bosniak neighborhoods. Outside Mostar's municipal boundaries, physical barriers did not mark the boundaries dividing Croatian and Bosniak territories during that latter phase of the war, though these were monitored and defended.

Materials	Asphalt, concrete, sandbags, barbed wire, ruined concrete structures, ruined machinery.
Status	Mostar has been unified since the creation of the Federation of Bosnia-Herzegovina on 18 March 1994. After that time, partition line fortifications and checkpoints were dismantled, but willingness to cross over the former boundary separating hostile forces in the city was very slow to evolve.
Actors	Designed and built by paramilitary combatants, subsidized by unofficial governments.

collected and put onto buses waiting below without a chance to collect any of their belongings, and they were told, according to Lejla, "Come, now . . . you have to get up from your beds if you want to live!"

Two buses took the Muslims who had been rounded up that night in western Mostar to the front line and ejected them there. Croatian soldiers forced them to walk across sandbagged military positions along the Boulevard in single file, calling out to the civilians as they went, "Just go! Go to your side!" Lejla described the atmosphere that night as approaching "total anarchy," but also observed that the expulsion process appeared to have been well planned in advance. Having been forced to abandon their home on Mostar's east side the year before, now Lejla's family were forced out of their new home on the west side by an informal militia comprised in part of their former allies and neighbors.

Because of the unexpected nature of these events, very few of Mostar's residents were aware of what was happening. When Lejla bumped into her grandmother the next day, she asked if Lejla wanted to join her for a cup of coffee, having heard nothing about the expulsion of Muslims the night before. The process of ethnic cleansing was incremental and secretive. Lejla described it as "something like just rolling and rolling and growing and going on" with the understanding that "no one wants you or gives you the chance to leave . . . just probably to disappear into the air."

Many of the Muslim residents forced into east Mostar that night told

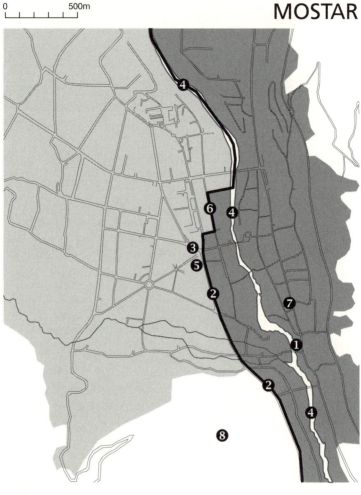

0   500m

East Mostar, predominantly Bosniak & Muslim

West Mostar, predominantly Croatian & Catholic

— partition line 1992-95

❶ Old Bridge   ❺ Central High School
❷ Boulevard   ❻ Santic Street
❸ Spanish Square   ❼ Karazdog-beg Mosque
❹ Neretva River   ❽ Hum Hill

Figure 6.1. Map of Mostar's partition, 1992–1995. Mostar is located at 43°20′N, 17°48′E, 45 km inland in the southeastern portion of Bosnia along the Neretva River. Bosnia-Herzegovina is bounded by Croatia to the southwest and by Serbia and Montenegro to the East. Mostar lies 464 km east of Rome and 552 km southeast of Vienna. Authors.

their story on a local radio station the next morning, but their efforts came too late. The tide of violence continued to push Muslim residents of western Mostar across the new ethnic divide, the Boulevard of National Revolution running parallel to and about 100 meters west of the Neretva River. Lejla and her family were fortunate. Their identification cards allowed them to travel back across the front line on a United Nations shuttle bus just before the front line was completely sealed to all further civilian traffic. From the west side of the city they were able to board a regular bus to Zagreb, where relatives lent them money for air tickets to Istanbul. Lejla spent the next two years in Turkey and moved back to Mostar in 1995, as soon as hostilities were halted by the signing of the Dayton Accords.

Upon her return, she found Mostar physically and socially shattered. The physical ruins of the city affect Mostar's residents in a mostly subconscious way, according to Lejla. She said it has been difficult to retain a positive and hopeful outlook due the sluggishness of the city's recovery. Most important, few of her friends and relatives remained or returned—perhaps fewer than 20 percent of the original residents could be found there by 1996. In the meantime, tens of thousands of Bosnian refugees from the countryside had appropriated apartments in Mostar, though they had never lived in the city before. Since the second phase of the war, Lejla observes, there are more Mostarians all over the world than there are in Mostar itself. Under such circumstances a person does not belong to a city but, Lejla observed, "you belong to your memories . . . and I wouldn't say that I was not disappointed" (Lejla C. 2001).

Background

Mostar was a quiet, provincial outpost of the Ottoman empire until the late nineteenth century. When the Treaty of Berlin gave the Austro-Hungarian monarchy control over Croatia and Bosnia-Herzegovina in 1878, an energetic and ambitious project of expansion and upgrading was immediately enacted. As foreign investment increased and local jobs multiplied, Bosniak and Croatian citizens received preferential treatment over Serbians, who were considered dangerous by colonial administrators due to their traditional desire for political autonomy and their traditional antipathy toward foreign powers.

In July 1908 the Young Turks established a constitutional government in Istanbul, and concerns were raised in Austria-Hungary that the new

Turkish leadership, with assistance from the Russians, might attempt to reclaim the formerly Ottoman territories in Austrian possession. Acting quickly to avoid the loss of its recent investments in Bosnia-Herzegovina, Austria-Hungary annexed the entire territory in October. This action generated strong negative reactions both internationally and regionally, especially among Serbian nationalists, who imagined a Serbian state with Mostar at its western edge.

These resentments and aspirations contributed to the Balkan War of 1912. Still, the 1908 annexation succeeded and rapid urban development in Mostar continued. Expanding westward away from the historic core and Neretva River, new commercial and residential areas were constructed according to Austrian standards calling for wide streets, landmark institutional structures, geometric planning, green public spaces, and modern infrastructure.

The largest and most important avenue in the city—later named the Boulevard of the National Revolution—functioned as a border between the new and old parts of the city. It also provided a corridor for economic growth more accessible to vehicles than the narrow and winding streets of the medieval Ottoman neighborhoods to the east. Between 1890 and 1910 Mostar experienced a building boom. Schools, libraries, hotels, and administrative offices were built in grand, formal styles common in Vienna but unfamiliar to Bosnians. Railroad tracks appeared along the Boulevard to facilitate streetcars and passenger trains from the Dalmatian coast.

Industrial expansion benefited from production methods and management techniques introduced by the Austrians. Mostar enjoyed a diverse, prosperous, and competitive economy for the last time in its history. The essential role played by Bosnia-Herzegovina in the outbreak of World War I is well known. The dissolution of the Austro-Hungarian Empire in 1918 coincided with the war's conclusion.

That same year Bosnia-Herzegovina joined the newly established Kingdom of Serbs, Croats, and Slovenians. In the decades that followed, leading nationalist politicians explored ways to carve sovereign states out of the Balkan kingdom. As the major European nations were immersed in their own concerns during the prologue to World War II, Croatian and Serbian leaders formalized their strategems with the signing of the Cvetković-Maček Agreement in 1939. This plan called for the partition of Bosnia and Herzegovina for subsequent annexation by Serbia and Croatia respectively. No provisions for nationhood were made for Bosniaks, though they constituted the majority of the citizens in the territory to be divided.

The end of World War II interrupted these plans for a compromise between regional rivals at the expense of the Bosniaks. Because Bosnia-Herzegovina was retained as a republic of equal standing in the new state of Yugoslavia, the republics of Croatia and Serbia were considerably smaller than the territories envisioned in the Cvetković-Maček partition scheme. All the same, that document had a lasting influence on the imaginations and ambitions of hard-line Serbian and Croatian nationalist leaders over the next fifty years. It asserted the physical partition of Bosnian territory as a feasible diplomatic objective, and it set a precedent for the purposeful neglect of Bosniak interests whenever programs for territorial expansion were engineered by their larger and more powerful neighbors.

Postwar president Marshal Josip Broz Tito staked his political career on his capacity to neutralize rivalry between the republics of Yugoslavia, which corresponded closely to the major ethnic communities in the country. The exception was Bosnia, notable for its tradition of social pluralism and tolerance despite a Muslim majority. For thirty years the combination of Tito's charismatic leadership and a national economy heavily subsidized by international aid allowed Yugoslavia to prosper and kept ethnic tensions in abeyance. With Tito's death in 1980 and the conclusion of the Cold War approximately nine years later, Yugoslavia was dispatched by circumstance as an orphan on the doorstep of Europe, with its international clout much diminished and large amounts of foreign debt.

Escalation

The separatist provocations of ultranationalist leaders active at the regional level, coinciding with a period of great uncertainty and instability, accelerated the disintegration of the former Yugoslavia after 1989. In February 1991, Croatian president Franjo Tudjman and Serbian president Slobodan Milošević turned back the political clock to 1939 by conducting a series of secret meetings to discuss the partition of Bosnia-Herzegovina; the territory was to be divided between their two would-be states in deference to the Cvetković-Maček Agreement.

During the next eighteen months, all the major republics announced their secession from the former Yugoslavia, ultimately comprising only the "rump" of Serbia and Montenegro. On 1 March 1992, a majority of Bosnian Muslims and Croats voted in favor of independence, despite strong opposition from many Bosnian Serbs. Serbians in Bosnia rapidly organized paramilitary units to consolidate and expand their control over as much territory as possible, using military aggression and intimidation to flush out members of rival ethnic groups from the various enclaves they intended to claim.

These activities marked the beginning of a civil war in Bosnia-Herzegovina. Personnel and heavy artillery belonging to the Yugoslav National Army were transferred from Slovenia to Bosnia in the summer of 1991 to support the hostile annexation of Bosnian land by Croatian and Serbian paramilitaries. Mostar assumed a central role in the ensuing conflict because it is located on the traditional boundary between predominantly Croatian territory to the west and predominantly Serbian territory to the east.

A famously beautiful and pleasant city along a major transportation route, it had served for centuries as a hub for commerce and administration in the region. Its eventual destruction was linked to the extraordinary social history of the city: mixed, cosmopolitan, and liberal. Prior to the civil war, Mostar's residents seemed to personify the spirit of peaceful coexistence among ethnic communities in the region. This multi-ethnic spirit was out of keeping with the territorial ambitions driving political events in the early 1990s.

By September 1991 the Yugoslav National Army was patrolling the streets of Mostar under an ominous and increasingly ambiguous mandate. In April 1992, one month after the decision to secede was reached by public referendum, the first battle of Mostar began, when Serbian forces under the aegis of the Yugoslav National Army attacked the city from elevated positions in the east. All Muslim and Croatian residents of east Mostar were immediately forced to abandon their homes and take up temporary quarters on the other side of the Neretva River, which served as a natural partition line during that initial period of hostilities. This conflict pitted Bosnians defending their autonomy against Serbian extremists trying to withhold it. Bosnians found solidarity in this cause, somehow succeeding in defending their homes despite the lopsided nature of the conflict and the loss of hundreds of lives.

Negotiations

While this struggle intensified, a second secret meeting allegedly took place between high level Serbian and Croatian authorities regarding the partition and annexation of Bosnia-Herzegovina. Late in April 1992, Bosnian Croat leader Mate Boban discussed the particulars of Bosnia's future physical partition at considerable length with Božidar Vučurević, the mayor of Trebinje and one of the key Serbian nationalist politicians in the eastern, Serbian-controlled part of Bosnia. Their meeting is significant because it occurred during the high point of hostilities between their respective paramilitary forces in the struggle for Bosnian territory. It postulated a new political alliance between active enemies based on shared Christian beliefs, and it is the first official conversation on record regarding the location of a physical border between ethnic communities in Mostar. It is instructive to review Mayor Vučurević's description of the discussion at length.

[Mate Boban and I] understood that our war was leading nowhere. Croats and Serbs are Christian peoples and original inhabitants of the country—our killing and expelling one another was leading nowhere. We both believed that there was enough space in this region for both peoples, and that only an unfortunate configuration of circumstances had brought us to war against each other. At our first meeting we discussed the final resolution of the war between Croats and Serbs in Herzegovina. . . . What we discussed quite concretely was the partition of Herzegovina. I proposed an end to the war and an agreement on how to establish a Serb-Croat border in our area. When Boban asked me where the border should run, I proposed the most natural one—the River Neretva. The Croats would get the right bank and the Serbs the left one. Boban asked me what about the Muslims. I answered that the place for this semi-people was in between—in the Neretva. We both laughed at my reply, drank coffee and agreed to continue negotiations about concrete questions for the benefit of our peoples. (Quoted in Barnsdale 2001)

The satisfactory progress made during this initial meeting led to a second conversation of an even more pragmatic nature, conducted once more in secrecy, at the Graz airport, between Boban and Radovan Karadžić, leader of the Serbian Democratic Party dedicated to the establishment of a Greater Serbia through the annexation of Bosnian territory. The point of the conversation was to determine an optimal boundary between Greater Croatia and Greater Serbia. The tricky part was how to divide Mostar.

It was tentatively agreed that instead of adopting the river as an international boundary—a decision that would cede full control of the historic city to Serbia—Marshall Tito Street, the main commercial artery of eastern Mostar, would be used as a partition line (Kumar 1997: 55). This concession left most of Mostar's most important historic places in Croatian hands and suggests that the Serbians were more concerned with territorial acquisition than with historic relics.

Consistent with the promises made at these meetings, by mid-June in

1992 Serbian forces had completed their withdrawal from Mostar to a new front line in the mountains about 20 km east of the city, corresponding closely with the eastern perimeter of the 1939 Cvetković-Maček Agreement. Having feigned pursuit and claimed credit for the successful ouster of the Yugoslav national army from Mostar, Boban quickly installed a political apparatus in the city sympathetic to his hard-line nationalism. Few Bosniak representatives were invited to participate in this newly formed municipal government.

Shortly afterward, roadblocks were established at the outskirts of the city to curtail the movement of Muslim residents in and out of the city. At this juncture, the nature and content of the secret meetings conducted with Serbian politicians were generally unknown to the Bosnian public. In Mostar people still assumed that Bosniaks and Croatians were unified in their desire for Bosnian autonomy and their distaste for Serbian expansionism.

This assumption was soon to be displaced by profound disillusionment. By late summer, reports of Bosnian concentration camps and ethnic cleansing campaigns were gradually filtering back to North America and Europe. By mid-August, the growing concern in the United States regarding the extreme vulnerability of Bosniak civilians had resulted in a report by the Senate Foreign Relations Committee regarding the de facto partition of Bosnia.

This concern accelerated efforts already underway by UN special envoy Cyrus Vance and EC representative Lord Owen to present a proposal designed to halt the juggernaut of interethnic violence that had already claimed thousands of civilian lives. Meanwhile hostilities slowed between Serbian and Croatian paramilitaries, since they had resolved most of their major differences with the Karadžić-Boban Agreement. By late autumn 1992 both forces turned their attentions to the rout of Bosniak resistance from the assorted territories slated for occupation.

In January 1993 Vance and Owen presented their scheme for the comprehensive territorial settlement through the creation of ten ethnically defined cantons knit together by a weak federal government (Kumar 1997: 63). The Vance-Owen plan had been crafted under duress, although with good intentions, and its failure was inseparable from its expediency. The quilt of ethnically homogenized enclaves they proposed contributed to the worsening of the situation on the ground in Bosnia.

To start with, by favoring the status quo in projections of a final territorial settlement, and affirming that ethnicity was to be the first principle of political organization, the plan sanctioned the results of the brutal ethnic cleansing campaigns already undertaken by Croatian and Serbian paramilitaries.

Second, by preserving scattered, homogeneous enclaves with the intention of precluding large-scale annexation, it multiplied the number of actively violent interfaces in the region and isolated Bosniak communities from potentially valuable allies.

Third, by giving the lion's share of civil power to politicians at the cantonal level, it permitted internecine conflicts to intensify as more resources were placed at the disposal of the same ethnonationalist leaders whose actions had provoked widespread prejudicial killing and insecurity in the first place.

Finally, as the plan adopted a tripartite partition strategy that had long been favored by Serbian and Croatian nationalists, it allowed the latter parties to became increasingly convinced that the major western nations had no stomach for untangling the riddles posed by civil war in Bosnia.

Bosniaks felt disappointed and betrayed by this compromise, which appeared to reward bald aggression with ill-gotten land. The subtext of the Vance-Owen plan suggested to them that they would have to rely on their own devices in the defense of Bosnia-Herzegovina as a free, democratic, and multi-ethnic sovereign state. Emboldened by these cues, Croatian paramilitaries in Bosnia launched a renewed assault on Bosniak forces in late April 1993. Regional Serbian commander Ratko Mladić confirmed popular conspiracy theories by publicly pledging to defend Croatian interests in the Mostar region—just six months after his last battles with Croatian Defense Council forces for the same territory.

In early May 1993, the second phase of major hostilities began in Mostar under circumstances significantly less favorable to the Bosniak position than the ones that had confronted them a year earlier.

Emergence

Many Muslim residents had returned to the eastern part of the city after the Serbian withdrawal, seeking to rebuild their property and explore the possibility of returning to normal life. By this time most middle-class Mostarians of every nationality with sufficient means had left the country in search of safety. Most of those who remained did not foresee the reversal of allegiances that unfolded when Croatian Council of Defense paramilitary soldiers began expelling Muslim residents from their apartments on the west side of the city. Almost overnight the Croatian and Bosniak communities that had hitherto been allies in their defense of the city against Serbian usurpation became bitter enemies.

Beginning on 9 May 1993, thousands of male Muslim civilians were collected and sent to detention camps while women, children, and elderly from the same families were forcibly removed from their homes and shuttled across the newly established front line with no more than their coats, shoes, and wallets.

That boundary was the Austro-Hungarian Boulevard of the National Revolution, the traditional threshold separating the Ottoman sector city in the east from the Austro-Hungarian one to the west. In the days that followed, this partition line became increasingly rigid and impassable. A resident of Mostar present during this period described the Boulevard in military terms:

That was a classic military front line, a division line, with everything that usually goes with that kind of line. At the time there were no vehicles moving, not only on the Boulevard but also in the whole Mostar. There was no food not to mention fuel for vehicles. Most of the barriers were made by the material of the buildings destroyed by the military war activities . . . At that time there was one check point, the only crossing point where you could go with your ID three days in advance to undergo some checking procedure. Only women and children could cross then. (Ferhad D. 2001)

In the early rounds of battle, Croatian paramilitary forces had attempted to push Bosniak defenders back to the river bank, but they progressed no farther than the Boulevard. Though their supplies and numbers were far superior to those of the Bosniak forces that repelled them, the choice by Croatian commanders to use unseasoned troops unfamiliar with the urban terrain probably gave Mostar's defenders a much needed advantage.

Had the Croatians reached the river, the Bosniaks could not have held their position in the eastern portion of the city because this would have ended their access to drinking water. For the duration of this second phase of hostilities, a swath of ruined buildings about 100 m wide separating the Boulevard from the river was all that stood between Mostar's remaining Muslim residents and Croatian occupation, with its predictable consequences. From this moment until the close of the war, two cities constituted

Figure 6.2. The Boulevard and former front line in Mostar, where apartments once housed hundreds of families of all ethnicities, remains in a state or relative dereliction as of 2004. Aida Omanovic, used by permission.

themselves and grew in parallel on either side of the partition, exchanging only hostilities.

Duration

Both sides of Mostar's widest avenue became heavily fortified with gun placements, sandbags, barbed wire, and fortified redoubts. Most of the large concrete apartment buildings, schools, and offices lining the Boulevard were ruined during early battles and subsequently converted into elaborate bunkers. Combatants on both sides of the Boulevard dug into their sandbagged positions in expectation of a prolonged siege, punctuated by occasional and mostly ineffective forays into enemy territory. While Croatian forces enjoyed virtually limitless access to materiel via Zagreb, Bosniak forces relied on a supply chain connecting Mostar with the Bosnian interior by way of mountainous footpaths that had to be traversed at night. Food, water, and heating fuel were all scarce in the eastern sectors of the city, where all normal aspects of urban life had disappeared in the wake of prolonged battle. Life for Mostar's Bosniak population was governed by the daily anxieties associated with survival.

The consternation of foreign governments and the international public reached a peak when they learned that Mostar's Old Bridge had been demolished by a Croatian tank on 9 November 1993. This episode dealt a devastating blow to the beleaguered residents of east Mostar, but as military strategy it proved faulty. Images of the missing bridge, coupled with news of assorted atrocities, circulated widely in the international media and galvanized negative feelings outside Bosnia-Herzegovina about the war. A tipping point with respect to popular opinion and passive foreign relations policies was reached by the beginning of 1994, prompting European governments hastily to empower a special administration in the region and approve the emergency disbursement of discretionary funds for postwar reconstruction.

Dismantling

By the middle of March 1994, Bosniaks and Croatians signed a treaty called the Washington Agreement. This functioned formally as a ceasefire, while establishing a set of initial specifications for the creation of the Federation of Bosnia-Herzegovina. With this promise of future cooperation, hostilities in Mostar officially ended and fortifications along the Boulevard were gradually dismantled as popular confidence in the slow peace process grew.

By 1995, the terms of this initial agreement were confirmed and legalized when the Dayton Agreement, largely the product of American diplomatic activity, was signed by Croatian, Serbian, and Bosniak representatives of Bosnia-Herzegovina, officially bringing civil strife to an end. Like many settlement arrangements before it, the Dayton plan relied on ethnic partition and decentralization rather than integration and unification to insure sustainability. The cessation of interethnic violence was taken to be the paramount consideration in the development of this agreement, while most internal displacements were accepted as faits accomplis, regardless of the means by which they were undertaken. This partial settlement left many of the injustices of the war frozen in place, and Mostar still deeply divided in the eyes of one resident:

I'd like to say that there is an international border between the states Bosnia and Herzegovina and the Republic of Croatia on the Mostarian Boulevard because once you cross the Boulevard, you are de facto in another state . . . these are still two cities. (Sead A. 2000)

Though the settlement brought relief to large segments of the Bosnian population and probably preserved hundreds or thousands of lives, the chances of its long-term success remain in doubt. The Dayton Accords addressed some of the symptoms but few of the causes of the debilitating struggle in Bosnia-Herzegovina. In the meantime, the partition of the city has been transformed:

First, it was a physical war division line, a front line, and now, it is not a border in a physical sense but is a border in a psychological sense. It is a psychological barrier: something which is always in one's mind. In other words, each crossing of the Boulevard refreshes one's memory. (Adnan M. 2001)

Impacts

The international community has treated Mostar as a barometer of political conditions in Bosnia since the outbreak of hostilities in 1992. The city has attracted disproportionate numbers of foreign diplomats and administrators along with significant waves of investment. Despite many elaborate and generally well-intentioned attempts to solve Mostar's problems, most remedies—including the "lesser evil" partition schemes embodied in the Vance-Owen plan and Dayton Accords—were designed to address symptoms rather than causes. The authors of these agreements were under pressure to end the hostilities and were hampered by a lack of reliable data regarding popular needs, fears, and attitudes.

This is true in part because the local governmental authorities that were capable of executing social surveys were either too distracted or too culpable to seek information that might be incriminating or inconvenient. Another complicating factor was the tendency of foreign interveners to enter the diplomatic fray so late in the conflict that systematic research and analysis were unaffordable luxuries. In any case, very few reliable studies have been conducted since the outbreak of war regarding its effects on Mostarians' health and productivity. Not even baseline demographic statistics reflecting its postwar conditions are available for the city. This is probably attributable to general disarray in the municipal government and a distaste for revised power-sharing schemes based on ethnic quotas.

Figure 6.3. Just inside the Boulevard and former front line in Mostar, psychological barriers persist and destroyed houses remain mostly in ruins, c. 2004. Aida Omanovic, used by permission.

It follows that only approximate quantitative assessments are possible regarding the overall costs of partition in Mostar. Rough estimates suggest that about 5,000 residents of Mostar died as a result of interethnic hostilities between 1992 and 1995, including both combatants and noncombatants. During the same period as many as 40,000 prewar residents left the city altogether in order to avoid the violence. About 10,000 male residents were forcibly detained in local prison camps; more than 30,000 remained in the city but were compelled to leave their homes.

In eastern Mostar between 1993 and 1995, supplies of food, heating fuels, and medicine were consistently low and irregular, leading to health problems. Citizens collecting drinking water along the eastern bank of the river ran two risks: exposure to sniper fire from the surrounding hills, which also threatened pedestrians crossing bridges or traversing open spaces on essential errands, and exposure to harmful bacteria from river water that was used as a public sewer in the eastern sector of the city and could not be purified due to a scarcity of heating fuel.

Flourishing black market activities in Mostar during and after the war ensured that residents had relatively easy access to addictive drugs, compounding existing mental health problems for the younger segment of an urban population already struggling with despondency and acute anxiety. Destabilization worsened and psychological insecurities deepened with the involuntary movement of people from hostile to friendly ethnic enclaves that began in May 1993. In the absence of longitudinal studies, the degree to which Mostarians suffered from such things as depression, post-traumatic stress disorders, malnutrition, and abnormal levels of domestic violence, is a mostly matter of speculation.

If the generalizations drawn from parallel research in Belfast can be considered potentially relevant in other divided cities, psychological trauma was probably greater in the eastern section of the city and close to the partition line on both sides. Though the number of residents physically injured or severely traumatized by the violence is not known, it can be assumed that few Mostarian families emerged from the war with all their members alive, unscathed, and residing in their prewar homes.

The costs of violence and separation between rival ethnic groups in Mostar are more readily calculated in material terms. The physical destruction or inaccessibility of many schools, offices, homes, factories, and public buildings during the course of hostilities left citizens in the eastern sector struggling for bare survival, while economic life in the western sector was dominated by illicit trade. Thousands of Bosnians forced to abandon the surrounding villages arrived in the city, occupying the empty apartments and straining the already overburdened infrastructure.

As a regional capital and one of Bosnia's major manufacturing cities, Mostar was harshly affected by general lapses in national productivity during the war. Economic growth rates were halved with the outbreak of interethnic hostilities, dipping toward –27 percent by the end of 1993, while the adjusted gross domestic product fell precipitously from $13.1 billion in 1990 to $6.2 billion in 1993. Theft, expulsion, and bombardment generated massive property losses. Hundreds of Bosniak families from western Mostar were obliged to abandon their homes with what they could carry, or less, leaving the bulk of their possessions behind for looters or black market profiteers.

Mostar emerged from civil war as a crippled industrial center and a pariah on the tourist map, having been stripped of its greatest prewar assets. Meager public revenues were squandered in the support of two parallel urban complexes where previously there had been one, and all major institutions and systems were duplicated on either side of the partition line during hostilities, continuing to function separately for several years after the Dayton Accords. In the years immediately following the war, unemployment in the city remained above 50 percent; it stayed high in subsequent years due to risk-adverse foreign investors awaiting reliable political partners. Displacement, lack of jobs, negative health factors, and cycles of education that had been interrupted by the war probably combined to impose opportunity costs on Mostar's residents that were more debilitating than the economic losses incurred directly.

Chapter 7
Nicosia

Introduction

In the 1980s a Turkish-speaking Cypriot civil engineer named Nevzat Öznel was sent to Canada for training, together with Greek-speaking Cypriot colleagues. Because it was assumed that Greek- and Turkish-speaking Cypriots would prefer to remain separate when abroad, as they were at home, expense accounts for the trip provided each traveler with a hotel room for the duration of the program. Each room had two beds and cost $50 per night. Nevzat thought of a more efficient scheme:

I said to my friend, "This is foolish to stay in different rooms! Why not share the same room, since there are two different beds? Instead of paying fifty-and-fifty, one hundred, let's pay $50 and share the money!" And I stayed with him thirty-five days. (Öznel 2001)

This arrangement proved advantageous and continued without incident until his Greek-speaking Cypriot roommate made a telephone call to his mother and described his unorthodox living conditions. Nevzat recalled her reaction with a grin: "'Ooh, heavens! How can you stay in the same room with a Turkish person? What about if he takes out his knife during the night?' Like that." Upon their return from Canada, the two engineers enjoyed a cordial acquaintance but had no further interaction.

Nevzat is a senior waste-management engineer in the northern part of Nicosia, where all the sewage from both sides of the city is treated, thanks to a famous cooperative initiative undertaken in the late 1970s (UNDP 1984). He points out that the city is divided above ground but unified below, because gravity and economics conspired to prevent the duplication of water and sewerage infrastructure. "For sewerage, there is no obstacle," he observes. This underground relationship between Turkish and Greek Cypriots is pragmatic; Greek-speaking Cypriots pay Turkish-speaking Cyp-

TABLE 7.1. BASIC FACTS REGARDING THE PHYSICAL PARTITION OF NICOSIA

Antagonisms	Greek Cypriots v. Turkish Cypriots
Name	Green Line, Attila Line, Mason-Dixon Line
Location	The Green Line is a swath cutting the entire island and comprises two "forward defensive position" lines separated by a buffer zone of varying width. The segment of the Green Line dividing Nicosia approaches from the northwest, narrowing as it passes through the western suburbs and bifurcating the medieval nucleus of the city before turning and widening sharply to the northeast beyond the circular walls near Famagusta Gate. Approaching the old city from the west, its path traced Nelson Street eastward to the west bank of the Pedieos River, following that south then turning east along Bach and Erechthion Streets then dipping south on Acropolis Street until the Mula Bastion; from there the partition follows the perimeter of the walls southward until the Paphos Gate, from there turning eastward along Paphos Street until the intersection with Tourounjiou Djami Street, were it dips to follow Hermes Street eastward until it meets Kara Ayios Iagovos and Constantine Streets, which are traced to the to northeast. As the partition approaches the Flatro Bastion it turns due east to meet its northern flank, then continues north along Aylos Demetrios Street and northeast along Olympus Street toward the northeastern suburbs and the municipal boundary.
Context	The Green Line is a de facto international boundary between the portion of Cyprus that is officially recognized as a sovereign state and the self-proclaimed but unrecognized Turkish Republic of Northern Cyprus. It runs mostly through open agricultural land, encountering urban communities of significant size only in Nicosia and Famagusta. Its course through Nicosia corresponds to the natural path of the Pedeios River through the center of the medieval city, later diverted and paved over to create the main commercial arteries of the city: Paphos and Hermes Streets. This path interrupts some of the most dense and historic parts of the city along with several traditionally mixed suburbs. The Green Line severs about twenty streets running perpendicular to it and swallows altogether about five streets with which it is aligned along an east-west axis. Its establishment consumed hundreds of buildings within or adjacent to the buffer zone. Formerly containing the city's most valuable commercial properties, the swath of the Green Line now is flanked by low-income residential

neighborhoods, light industrial facilities, and a red light district.

Size   The partition line, as it passes through Nicosia and its suburbs is about 10 km long. Its width in the historic city is as large as 20 m and as narrow as 4 m, including the structures within it. The walls and fences forming its northern and southern edges vary in size, but are typically 4.5 m high and 1 m wide at their base. As the Green Line passes through suburban and rural terrain, the width of its buffer zone increases substantially and border fencing becomes minimal or nonexistent.

Porosity   During the first phases of the partition's existence from 1955 until 1963, it was known as the Mason-Dixon Line and was a largely voluntary threshold between the Turkish and Greek quarters of the old city. During its second phase from 1963 until 1974, it was called the Green Line, and expanded to include a *cordon sanitaire*. It was generally open for pedestrian and vehicular crossings through checkpoints monitored by police and British military personnel, fortified only in especially sensitive areas or during violent episodes. After the Turkish invasion of 1974 the Green Line entered a third phase, during which it became heavily fortified within Nicosia, constantly monitored by United Nations peacekeepers in the buffer zone, and passable only through a single checkpoint near the United Nations headquarters in the Ledra Palace Hotel along Leoforos Markou Drakou Street. Since 2003 restrictions on Turkish Cypriot civilian crossings have been eased, leading to millions of unprecedented crossings through the Ledra Palace and Ledra Street checkpoints.

Materials   Sand bags, oil barrels, concrete, corrugated iron, brick, barbed wire, remnant architecture.

Status   Nicosia remains physically and functionally divided, and a plan for its unification included in the revised United Nations settlement plan for Cyprus put forward in February 2003 faltered in 2004.

Actors   Authored by British military personnel and Cypriot political representatives in light of traditional social boundaries and existing military forward positions held by domestic forces, the Green Line was constructed by Greek and Turkish Cypriot military and paramilitary units, respectively, and monitored by United Nations peacekeepers.

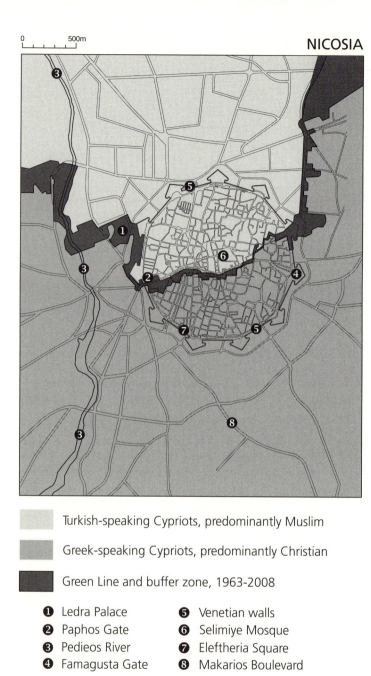

Figure 7.1. Map of Nicosia's partition 1963–2008. Cyprus is the third largest island in the Mediterranean Sea and lies off the southern coast of Turkey and the western shore of Syria. The capital Nicosia is located at 35°10′N, 33°21′E at along the Pedieos River and situated almost in the center of the island. Nicosia lies 327 km northwest of Damascus and 661 km southeast of Izmir. Authors.

riots to process their solid waste, while Turkish-speaking Cypriots use the gray water for agricultural purposes during the long, hot summers when irrigation is costly.

In relation to such a project, Nevzat observes, "You don't have to talk about nationality; you just have to say, 'I am a human being and I love my country. I love my environment.'" Nicosia's shared waste treatment system is one of a handful of successful and ongoing bicommunal urban programs, but demonstrates some of the conditions under which cooperation in a divided city is most likely: when only one system in a given category is needed, when the nature of the system is apolitical, and when the prospect of duplication is unaffordable.

Why is symbiosis so elusive and inefficiency so common? Nevzat suggests that a popular obsession with history and vendettas holds divided communities back from forms of progress that would be mutually beneficial. "Don't touch the history, forget the history," he said. "For me, history is going to be a lesson in order to move forward" (Öznel 2001). Though his father-in-law and only brother were killed by Greek paramilitary soldiers during civil disturbances of the 1960s, Nevzat refuses to condemn Greek-speaking Cypriots as a whole or reject the idea of a unified future. He remains a firm believer in the restorative power of joint ventures like the sewage treatment network that has transformed him from an engineer into some kind of diplomat.

Background

The Ottoman Empire conquered Cyprus in 1571 and endured there for three centuries. Under Ottoman rule, an ethnic distinction was created in Cyprus based on religious and cultural affiliations; a privileged Muslim minority community gradually distinguished its interests from the traditionally hellenic, non-Muslim population. Commercial and social relations between ethnic groups were open and active. During the Ottoman period Nicosia developed distinct ethnic neighborhoods, with Turkish-speaking residents primarily in the north and Greek-speaking residents in the south of the city. These two residential quarters were joined by a mixed commercial zone in the center of the city.

Though all Cypriots could prosper under the Ottoman administration, the millet system favored Muslims and institutionalized ethnic segregation in Cyprus. The Greeks of Cyprus were politically consolidated under the umbrella of the Orthodox Church, which became the "unchallenged spokesman in the political, social, educational and religious affairs of the Greek Cypriot community" in the late sixteenth century (Coufoudakis 1976: 31).

By the start of British occupation and administration in 1878, increasing emphasis on ethnicity in Cypriot political affairs gave Church leaders a monopoly over decision making for more than three-quarters of the population. This was a welcome development in Greece, where the Megali Idea for reclaiming Byzantine territories exerted a powerful influence over foreign policy in the early twentieth century. A component of this larger reclamation process, the campaign to annex Cyprus called *enosis*—the Greek word for "union"—was a popular response to both British occupation and the conclusion of Ottoman sovereignty on the island. Meanwhile, the Young Turks' revolution took place in 1908 as the Ottoman Empire entered its death throes, in part a response to irredentist stirrings in Greece.

Inspired in part by the Young Turks, the nationalistic aspirations of Turkish-speaking Cypriots began to find more organized and popular expression. Recognizing the shifting nationalistic ambitions that were beginning to polarize Greek- and Turkish-speaking Cypriots under their authority, British mandate officials were quick to adopt the Greek-Turkish dichotomy as a cipher for social relations on the island. With respect to political dynamics in the region, they tended to view the two Cypriot communities as natural extensions of the island's two neighboring countries, ethnic rivals in need of a civilizing intermediary. The outcome of World War I allowed Britain to consolidate its holdings in the former Ottoman empire; Cyprus was formally annexed to the United Kingdon in 1914 and declared a Crown colony in 1925.

Greek-speaking Cypriots in favor of *enosis* and critical of colonial taxation policy rioted against the British in October of 1931, burning the British governor's residence in the process. Punitive measures followed, including deportation of resistance leaders in the *enosis* movement and the national Communist party, AKEL. Despite pronounced tensions, approximately 37,000 Greek- and Turkish-speaking Cypriot volunteers served in several branches of the British armed forces during World War II, hoping their contributions might earn Cyprus an opportunity for self-determination. Many were encouraged by the wartime British recruitment slogan in Cyprus: "For Greece and Freedom" (Mallinson 2005: 11).

In the aftermath of the war, these expectations were not realized. While conscription-for-independence bargains were struck successfully elsewhere in the British Empire at the time, the war only reinforced Britain's conviction that Cyprus was vital to its ongoing strategic interests in the region. Seeking to legitimize a permanent presence on the island, the British colonial authorities pursued policies in Cyprus that emphasized and formalized ethnic divisions, contributing significantly to the accelerated development of nationalist agendas and interethnic rivalries.

From the early 1950s until 1974, influential foreign diplomats used a powerful blend of antipathy, indifference, and manipulation to counteract the Cypriots' natural affinity for tolerance and contribute to the provocation of interethnic rivalry. Had the country not occupied such an important strategic location with respect to the Middle East, it might not have been subjected to the relentless and often destabilizing foreign interventions that dramatically changed its political destiny. These external influences tended to disrupt the natural evolution of self-determination and the emergence of an inclusive national identity, aggravating latent antagonisms between Greek- and Turkish-speaking Cypriots.

Escalation

Anti-British sentiment among Greek-speaking Cypriots intensified in 1954, the year the British transferred their Middle Eastern headquarters from Egypt to Cyprus. Now a major fixture in the middle eastern defense network for Britain and America, this shift dramatically decreased the likelihood of Cyprus's union with Greece. From 1955 onward, Greek and Greek-speaking Cypriot paramilitary activities focused on disrupting the British colonial administration through a campaign of bombings and assassinations. Beginning in early April, these efforts were orchestrated largely by George Grivas, a Cypriot from Nicosia who had studied at the Athens Military Academy. Grivas was an apostle of *enosis* and the leader of the National Organization of Cypriot Fighters (EOKA), the paramilitary instrument of right-wing Greek-speaking Cypriot politics at that time.

Alarmed by escalating violence on the island, British foreign secretary Harold Macmillan convened a closed-door tripartite discussion with Turkey and Greece during the London Conference of August 1955. This meeting, to which Cypriot leaders were not invited, did not result in de-escalation. Rather, it intensified Turkish concerns regarding the future of Cyprus and the safety of Turkish-speaking Cypriot citizens in the event that *enosis* was realized through military force. It also framed the growing crisis in Cyprus in terms of Greek-Turkish enmity, rather than addressing the mounting tensions between British authorities and the anti-colonial resistance.

In May 1955 EOKA attacked police stations in Nicosia and Kyrenia, killing fourteen people. These events, especially given the willingness of paramilitary personnel to attack civilians, confirmed the worst fears of foreign onlookers; these attacks pointed to weakening authority of the British colonial government in Cyprus and promised to provoke large-scale interethnic bloodletting. It is useful to note that until the middle of 1955, violence between Cypriots was minimal; Grivas, in fact, initially forbid attacks on Turkish-speaking citizens. Though he eventually reversed this policy, it illustrates the predominantly anticolonial character of violence in Cypus during the early 1950s.

Finally awake to the potentially disruptive impact of *enosis* and EOKA on the regional political equilibrium, Britain offered more vocal support for Turkish claims in order to counterbalance the increasingly radical nationalistic sentiments among Greek-speaking Cypriots. Gradually, this effort to dilute anticolonial violence with intercommunal violence succeeded: "Greek and Turkish Cypriots were progressively sealed off from each other, allowing suspicion and even hatred to fester" (Holland 1998: 66). This progression seems to have been consistent with unofficial British policy at the time, which "was simply to do what it could to undermine Graeco-Turkish relations" (Mallinson 2005: 25).

Because the British had recruited Turkish-speaking Cypriot police officers as members of an auxiliary force assigned to contain EOKA attacks, anticolonial violence directed at local police was sometimes indistinguishable from interethnic violence. Accordingly, the first serious attacks between Turkish- and Greek-speaking Cypriots took place in 1956 after a Turkish-speaking police officer was killed by EOKA (Ehrlich 1974: 19), resulting in reciprocal violence and the formation of VOLKAN in the north of the island, a paramilitary group later reconstituted as the Turkish Resistance Organization, or TMT.

Punctuating the first signs of a shift from anticolonial to intercommunal discord, British military personnel installed barbed wire fencing and five checkpoints in late May 1956 to "prevent clashes between the Turkish and Greek factions" in the wake of riots and looting in the capital (Haff 1956). The barricades followed Hermes Street, the commercial artery running east-to-west through the center of the old city following the original course of the Pedieos River. It was the first in a lengthy series of steps leading to the permanent, physical division of Nicosia.

The resulting interface was known informally as the Mason-Dixon Line, a temporary, semi-official boundary dividing Greek- and Turkish-speaking Cypriots as civil hostilities began and anti-colonial violence continued. (Harbottle 1970: 63) It corresponded almost exactly to the recommended division line specified two years later by the Surridge Report of 1958 and to the segment of the Green Line drawn through Nicosia seven years later, strongly suggesting that each formal partition was informed by the divisive strokes which preceded it.

Foreign diplomats scrambled to construct proposals that might result in a durable settlement without provoking further animosities between Greece and Turkey—both traditional rivals were members of NATO. At least five distinct diplomatic strands contributed to the tangle of conflicting interests surrounding Cyprus at the time:

- Britain's efforts to retain its strategic position in Cyprus and avoid a wider regional conflict;
- Cyprus's efforts from both sides of the ethnic divide to shed the British administration;
- Greece's efforts to retain cultural and political influence in Cyprus;
- Turkey's efforts to protect its southern border;
- American efforts to block the ascendency of the Communist party in Cyprus and preserve unfettered access to its surveillance facilities and military installations on the island.

Throughout the summer of 1958, violence between Greek- and Turkish-speaking Cypriots worsened. In early June riots followed a bomb explosion at the Turkish Press Office in Nicosia, police stations were attacked, and eight Greek-speaking Cypriots were killed near the Turkish village of Geunyeli. Tensions in and around the capital were high, prompting British military personnel to impose evening curfews and maintain strict separation along the Mason-Dixon line.

In June 1958 British prime minister Harold Macmillan made public the main elements of his settlement scheme calling for bifurcated political institutions during a seven-year transition period that could lead to a more integrated national government. One major component was the administrative division of five major cities, including Nicosia, into geographically distinct areas served by autonomous Turkish-speaking Cypriot and Greek-speaking Cypriot municipal councils. A special advisory commision was appointed in September of 1958 to examine implementation strategies in detail, chaired by B. J. Surridge. The "Report of the Municipal Commission" noted substantive problems with functional partition, but ultimately affirmed, due to extraordinary circumstances, separate and communcal municipalities for the largest mixed towns in Cyprus.

The unpublished 1958 Commission map showing a proposed administrative boundary between northern and southern sections of Nicosia is probably the first graphic representation of the capital's formal, negotiated division along ethnic lines. It corresponds closely to the so-called Mason-Dixon line of 1956 and must be considered a precursor to the Green Line drawn officially in December 1963. Accordingly, it can be considered a rehearsal of the partition that became far more permanent in 1974.

So inflammatory were the Commission report's maps and segregationist recommendations that British governor Sir Hugh Foot anticipated riots, and accordingly the document was never published. Meanwhile, illegal Turkish-speaking Cypriot municipalities continued to function in the capital, collecting tariffs and taxes from Turkish-speaking residents and providing basic public services in areas where Greek-speaking civil servants of the legal municipality no longer dared enter.

When the Macmillan Plan was promptly rejected by Greece and Greek-speaking Cypriots, the United Nations initiated a debate on the subject of a settlement in Cyprus that raised expectations for a quick resolution of what was dubbed the "Cyprus Problem." As new plans and discussions unfolded, fighting between Greek- and Turkish-speaking Cypriots grew more vigorous. By 1959, as Britain showed signs of capitulation and both ethnic factions sought preemptive advantage through military means, the first phase of the Cypriot civil conflict officially began.

Negotiations

Despite the bitterness of interethnic relations in Cyprus at that time, many Greek- and Turkish-speaking Cypriot political representatives recognized that their differences were overshadowed by a shared desire to achieve independence from Britain. Those favoring *enosis* probably considered their chances for success better in the absence of British mediation, and those favoring partition probably assumed that Turkish military intervention on their behalf would be more plausible without the prospect of direct engagement with British forces.

Whatever their motivations, the military dispute between Cyprus's two rival ethnic communities swiftly concluded in February 1959 with the signing of the London and Zurich Agreements, the result of intensive negotiations between Greek, Turkish, and British diplomats. Eighteen months later Cyprus formally asserted its sovereignty as a member of the United Nations and the Council of Europe under the leadership of the Greek Orthodox archbishop, Makarios III, first president of the independent Republic of Cyprus. This settlement gave Cyprus autonomy as a sovereign nation to be governed democratically according to a Constitution that distributed power at the national level according to ethnic quotas.

Along with independence, substantial but limited authority was granted to external guarantor powers regarding the future of the fledgling republic, and Britain retained two large sovereign military bases at Dhekelia and Akrotiri-Episkopi. The organizing principles and institutional structure of the new Cypriot government proved expedient in the short term. British influence on national affairs was minimized, issues regarding Greek and Turkish irredentism were taken off the negotiating table, and a permanent institutional framework was provided for the resolution of existing interethnic conflicts.

The expediency of this political formula, hastily crafted at the height of a civil conflict, did not prove durable. Cyprus backed into political independence from a position of weakness and desperation. It adopted a democratic framework for national government without having first achieved national integration. Rigid quotas and hierarchies embedded in the Constitution institutionalized ethnic rivalries, effectively poisoning the political groundwater before Cypriots could drink.

For all practical purposes the constitutional government of Cyprus was stillborn, a short-lived compromise brokered under pressure between moderate parliamentarians and militant nationalists. Instead of redeeming the country, the Cypriot Constitution acted as a springboard toward the darkest period of civil strife in the island's history. By late 1963, the constitutional frameworks provided by the London and Zurich Agreements had been effectively abandoned in the wake of intense political turmoil regarding proposed constitutional amendments and renewed violence between Greek Cypriot and Turkish Cypriot paramilitary personnel.

Among the most controversial issues in play at this time was the question of separate municipalities, provided for in the Constitution and rationalized by the Surridge report of 1958. Though de facto separation of municipal functions existed in Nicosia and elsewhere, legal implementation of the constitutional mandate was never achieved. A split verdict on this matter led to the dissolution of the fledgling Supreme Court. Amendment of the constitutional provisions for separate municipalities, along with other controversial changes to the 1960 framework, were put forward by President Makarios in November 1963 and resulted in further destabilization of the political situation.

Mounting tensions overflowed on 21 December 1963, when two Turkish-speaking Cypriots were killed by Greek-speaking Cypriot police officers in the red light district of Nicosia, located along the border between the increasingly homogenized Greek- and Turkish-speaking quarters of the city. Though the killings may not have been motivated by politics or interethnic rivalry, they were widely interpreted as a threat to the Turkish-speaking Cypriot community as a whole. Widespread rioting resulted from this episode, especially in mixed suburbs of Nicosia such as Omorphita and Trakhonas, prompting intervention by the British forces stationed at the sovereign bases.

As in 1955, chaotic conditions and the seemingly spontaneous nature of interethnic violence in late 1963 prompted the British soldiers to erect temporary physical barricades along the Mason-Dixon line. By Christmas a ceasefire had been arranged, and on 26 December British commanders recommended to President Makarios the creation of a corpus separatum along the length of Nicosia's ethnic interface—already seven years old.

Emergence

The Mason-Dixon line—previously the main commercial street of the medieval city, and even earlier the Pedieos River bed—became the Green Line during the early morning hours of 29 December 1963 at the British High Commissioner's residence on Shakespeare Avenue in Nicosia. British major-general Peter Young, commander of the British units in Cyprus, convened a meeting late in the evening of 28 December to reach a consensus regarding the exact placement of a temporary ceasefire boundary between the two embattled groups in Nicosia.

Crafting a stable and mutually acceptable military border that would bifurcate Nicosia required special consideration due to its practical and emblematic importance. High-ranking representatives of all interested parties to the Cypriot conflict were in attendance. They included president of the House of Representatives Glafkos Clerides and minister of the interior Polycarpos Georghadjis on behalf of the Greek-speaking Cypriot community, chairman of the Turkish Communal Chamber Rauf Denktash and minister of defense, Osman Orek on behalf of the Turkish-speaking Cypriot community, the Greek and Turkish ambassadors to Cyprus, British high commissioner for Cyprus Sir Arthur Clark, British minister for commonwealth affairs Duncan Sandys, and British military adviser major-general Peter Young.

By 4 a.m. on 29 December 1963, after much discussion and revision, two forward positions were etched onto the map of Nicosia with a green chinagraph pencil by Major General Young. This line constituted the double-layered partition line between Greek and Turkish Cypriots with a substantial no man's land in between. This "chinagraph frontier," hastily drawn as a temporary ceasefire measure, was converted into an impermeable physical partition in 1974 and remains "an unremitting obstacle to progress toward normalization" in Cyprus more than forty years later (Harbottle 1970: 66–68). For its creators in 1963, the prospect of Nicosia's Green Line enduring for more than forty years would have been inconceivable. The Green Line was meant only to halt hostilities and save lives during the uncertain period between a ceasefire and a more permanent negotiated settlement between the two rival ethnic communities.

While the formal establishment of the Green Line certainly lowered the intensity and frequency of intercommunal violence in the capital, tensions between Greek- and Turkish-speaking Cypriots remained high throughout the 1960s. Prospects for a lasting settlement seemed remote. Tens of thousands of Cypriot refugees were created when the boundary was formally established. Greek-speaking Cypriots in the north and Turkish-speaking Cypriots in the south abandoned their homes in order to seek the security of a friendly enclave. In most cases this meant crossing the Green Line, leaving their property to looters or squatters.

Foreign diplomats, fearful of instability and political opportunism in such a sensitive region, again scrambled to respond to the crisis. The London conference of 1964 spearheaded by British and American negotiators recommended the creation of a NATO peacekeeping force in Cyprus, a scheme rejected by President Makarios. Likewise, the "double-enosis" plan put forward in July 1964 by former U.S. secretary of state Dean Acheson—calling for the permanent division and the simultaneous annexation of the northern and southern sectors of Cyprus by Turkey and Greece respectively—was roundly rejected.

Both these plans emphasized the control of NATO over Cypriot political affairs and demonstrated their political sponsors' anxieties regarding expansion of Cold War spheres of influence in the Middle East. Meanwhile a United Nations peacekeeping force in Cyprus had been established in March 1964 at the request of British and Cypriot representatives with Security Council Resolution 186, providing mostly Dutch and British troops to monitor the ceasefire and to control sensitive boundary areas in an effort to "contribute to the maintenance and restoration of law and order and a return to normal conditions." Their arrival was punctuated with the construction of barbed wire fences, road blocks, trenches, and other fortifications crisscrossing the island, with a special emphasis on the Green Line as it passed through Nicosia. This fortification process followed standard military protocols in order to minimize contact between the two rival communities and to maximize the efficiency of the monitoring operations to be undertaken by the peacekeeping forces.

Duration

Rather than fulfilling its ostensible purpose—to provide time and space for gradual reconciliation and negotiation—partition seemed to encourage further animosity and segregation between the two rival communities. The political atmosphere in the years that followed the establishment of the Green Line was increasingly polluted by mutual suspicion and instability. By 1967, a military coup in Athens resulted in renewed support for *enosis*. American special envoy Cyrus Vance was dispatched to outline a settlement, but like his predecessors he returned home emptyhanded due to the multiplying complexities of the situation on the ground: violence perpetrated by EOKA B, assassination attempts against President Makarios, and the ongoing intransigence of communal leaders.

By 1974 circumstances had reached a breaking point once again. The military junta government in Athens engineered a coup against President Makarios on 15 July, installing former paramilitary commander Nicos Sampson in his place. Sampson was a zealous advocate of *enosis* and was widely assumed to have been responsible for the murder of many Turkish Cypriot civilians during earlier stages of the civil conflict. The Turkish government was troubled by the swift progress of events in Nicosia and promptly invoked its concern for the welfare of isolated Turkish Cypriot enclaves. Invoking its responsibilities as one of the three guarantors to the 1960 Constitution and despairing of any intervention by Greece or Britain, Turkey decided to apply military force.

By 22 July 1974, just days after launching a unilateral military intervention nicknamed Operation Attila, Turkish forces occupied a large territory extending southward from their beachhead in Kyrenia to forward positions along the buffer zone, including the northern half of Nicosia. Within weeks they controlled about 37 percent of the island. Their success, along with President Makarios's unlikely escape from Greek assassins, spurred the collapse of the junta government in Athens and the demise of Sampson's administration in Nicosia. Hundreds of thousands of Cypriot civilians still living on a potentially hostile side of the Green Line were compelled to cross it, the last push in a massive campaign of internal displacement resulting in near-perfect ethnic homogeneity of northern and southern sectors of the island.

By the time a durable ceasefire had been arranged on 16 August 1974, Turkish forces had established a forward position which they called the "Attila Line" (Grundy-Warr 1987: 75), running from Morphou Bay in the northwest to Famagusta in the east. Its path corresponded in large part to the Green Line established eleven years before.

Before foreign governments could formulate even a rudimentary diplomatic response to these events, the political landscape in Cyprus had shifted dramatically. The constitutional government established in 1960 had disintegrated, the president was lucky to be alive in London, and the world had witnessed the unprecedented military invasion of a neutral country by a NATO member state on behalf of a minority ethnic group. Several authors have suggested that these events were unofficially sanctioned, or even supported, by the U.S. State Department and that Secretary of State Henry Kissinger considered the Cyprus Problem resolved with the de facto partition imposed by the Turkish invasion (Hitchens 1989; O'Malley 1999).

From 1974 onward, United Nations peacekeepers assigned to patrol the buffer zone were joined by Greek- and Turkish-speaking Cypriot soldiers stationed at regular intervals along the fortified walls marking their forward positions in the capital and beyond. The Turkish intervention continues to be viewed by advocates as a defensive maneuver on behalf of Turkish-speaking Cypriots, while detractors consider it an illegal act of foreign aggression against a sovereign, nonaligned nation.

The 1974 invasion completed a process of ethnic partition in Nicosia that evolved over a period of 18 years. It cemented the terms of a prolonged political stalemate in Cyprus that has yet to be broken. A vigorous renewal of diplomatic efforts toward a comprehensive settlement was prompted by the prospect of European Union membership for Cyprus and the assertion

Figure 7.2. The Green Line as it cuts through streets in southern Nicosia, 2002.
Authors.

Figure 7.3. The Green Line as it cuts through streets in northern Nicosia, 2007.
Authors.

Figure 7.4. A glimpse into the buffer zone in the heart of Nicosia's old city, 2002. Authors.

of a comprehensive settlement plan by former United Nations secretary general Kofi Annan in 2004. A sea change in Cypriot politics appeared imminent due to pressure toward unification from Ankara, widespread economic stagnation in the north, and the enormous incentives presented to the island by attaining membership of the European Union.

Positive indications of this kind of became visible in the spring of 2003, when a major thaw in diplomatic relations led to the easing of transit restrictions across the Green Line for Cypriot civilians. During the remainder of that year about two million Cypriots, mostly citizens from the north traveling south, crossed the line to visit their homes and friends without being disturbed. With the referendum of April 2004 it became clear that the incentives offered by foreign diplomats were insufficient to unify Cyprus. Though more than 64 percent of Turkish Cypriot voters endorsed Annan's reunification plan, more than 75 percent of Greek Cypriot voters rejected it. Prospects are bright in 2008, but a durable settlement still eludes the best political minds in Cyprus and beyond.

Impacts

Like most of the divided cities considered in this book, very few reliable studies regarding the impact of partition on Nicosia have been conducted since the Green Line was established in 1963. While both parties to the conflict have collected statistics regarding the losses of life and property, it is typical for each group to count only the losses incurred in its own ethnic community while ignoring and minimizing the losses resulting from the violence for which they are responsible. When comprehensive estimates are offered, the numbers generated on one side of the Green Line rarely agree with those generated on the other. For this reason, extrapolation from a handful of imprecise statistics must suffice to estimate the cost of the Cyprus Problem since 1963.

Loss of life among Cypriots, Turkish military personnel and British military personnel since the beginning of civil strife in the mid-1950s was substantial. The first deaths attributed to inter-ethnic conflict in Cyprus following World War II occurred in June 1955 when EOKA began its operations in support of *enosis*. Three years later, as many as 600 Greek Cypriot families were forced to abandon their houses in the mixed Nicosia suburb of Omorphita when Turkish Cypriot riots generated widespread intimidation in the civilian population. Between 1955 and 1959 as many as 600 deaths

Figure 7.5. Turkish-speaking Cypriots gaze through a fence along the Green Line into southern Nicosia, the closest point of contact between the two segregated communities, 2002. Authors.

have been attributed to intercommunal violence, and as many as 1,000 deaths resulted from the hostilities in the wake of formal partition in 1963. Military intervention by Turkey in three phases beginning in July 1974 resulted in about 5,000 deaths, more than half of them nonmilitary (White 2003).

Very few studies related to the citizens' physical and mental health in the aftermath of intergroup violence appear to have been conducted in Cyprus since the beginning of hostilities in the mid-1950s. What can be safely assumed is that the same degree of stress, anxiety, and trauma documented in similar situations was experienced by the thousands of Cypriots whose lives were impacted by violence. The unusually long duration of unresolved intergroup tension in Cyprus probably introduced low-intensity mental health impacts that are widespread but difficult to measure.

One Cypriot anthropologist observed that the aftermath of a political settlement could be complicated by the accumulation of ill will and psychological trauma. "That is what worries me about the day after," he said, "since if we still see ourselves as victims and do not acknowledge the pain of others, it could be very scary . . . we have both been aggressors" (Papadakis 2002). It seems likely that the full extent of these complications will not be known until they are put to the test of a full political settlement.

Along with loss of life and physical health, a large percentage of Cypriots lost property and access to resources central to their livelihoods in the course of interethnic hostilities. Beginning in 1963, major population movements took place in Cyprus as citizens abandoned their homes in an area where they belonged to an ethnic minority to join larger and more secure enclaves elsewhere. As the Green Line grew more permanent and the scope of intergroup violence widened in the years that followed, the number of refugees compelled to cross it grew in a commensurate fashion. This displacement process reached a peak immediately following the Turkish invasion of 1974, when political events no longer allowed for mixed communities of any kind, and ethnic homogenization on either side of the Green Line became almost total. According to the 1960 census, about 40,000 Turkish Cypriots lived south of the future boundary, and approximately 200,000 Greek Cypriots north of it: by 1975 fewer than a hundred members of these statistical categories remained. Most of the nearly 250,000 refugees participating in this demographic reengineering exercise—about 40 percent of the prepartition population of Cyprus as a whole—received no compensation for loss of their possessions, houses, and jobs.

The partition was most pronounced in Nicosia, because its physically disruptive impact on the fabric of the city led directly to inefficiency and demoralization for urban residents. The Green Line had transformed the center of the historic city, its most vibrant and cooperative sector, into a no man's land. Beginning in 1964 and accelerating after 1974, increasingly separate Greek and Turkish municipal authorities in Nicosia were obliged to develop new commercial centers in the southern and northern outskirts of the city. This duplication of institutions, facilities and services is a defining characteristic of the divided city. The inevitable results are hasty and redundant urban development undertaken to accommodate ethnic apartheid. Segregated education systems and minimal communication across the partition line after 1974 created an atmosphere of stagnant and widespread bigotry in which the new generations of Cypriots were raised.

The municipal revenues used to convert one city into two could hardly be afforded, since the national rate of adjusted economic growth had steadily declined since the early 1970s, dropping to −18 percent in the year immediately following the Turkish invasion. Interethnic violence was devastating for a Cypriot economy that had relied on industries like tourism and agriculture that are especially sensitive to political instability and dependent on fickle markets.

The internal displacement of a large segment of the workforce only compounded the problem. Economic decline was sharply felt in the capital, where many residents lost their white-collar jobs and manufacturers on both sides of the Green Line suffered from the drastic erosion of their urban markets. These negative economic impacts were generally felt more intensely by Turkish Cypriots, whose government was not recognized outside Turkey and was barred from normal trade relations as a result.

By 2004 the major incentives for a comprehensive peace settlement and eventual unification were tied directly to the economic advantages of membership in the European Union. The prospect of increased productivity and higher standards of living, especially in the north, had become so attractive to ordinary Cypriots that the trepidation traditionally associated with unification faded from the foreground political discourse. Though many psychological and emotional scars may have healed, albeit poorly, during the last forty years, the material costs of partition—more than moral objections to ethnic apartheid—appear most likely to prompt a reversal of longstanding political antagonisms.

Chapter 8
Breaching the Urban Contract

Introduction

Urban walls have long constituted an outward sign and guarantee of the social contract binding city managers to citizens. Historically, perimeter walls promised a stable, passive security infrastructure as a prerequisite for sustained economic and cultural development. Citizens of such hemmed in cities offered their services in a dense, diversified, relatively expensive environment in return for the provision of reliable public services, social opportunities and sanctuary. In its most basic form, this exchange might be understood as the "urban contract."

In exchange for a livelihood within the walls, urban residents made substantial concessions: they submitted to taxation, they gave their allegiance to abstract political systems based on indirect representation, they provided labor and specialized resources to the city, they lived in expensive and crowded spaces, and they generally allowed their traditional cultural identities to be subordinated to the corporate identity of the city as a whole. All this and more is paid to fulfil the urban contract with urban managers, who promise in return to provide secure and stable conditions for development.

When this contract is threatened or broken, the fabric of the city is sometimes tailored until baseline security needs are met. Chapter 2 argued that this basic process is not new. The urban wall has always been the result of an ongoing, often volatile, process of negotiation between the city and its enemies, its allies, its elites, and its marginalized residents. Minimizing real and perceived group vulnerability is a primary force shaping city-making and partitioning.

According to one Belfast resident, "It's about a feeling of security." Real or imaginary, it is the fears of normal citizens residing near ethnic interfaces that drive the process of involuntary segregation, violence, and ultimately physical partition in formerly open and integrated cities. Urban residents, as consumers of policies generated by urban managers, take the measure of their overall security and prosperity and seek to adjust the terms of their urban contract accordingly. They are the ones for whom passive physical security matters most.

This chapter provides the framework for understanding physical partitions as indicators of a failure to provide security at the municipal scale—a broken contract between vulnerable ethnic communities and the city managers. Physical partitions strongly suggest that the need for collective security, especially for minority groups that are already marginalized, can overshadow many conventional social and practical concerns. When considering the problems generated by the divided city condition, important questions focus on how and why urban managers meet—or fail to meet—the security and development needs of resident communities. Reliance on walls often postpones the answer, as observed by a community worker in Belfast:

We find that peacelines address a symptom, but not the problem. If my windows are being broken every night, putting a twenty foot fence in front of my windows can stop them from being broken. It doesn't do anything to address what it is that makes that person want to break my windows. (David O., 2001)

Walls promise to limit the negative consequences of intergroup conflict and may even preempt it by restricting access to urban terrain with special historic, symbolic, or psychological value. In Belfast popular slogans within the contested enclaves—such as "not one inch" and "this far and no farther"—have a lot to say about the consecration of urban territory and the myths surrounding that process, but they also underscore the faith residents of divided cities place in physical partitions. Fortified clusters are considered necessary by those who create them in the light of the security concerns they believe are insufficiently addressed by their urban managers. Physical partition can be understood as a minority community's reaction to forms of urban expansion that threaten group identity.

Walls and the Revised Urban Contract

Partitioning along ethnic lines is not assumed to be the worst possible outcome for cities experiencing a prolonged crisis of spoiled ethnic relations. It is necessary to ask: What is broken and lost when a city splits along its customary ethnic thresholds? The answer calls for a fair assessment of prepartition conditions and the city's fluctuating capacity to meet the security and development needs of resident communities—especially those that constitute a minority or have been traditionally marginalized. Some of these conditions were examined in chapters three to seven. A number of counter-intuitive observations result from this examination and are briefly summarized below.

1. Segregated ethnic communities do not require reconciliation.

One community organizer in Belfast asserts that strength and security are prerequisites for successful negotiation between rival communities:

> Those who approached reconciliation did so from a point of weakness, not strength. If you are willing to do anything for peace and good will . . . you've thrown it all away on the way . . . you arrive with an empty boat. (Richard S., 2000)

The problem of security and the onerous presence of walls are not new or contemporary urban problems. Chapter 2 outlined a legacy of fortification that reaches back to dynastic Egypt. In the course of his analysis of the medieval period of urban development, Lewis Mumford points out that "five centuries of violence, paralysis, and uncertainty had created in the European heart a profound desire for security" (Mumford 1960: 14). This desire was often answered by the urban perimeter wall, which, as has already been noted, satisfied the urban residents' desire for passive protection from external enemies with a significant degree of success for several centuries.

Though most cities subsequently outgrew their girdling walls and the external threats to the urban populace gradually diminished, the need for security never faded. Though good fences rarely make good neighbors where they are the product of chronic discrimination, in many instances they protect community interests in ways that laws and the police do not. The urban cluster that results from interethnic partition bears a strong resemblance to the urban nucleus that characterized the earliest stages of urban development, as noted in chapter two. It more closely resembles in scale and spirit the majority of cities since the birth of the urban settlement than the larger, pluralistic cities that came later.

Within both the enclave and the earliest fortified urban settlement, exclusion, safety and solidarity were the hallmarks of success. As cities grow larger the difficulty and cost of maintaining intergroup cohesion increases, so that partition in some cases can be considered "the spatial expression of inherently conflicting current conditions that characterize plural societies" (Benvenisti 1986: 87) . The result may be urban enclaves that are perceived locally as uncompromised, autonomous urban units.

One Palestinian resident of East Jerusalem sees no division, since his city never included the Israeli West:

I can't compare Jerusalem to Mostar, to Berlin, to Sarajevo, to any of these cities that were divided. No, it is the opposite, actually. It is divided. If they try to say, "it's not divided," they are wrong in the opinions of the majority of Palestinians. Let's say: "it's not one city any way. It's two cities; there are two Jerusalems." Put it that way. Probably it will sound better to the international community. It has always been the case that these are two cities. You can't try to say, "no, it's one city." If we both decide to make it one city and then come together and say, "let's make it one city," then okay, probably, but that will take hundreds of years until we fully trust the Israelis and they fully trust us. (Hakim B., 2003)

In Belfast, one enclave resident pointed out the local advantages of the ongoing rivalry in the Upper Ardoyne Protestant enclave:

It's all about pulling together. I must be honest with you; if anything, [the Catholics] have done us a favor. Because this community is split up into four pockets . . . you have Hescuth, Wheatfield, Alliance, and Glenbrunn, and they could never agree before this. But now they're totally united, you know, in their stance, to stand up to these people. (Henry M., 2001)

In practical terms, the divided city may present a less desirable but more stable model for the accommodation of social stresses in the urban environment than the unpartitioned city in many of its mismanaged forms. It promises, in many cases, at least a temporary resolution of stalemate forces acting between rival communities in its boundaries.

2. Some urban residents benefit from physical barriers.

Most often, urban walls separating rival ethnic communities fall short of expectations and constitute an inadequate response to civilian violence. All the same, their existence is often both functionally and symbolically meaningful to the people living and working nearby. In Jerusalem, for example, walls dividing the city from 1948 until 1967 provided relief for both the Israeli and Palestinian communities who had been traumatized by civil war and massive internal relocations. They brought an immediate decrease in intergroup violence and an opportunity to develop intragroup cohesion by channeling their energies toward a common enemy. The process was a dramatic illustration of the idea that "spatial and cultural segregation reflect the fundamental needs of the two communities for physical security and preservation of their collective identities" (Benvenisti 1996: 200).

Though it is contrary to conventional assumptions about how a city should respond to and accommodate social conflict, the physical segregation of ethnically heterogeneous cities is considered by some to be a natural and even inevitable reaction to stress. From this perspective, urban partitioning that is driven by ethnic conflict functions in part as a renewal of the urban contract, revised to accommodate the needs of smaller, more defensible social units in the city. A Turkish Cypriot politician noted the ready acceptance of the dividing wall:

People say, "We are used to this. We want to live like this." Subconsciously, they are telling you something else: they are saying "We prefer this because we are safe now." (Halit O., 2001)

Carried too far, these observations seem to suggest that good fences make good neighbors among traditional rivals. In practice, fences rarely stabilize or enhance intergroup relations when they are the product of chronic discrimination. When assessing the real impacts of urban partitions in the divided city context, it is usually the case that what is good for the few is detrimental to the many. That is, while in many instances these walls protect local community interests for the disenfranchised in ways that discriminatory laws and compromised police practices cannot, they meanwhile serve to deepen and intensify the antagonisms that prompted their construction in the first place. It is difficult to condemn or condone urban partitions categorically, but it is useful to identify concretely those who benefit from physical partition and those who do not.

3. Unified cities may not be superior to divided cities.

Divided cities force a critical distinction to be made between arbitrary municipal boundaries and social boundaries created by inhabitants seeking security, solidarity, sovereignty, and so forth.

In some cases, boundaries that appear arbitrary are actually constructed to frustrate a minority ethnic community with legitimate claims to the city's resources. Jerusalem provides an instructive example. Palestinian communities in the eastern sectors of the city have traditionally been denied municipal services and resources not available outside municipal boundaries that appear mundane and rational but are not, since they have been drawn and adjusted by Israeli policymakers "keenly aware that they have much to gain from the acceptance of such actions as routinized and 'municipal'" (Bollens 2000: 87).

It is not only urban managers who emphasize the merits of division. One architect in Beirut notes the shortsightedness of many attempts to bridge divides in Lebanon without a full appreciation of the nature and consequences of the conflict: "Everybody automatically valorizes unification and pluralism but it's not clear to me that this is a starting point for discussion. I'm not even sure that it is idyllic in every respect" (John S., 2000). This valorization frequently colors external perceptions of divided cities, and it deserves to be questioned.

The terms that govern how well, and under what conditions, the needs of urban residents are met shape an unwritten urban contract that is constantly renegotiated according to circumstance. Because they can be viewed as a practical solution in cities that have expanded to a point where communal identity is routinely threatened, partitions can be understood as both a breach and a fulfillment of the urban contract.

4. Ethnic rivalries can result from reasonable insecurities.

Examination of the divided city condition often relies on the pretext that urban division is the product of intractable intergroup conflicts that cannot be successfully rationalized by those who favor the norms of conventional society (see Perowne 1954; Hastings 1970). A stable counterargument is generated by concentrating on the erosion of the urban contract rather than on theories of endemic violence between neighboring urban communities.

Explaining the complex dynamics linking local and external interests in a divided city requires a careful appraisal of the rivalries that lead to urban violence between resident groups. While all the cities examined in this book are outwardly defined by conflict between rival religious communities, none reveals upon close inspection the skeleton of a theological or even ideological dispute. It thus appears likely that religious affiliation provided a convenient vehicle for struggles tied to sovereignty, political influence, territory, property, and opportunity. Seeking an alternative framework for understanding, some contend that cities split between those who cherish urban values and those who disdain them.

It is interesting to note in this regard that some radical intellectuals have rejected the idea that the city is an incubator for social progress. The early Zionists' disparaging view of urban culture in general and Jerusalem in particular demonstrates this tendency well. Once superficial and erroneous explanations of intercommunal conflict are rejected, it becomes clear that urban residents frequently participate at a local level in battles that are neither of their making nor in their interests. They frequently suffer the consequences of a broken contract with urban managers so that others might benefit.

5. Urban partition is not always the result of faulty public policy.

Several highly capable students of ethnic conflict and divided cities assign responsibility for discord and partition in large measure to the highest levels of national or international governance (see Dumper 1997; Schaeffer 1990; Khalaf 1993; Bollens 2000; Wasserstein 2001).

There is little doubt that local politicians often play a pivotal role in the creation and maintenance of interethnic tensions, as observed by a former soldier in Mostar:

The politicians on both sides in greater or lesser degree preserve their positions by determining which particular spots located on "their" side of the city are to be restored. That way they appeal on people's emotions and, thus, consciously confirm and keep alive this psychological border. . . . It can be said that the politicians keep emphasizing the psychological border just to avoid the real problems such as the unemployment issue, for instance. Concretely, in Mostar, this problem of avoidance to reconstruct the Boulevard is the clear sign of such an approach. (Ferhad D., 2001)

Without question, the cascade of problems stemming from bad policy is a driving force behind the eventual emergence of urban partitions. In Belfast, urban managers frequently favor walls because of their expediency while recognizing the need to generate popular consensus in order to satisfy public opinion. One police officer there made this train of thought clear:

To say that [an interface barricade] would make it easier for us to deploy our resources is not a reason. It may well do. And walls all over the place would be great for policing, because we could take all the officers we have doing security duty and look at burglaries and drug dealing and all of that stuff, but that's not the reason we use. So if there are sufficient incidents, and there's no template that says how many incidents you need . . . and if there's cross-community support . . . you get a wall. You get what protection both communities want. (Edmund S., 2001)

Accordingly, policy-driven models of partition and reconciliation underlie much of the critical literature on the subject of divided societies. Such studies typically assert that discriminatory policies lead to social strife, failed attempts to mitigate this strife generate a crisis, partition temporarily contains that crisis, and finally, reformed policy is the only way in which to attain urban unification. A social worker in Beirut confirmed the value of political readings of local conflict that seem to be rooted in class or ethnic tensions:

the majority of the people who turned out to be from other religions didn't have access to such jobs or rights concerning the state of Lebanon. So I certainly feel that it's not a war between rich and poor but [a struggle with] people who don't want to share their rights with others. People are scared because they are a minority, at least in comparison to the Arab world that surrounds them. And you always can stereotype people in a certain direction. You can make it religious and make the majority support you. I don't think it's a religious matter. Its basis is more about laws and negotiations. (Nora H., 2000)

Determined emphasis on a policy-driven model tends to neglect the historic context of segregation and the ways in which cultural identity becomes politicized over time. Worse, it discounts legacies of intercommunal competition and the ways these legacies frequently make episodes of division seem inevitable. A cursory examination of the social and cultural currents shaping these cities in the centuries and decades prior to their division supports two conclusions: that every urban wall has been the product of a long and incremental process of intensifying physical segregation, and that no erection of an urban wall can be considered predestined or inevitable.

Nicosia provides an excellent example. Where the Green Line now bifurcates the historic core of the city, a river originally passed and was later diverted and filled to create the central commercial thoroughfares—Paphos and Hermes Streets—active from the eighteenth century on. In 1963, the same streets became a de facto ethnic partition between Turkish and Greek Cypriots and were transformed into an impermeable wall about ten years later. While the path of the Green Line was etched physically in the city's surface for centuries, it was activated as a tool of social segregation only in stages and in the wake of political events that can be easily characterized as unlikely and avoidable.

Many scholars have traced the evolution of the flawed and bigoted policies that came to characterize the system of political representation in Cyprus before and after it achieved independence in 1960. One of the most

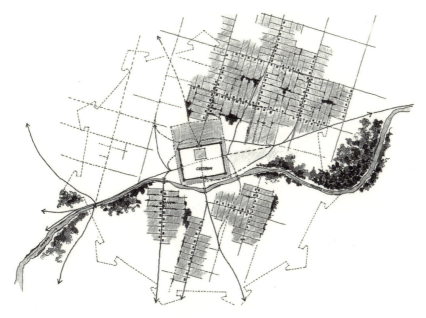

Figure 8.1. The path of the Pedeios River through the original Roman settlement, later an artery of the medieval city (walls indicated by a dotted line) and eventually filled in to create Paphos and Hermes Streets, which were transformed into the Green Line in 1963. Danilo Demi, used by permission from a 1997 typology study in support of the UNDP-assisted Nicosia Master Plan Bicommunal Project.

notable and damaging aspects of the Cypriot system during that period was its tendency to uphold models of political affiliation based on ethnicity, to the point where high political offices were permanently allocated according to ethnic quotas. This quota system was unfortunately protected by the Constitution and, as it was nearly impossible to adjudicate fairly on the shifting sands of interethnic rivalry, it became a major bone of contention throughout the 1960s. In this sense, faulty policy led directly to the bifurcation of Cypriot society along ethnic lines and, in turn, to the gradual segregation of the island and its capital along physical lines. Though the correlations between political systems and physical outcomes is both direct and linear in this case, strictly enforced ethnic quotas in the political realm did not entirely account for the recurrent violence and subsequent partitioning that has plagued Greek and Turkish Cypriots alike for decades.

Many other forces bubbling up from the community level are also to blame for the virulent ethnic segregation found in Cyprus, and many of these influences mounted incrementally decades before the impact of flawed government policies plunged the country into crisis. For years prior to independence and for many years after, military and paramilitary groups with a strong allegiance to Greece were active on the island in an effort to intimidate Turkish Cypriots and ignite the scattered embers of tension between the two ethnic groups. History has provided ample fuel for this gradual conflagration, since the memories and remnants of Ottoman occupation were near at hand for those who wished to exploit them.

At the same time, church leaders sometimes lent their moral authority to a nationalist chorus calling for union with Greece. From the mid-1950s forward, countless episodes of small-scale intimidation and violence marred peaceful relations between ethnic groups on the island. The ambivalence of British administrators did little to stem this tide of ill will and insecurity between Turkish and Greek Cypriots, and the informal channels through which these bigoted campaigns were implemented did not allow for their full impacts to be easily assessed by outside observers. The result was a deepening sense of mistrust and paranoia among ordinary Cypriots. This process was shaped by vested external interests but was designed to appear as the organic product of the popular imagination.

Similar manipulations can be easily recognized in the programs of intimidation and terror preceding major episodes of violence in Northern Ireland, the former Yugoslavia, and Lebanon. In each instance, actors anticipating gains from ethnic partition revived the memory of historic grievances and previous episodes of exploitation between native ethnic groups in order to generate mutual distrust. In this way they brought back to life long-dormant suspicions and provoked the violence that was ultimately propelled forward by a vengeful logic of its own.

All these influences operating at the local community level—the accidental, the intentional, and the residual—provided a foundation for violent episodes of recrimination between ethnic groups that had formerly coexisted in a cooperative manner. Political reactions led to policies that reinforced ethnic difference and took for granted the incompatibility of neighboring groups. Historic, local, political, and foreign influences converged to create what appeared to outside observers to be an intractable stalemate between rival ethnic communities.

Which influences were primary and which were secondary is a difficult question to answer, and the question is perhaps unimportant. The key observation is that complex and reciprocal influences exist in each case of urban division. Because political processes do not exclusively drive the causes and remedies of urban partition, the effort to avoid or mitigate it can in some cases be augmented by social intervention at the local level as well as by legal intervention at the institutional level. This places new opportunities and responsibilities before nonpolitical actors concerned with the health of urban communities thus entangled in conflict. The ways in which professionals can address these challenges are examined in Chapter 9.

Erosion of the Urban Contract

By the time urban partitions appear, at least one urban community has experienced a loss of security so severe that the cost of vulnerability outweighs the benefits of cooperation. At this juncture, urban managers are often viewed as untrustworthy or incompetent. In general, it is the minority ethnic groups who are the first to abandon the urban contract, though in many instances several groups don the cloak of the martyr, in accordance with Benvenisti's "double minority syndrome" discussed in chapter ten. Israel provides the archetypal example. Israeli Jews often portray themselves as a religious minority in the region, while Palestinians see themselves as an ethnic minority in the state of Israel.

When urban residents find that their vulnerability has reached intolerable levels in the urban environment, a core component of the conventional urban contract is missing. Some form of compensation must then be identified. A common cycle was described by a Belfast interface resident in straightforward terms:

It is frustrating. You have no where to go on it. Petrol bombs thrown into the street . . . reports about who started it . . . police saying that the Catholics put scorch marks on the ground to have an excuse for fighting. What would I do? Go to complain at the police station? They would tell me to get lost. If there were a problem, the police wouldn't come out. The police come and put their spotlights on us. Never arrest any of the Protestants . . . I think that's where the problem is. I think if you said, "Look, we're going to start taking walls down around here" people would say, "Hmm. Who's going to protect us?" Because nobody trusts the police to protect us. Not that police force anyway. (Paul M., 2001)

Urban managers are obliged to provide positive conditions for personal and commercial prosperity at a cost that does not burden the public budget. Seeking to construct and maintain an efficient social mechanism, they aim to promote the highest levels of prosperity at the lowest social costs in terms of poverty and discord. In most cities, this equilibrium is achieved without disrupting the physical and functional unity of the whole entity.

The ethnic violence that generally characterizes divided cities presents urban managers with an equation that is difficult to balance. They must try to preserve favorable conditions for the majority of urban residents without leading the city into bankruptcy. In this context, the economic value of dividing lines in relation to limited municipal budgets can be seen to contribute this to their popularity as a short-term solution to security crises.

It was necessary. The alternative would have been to flood the area with police: the walls serve the same function. There is very little else you can do as a quick fix. You always hope they will no longer be required. It gets down to security at the end the day. Gated communities of Miami—reduces their insurance costs. Invisible hand, trickle down. In Belfast, the government pays the insurance cost, so they put in the walls. But they do frustrate dialogue, there's no doubt about that. (James L., 2000)

Where intercommunal violence is rife, partitions are sometimes used as policing tools by local governments that lack the resources to support continuous police surveillance or lack political motivation to devise less socially disruptive solutions.

Where physical partitioning occurs, a kind of equilibrium is achieved by sacrificing the integrity of the city as a whole to the interests of discrete, often beleaguered, ethnic communities within:

If there was trouble at what we call an interface area, what you would find is that people living on one side would maybe go to the police would say, "Look, our houses are being attacked every night." And the police, if you like, can't be there 24 hours a day because of limited resources. So the people might say then, "I think you should build a wall or a fence there to give us protection so that we can feel safe in our beds at night." (Stephen N., 2001)

For residents of partitioned enclaves in Belfast, taking the long view is a luxury:

Some people want a wall up and some people don't. I prefer a wall up, but that's only because I have a young family. I'd be happy in a minute if they just put a wall up and just blocked it up completely. Because there's nothing that's going to happen between us and them up there. . . . I prefer a wall. (Paul M., 2001)

Breakdown of the Urban Contract

Strong incentives for urban partitioning emerge only in relation to specific combinations of spatial and political circumstance. These conditions in-

Figure 8.2. Carefully engineered, layered partition walls in Belfast, 2002. Authors.

clude longstanding associations between ethnic groups and distinct sections of urban territory, legacies of spatial segregation within the city, cataclysmic episodes of social and economic destabilization, and history of political affiliation bound closely and involuntarily to ethnicity. When these preconditions are compounded by unusual stresses encountered at the local level and the manipulations of nationalist politicians at the municipal level, intensified forms of physical segregation can be anticipated in the urban domain leading to the breakdown of the urban contract.

When breaches or compromises with respect to security take place, urban residents are forced to accommodate the resulting violence or trauma directly. Some observers have noted that violently alienated and dichotomized ethnic groups "strive to concretize the dichotomy by creating a dual physical and social environment" (Benvenisti 1982: 4). The urban wall clearly assists with this process of accommodation.

This fact is central to a discussion of why urban walls, which are undesirable in so many respects, have proven so durable. It points to a pragmatic logic that goes a long way toward explaining the tendency of urban managers to subsidize ethnic partition and can be considered separate from broader questions of causation and responsibility. Urban walls have been utilized repeatedly, the products of careful deliberation, by many urban managers seeking to shore up chronic ethnic violence in their jurisdiction. In Belfast, for example, one critic notes that "partition was the most practical and inevitable solution the British could devise when confronted with intractable troubles and the desire to minimize risk and investment" (Schaeffer 1990: 87). The same logic applies to all divided cities, since the cost of policing long, volatile boundaries is high.

Space becomes territory to be defended for its own sake when it has been politicized and converted into a symbolic commodity. In this way political legitimacy is often conflated with urban territory. For example, Croatians in the western sector of Mostar and Protestants in Belfast's Shankhill enclave choose not to profit by renting their empty housing units to members of a rival community, and they do not leave readily.

Ardoyne is a very tight-knit community. I'm forty-seven years old, I've lived here all my life and there's no way I would move out in a million years now, no matter how bad things get. I don't know where it actually comes from. You just feel part of it. To leave it would be dishonorable. (Craig W., 2001)

The infusion of urban space with special meanings is a conscious process that tends to mask or obscure the larger, more essential elements of a social crisis.

One common characteristic of all five divided cities is a precipitous and unexpected downturn in regional economic prospects during the years prior to the imposition of coercive internal segregation. In some cases, as in Jerusalem and Beirut, local security concerns were rapidly eclipsed by regional power struggles that disrupted a social equilibrium and created power vacuums ultimately filled by ultranationalist political entrepreneurs.

In Belfast and Mostar, political instability was compounded by industry closures that weakened employment and morale among working-class urban residents. Collective feelings of alienation, humiliation, and deprivation prompted many underprivileged ethnic minority communities to question the benefits they could expect from the urban contract. In some instances, the terms of the contract had shifted with political events; in others, the contract remained intact while new circumstances shed light on longstanding iniquities.

Urban managers with large-scale responsibilities for partitioned cities often justify them as a security scheme of last resort:

People don't want peacelines in general. If you don't live there, then you might think, "Peacelines are no use, we should be bringing down walls" and all this nice stuff you say. But the reality is that if you live there you want a peaceline. On the one hand you want to be moving away from the conflict situation, but the reality is you're not. It's still there to a certain extent so you need to deal with it. And peacelines are there, and essential. (Edmund S., 2001)

These actors tend to view the walls as a product of failed socialization and lawlessness that no reasonable government could predict or contain. While many regret the presence of these partitions in their cities and even campaign for their removal, most view them as a necessary if unwelcome solution to longstanding social ills:

You get a situation where somebody throws a brick through a window, then they put up a wire mesh over it, then you have a situation where maybe one of them gets burned, or whatever, and then people move out of the area and you get dereliction. So that usually is what causes the initial problem. Now how do they stabilize that? If you can't police it, or whatever, then the general idea is, okay, let's just accept the inevitable and put a wall up the middle. (James L., 2000)

Spatial remedies responding to interethnic tension without accompanying social remedies have not produced good results where they have been tested on a large scale over extended periods of time. As a local politician in Belfast observed:

the historic, the cultural, the economic, the social . . . none of it deals with any of those. So unless we have a multi-faceted approach to what our problem is, then I don't think we will be able to remotely deal with it. (Ervine 2001)

When this broad approach is rejected, new problems often result from the imposition of partitions. Individual and household deprivation generally rise in proximity to sectarian interfaces in divided cities. Property values tend to go down near the boundaries of contested areas regardless of, and often due to, the presence of walls. Those who live along these interfaces typically lack better housing options.

Most residents of divided cities have a hard time explaining the origins and necessity of the barricades that separate them from their neighbors. If they were to trace the roots of these conflicts they would often find that their physical segregation crisis stems from conflicts and rivalries so distant as to be unrecognizable. In this way different conflicts are projected into a violent urban interface: international tensions, regional wars, class struggles, ethnic rivalries, and neighborhood riots. One result is that local tensions become disproportionate to local problems.

In Palestinian Jerusalem, one social worker observed that it may be easier to cross the Atlantic than the former Green Line in order to foster constructive dialogue:

I would prefer to seek youth exchanges with the Israeli side, but we cannot do it, you see. They're living beside us. I want to send [Palestinian teenagers] out to exchange ideas and talk about the future and to know how they think. We cannot do it. It is easy for us to have exchanges with Western Europe and with the United States. It's very difficult to do it within Israel, with the Israelis. We're living together. We cannot do it. There is a red line, okay? (Maria B., 2003)

This invisible line is also felt in Belfast, where paramilitary forces appear to be acting with the approval of larger political interests. A Member of Parliament for Belfast observes:

Well I think they're beginning to realize that it's more than just a riot here or there. That there's something more fundamental that keeps people apart. But people want to stay apart, you know? And some politicians want people to stay apart. That's their agenda. (Maginness 2001)

As they emerge in the popular consciousness, chronic insecurities and a willingness to consider desperate remedies are often harnessed by politicians pledging reform through resistance and segregation. The frameworks they advocate generally ensure that political affiliation is bound to heredity so that ethnic identity becomes "the principle of incorporation into the political community" since "ethnicity is based on a myth of collective ancestry, which usually carries with it traits believed to be innate" (Horowitz 1985: 52). This exploitative dynamic between marginalized minority ethnic groups and racist politicians has direct implications on core issues like resource allocation and participation in municipal decision making. It emerges frequently in the late stages of a divided city's evolution.

As long as disadvantaged minority groups do not exert a destabilizing influence on the city as a whole, the urban contract remains intact. While they maintain a system with these inherent inequalities, urban managers are obliged to minimize tension in the urban arena while minimizing public expenditures on policing and public relations. The decision to utilize physical barriers was rationalized this way by a police officer in Belfast:

But whilst it is not the ultimate solution—building walls and fences—if the people on both sides request it, and they're in support of it, you know, what can you do? Because if the idea is supported by both communities, and the wall is not erected, and let's say there's a petrol bomb attack and someone loses their life on whatever side, you know all too quickly the finger of accusation is pointed: "Right, if you had built that wall, this wouldn't have happened." You have to be very, very cautious and careful. (Stephen N., 2001)

Stripping away the stereotypical notion that Protestants naturally despise Catholics in Northern Ireland, or that Croatians are consumed by their historic vendetta against Muslims in the Balkans, perception of intergroup competition as a zero-sum game is typically linked to longstanding discrimination and a scarcity of essential economic resources.

Residents impacted directly by fluctuating economic conditions are the most likely to suffer the negative impacts of ethnic partition, highlighting the class-based component of many divided city scenarios. This theme was explored at some length by scholars of Irish history regarding Belfast during the mid-1920s:

Working-class leaders sought to advance the political and economic interests of their class by uniting Protestant and Catholic workers in trade unions and challenging the absolute power of the industrialists and gentry. The Tory elite sought to preserve its prerogatives by fostering sectarian strife among its opponents. . . . The Orange Lodge, financed by Belfast industrialists and dedicated to the preservation of Protestant supremacy, had become the dominant institution of the Protestant working class. Fearing the imagined horrors of Catholic power (Home Rule equals

Rome rule) and jealous of their marginal advantages over Catholics, Protestant workers ignored their real economic interests and gave their support to the Unionist party. (Henderson, Lebow, and Stoessinger 1974: 209)

The same forces were still at work half a century later in Belfast:

There is a greater degree of conflict between the two ethnic groups in the working-class context . . . generated by situations of scarcity and competition, particularly in housing and jobs. (Murtagh 1995: 211)

Another example of class conflict obscured by ethnic rivalry is found in Cyprus, where Communist organizers on both sides of the island attempted to forge lines of communication and cooperation as tensions grew in the 1950s. An anthropologist in Nicosia described this attempt to create cross-cutting linkages based on shared economic interests in detail:

Another very serious rift is the conflict between the left and the right. The left had created very important bi-communal structures of cooperation in the past, through labor organizing and trade unions. But as the two sides were drifting apart—with Enosis versus Taksim—those who tried to co-operate were deemed traitors by both sides because they were supposed to cooperate with the people of the other community. This is why many leftists were killed by people on their own side, on both sides of the island, and this is why now the two left wing parties are still in very close solidarity. (Papadakis 2002)

As in Northern Ireland, early attempts to avoid interethnic conflict failed in large part due to competing political forces, leaving the economic foundation of much social upheaval largely unexamined.

The annals of divided cities are full of similar instances in which promising avenues of negotiation and cooperation were blocked while policymakers accepted the view that intra-class, intergroup conflicts were intractable. Such shortsighted interpretations consolidate habits of discrimination and encourage the institutionalization of difference within municipal government. Ethnic partition sometimes follows, appearing to affirm a self-fulfilling prophecy of violence, distrust and endemic conflict.

If you asked, in a rough kind of way, whether you thought the things people call peacelines should stay or not, you could probably draw a fairly decent curve where the percentage saying "keep them" would simply decline as your sample resided farther from the wall, but if you lived anywhere nearby, then, no way you want it down, you're not going to have those come down until other things changed, and then you might have enough confidence for the walls to go. So there's no doubt about it, there is massive and continued support for it, particularly among the people who live close to them. (Boal 2000)

It follows that many ethnic rivalries in divided cities stem, directly or indirectly, from broad-based class conflict. The preconflict histories of Beirut, Belfast, Mostar, Nicosia, and Jerusalem show that social tensions were as much a reflection of economic strife as of ancient ethnic rivalry, yet in each case class conflicts were successfully forestalled or diverted.

Other forms of third-party intervention tend to undermine the urban contract. Chapters three to seven have shown how the involvement of foreign governments frequently sanctioned interethnic urban violence in divided cities. It is thus clear that the involvement of Israel, the PLO and Syria in the Lebanese conflict prolonged civil strife in Beirut.

Likewise, the British influence in Palestine and Northern Ireland, the Greek and Turkish involvement in Cyprus, and the American intervention in Bosnia have all had profound effects on how local, interethnic disputes played out. Not all interventions had negative consequences. It can be argued, for example, that American pressure turned the tide of the Bosnian civil war in favor of the beleaguered Bosniaks, that the United Nations monitoring of the Cypriot Green Line brought stability to the border, and that British soldiers provided vital protection to Catholic residents of Belfast when Protestant paramilitaries attempted to displace them.

Nevertheless, manipulations of foreign governments with vested interests in the outcome of regional disputes tends to undermine the legitimacy of local political institutions and trivialize the legitimate concerns of disenfranchised ethnic groups. British protection of Catholic residents of Belfast addressed a crisis but simultaneously encouraged the expansion of Protestant paramilitaries as a compensatory measure. The American government's desire to avoid confrontation between Greece and Turkey certainly encouraged the United Nations and others to move slowly toward a condemnation of the violent abuses perpetrated against Turkish-speaking Cypriots from 1958 until 1974. Even when the motives of these third parties are relatively pure, however, they occasionally feel obliged to stand between antagonistic groups in order to save lives. In doing so, the bloom of a crisis is often mistaken for its root.

Violence and discrimination are not the causes of interethnic strife, but its symptoms. Being eager for quick and economical progress, third party interveners have a tendency to address the symptoms alone, leaving the creation of a long-term solution to the next wave of mediation, a wave that often never materializes.

Consequences of Breakdown

Urban partitions, regardless of their origins or their age, dominate local concerns and siphon precious energies away from social development concerns. They deflect attention away from causes and toward effects. Public debate is often restricted to optimal modes of damage control, so that a gradual accommodation of abnormal and gratuitous forms of communal violence takes place within the popular imagination.

I think basically what you're asking is: Why do we opt for self-imposed apartheid? That's basically what we have. And what people are demanding almost on a daily basis is more and more self-imposed apartheid. And I think that's not an answer to our long-term problem. I think it is . . . firefighting: you have an initial diffusion of difficulty. But if exclusion is at the core of our political difficulty, how can we advocate further exclusion? (Ervine 2001)

Defensive walls in cities are both a response to chronic social ills and a source of new cycles of violence. For this reason, the costs and consequences of urban partition must be calculated terms of exposure to direct and indirect liabilities: those felt in the presence of violence and anxiety, and those felt in the absence of opportunity and social health.

Despite the short-term advantages mentioned previously, urban partitions propel a morbid cycle. Thirty-five years after the Troubles began in Belfast, and a decade after the process of full political reconciliation began, faith in urban barricades remains firm. Popular petitions for new walls, or the extension of old ones, are regularly delivered to Members of Parliament by communities that believe themselves to be vulnerable.

Since permanent and semipermanent walls appear to validate interethnic boundaries, their construction often spurs violent reprisals from rival groups contending for the same urban territory. The fact that barricades so frequently exacerbate territorial disputes seems to have cooled appetites for them very little in Belfast. In this way, a last resort becomes the first and only recourse for communities that fall through the safety net of the conventional urban contract.

A patterned sequence of events leads healthy cities toward physical segregation and institutionalized discrimination. The catalyst is insecurity and widespread xenophobia in response to conditions of political and economic instability. These dynamics are common to most cities. When medieval European cities were hastening toward total fortification as a re-

Figure 8.3. Local papers in Belfast attested to the ongoing popularity of peacelines in 2002. Barricades are constructed and extended according to an orderly process of neighborhood consensus-building and Parliamentary petition. Authors.

sponse to political upheaval and hinterland attackers, physical transformation often required a Faustian bargain as

the need for more costly sinews of war put the cities into the hands of serious oligarchies that financed the ruler's mischievous policies, lived sumptuously on the profits and loot, and sought to entrench their positions by backing the ensuing despotism. (Mumford 1960: 87)

The case of the divided city is consistent with this legacy. Divided cities demonstrate the same fear and systemic corruption turned inward, compelling the city to lay siege to itself. Like Mumford's "war metropolis," the divided city is often crowded with opportunistic politicians who exacerbate popular suspicions, fan violence into ceaseless cycles of retribution, and sap the resources of ordinary citizens whose lives are transformed by interethnic rivalries from which they have little to gain.

Faced with institutionalized discrimination over lengthy periods, the most vulnerable urban residents may increase their reliance on formerly subordinate affiliations such as clan, caste, ethnicity, or nationality. When this happens, the linkage between inherited group identity and urban territory often becomes literal and concrete. Walls become precious emblems of both territory and identity for urban communities who feel besieged by neighboring rivals, whether or not they hold any practical value as security devices.

Urban managers are often sanguine about this process, since the costs of constructing partitions and the loss of rent, tax and income on the land they occupy may be minimal in comparison with the cost of containing chronic violence with conventional policing mechanisms. A Belfast police officer observes,

There are other ways we could provide additional security for that area. We could assign a special patrol to the area. We would have to find additional funding to do that, though, since it is very expensive. (Edmund S., 2001)

While a thorough comparative analysis of these economic considerations has yet to be undertaken in any divided city to date, it is likely that in many contexts walls and fences remain more economical than other forms of conflict management when judged from a purely pragmatic point of view. When these practical considerations are linked with other intangibles, the presence and persistence of urban partitions can be explained without resorting to notions of endemic ethnic rivalry.

Interpretations

Violence, partition, and deepening forms of discrimination in many cases constitute an attempt to compensate for the broken urban contract. When this contract between urban managers and urban residents is broken, the physical and social fabric of the city is often torn and tailored until baseline security conditions are met.

Urban walls indicate failure of conventional systems to uphold their traditional obligations to residents who are members of ethnic minority communities. Partitions are sometimes embraced by rival communities and urban managers as a practical alternative to chronic violence. In none of the five cities examined here was a respite from hardship and insecurity fully realized.

Physical barricades address the symptoms rather than causes of intergroup rivalries. Municipal governments hoping to preserve public trust may fear that their neutrality will be compromised if they intervene, leaving them unable to do much more than react to the most severe consequences of the problem. One good example is found in Mostar, where the central municipality is limited to decisions that reflect a consensus between the mayor and deputy mayor—each representing one of the rival ethnic communities in the city—and accordingly seems unable to make significant strides forward toward reconciliation.

In Belfast the refusal of the municipal government to acknowledge formally the need for ethnically homogeneous public housing estates forces it to mitigate chronic disputes that do not officially exist. Rather than strengthen the government's credibility, these "color-blind" planning policies have pitted Catholic and Protestant communities against each other. Catholics living in crowded neighborhoods often assume that vacancies in Protestant neighborhoods demonstrate the political allegiance of the city government to the United Kingdom, while Protestants assume that their claims to urban territory are being undermined by the municipality's accommodation of a growing Catholic population.

In the midst of these speculations, the British civil servants assigned to Northern Irish affairs during and after the outbreak of the Troubles worked with the assumption that fair, unbiased intervention was possible. They were not keen to hear from local administrators that institutionalized segregation offered the best prospects for progress because it contradicted their view of British involvement as both rational and equitable. Neutrality and effectiveness very rarely go together in the context of the divided city.

The recent history of urban partition supports the suggestion that walls built between ethnic groups can result in short-term improvements in social stability. In Belfast, a divisional urban planner with the Housing Executive clarified this linkage:

I can see that the wall, when it is put up because both communities want it, introduces a first key ingredient in the long way back, the path back that starts with stability. If you can create stability, then you have something you can build on in both communities, and ultimately it will lead to a position where maybe the walls do come down. (Morrison, 2000)

Advocates of physical division as a diplomatic last resort assume that "the greater the degree of territorial homogeneity, the better the chances for some form of inter and intrastate stability in the long term" (Newman 1994: 94).

The actual security performance record of these partitions only partly bears out this assumption. In Belfast, the impact on overall neighborhood security may be negative: "Peacelines are there to stop violence. Look at where all the violence is taking place: right around interface areas. You'll find those are the least policed part of that community" (Philip J., 2001). Lack of surveillance and blight near peacelines create an optimal staging ground for local and proxy wars. One Belfast community worker observed that "the interface becomes the focus for the violence, and it's the hinterland—it's the people from beyond the interfaces that come and perpetuate the violence. It's not that people on the interfaces are coming out and rioting" (McGlone 2001).

While improved stability has been achieved in many cases, most notably in Nicosia and Jerusalem, it may have been purchased at too a high price. The suppression of violent threats that are near at hand may be ultimately overshadowed by the dividends of fear and mutual suspicion that are an inevitable byproduct of involuntary separation.

Chapter 9
Professional Responses to Partition

Introduction

Effective and equitable professional responses to urban partition are rare. For experts trained to solve problems in the built environment—urban planners, architects, and conservators—the divided city presents a nightmare scenario for which surefire remedies do not exist.

Split, suffocating cities do not frequently appear in textbooks, and the complications of ethnic violence are generally assumed to be the concern of other disciplines. Academic training for planners and architects usually serves these polarized circumstances poorly, since segregation is typically lumped together with other forms of urban blight without considering the specific economic pressures and social weaknesses that divided cities reveal.

Built environment professionals are easily lost in the gap that separates anticipated problems from actual ones in the context of a divided city. They often lack vital skills, such as being able to negotiate diplomatically among rival groups; perform social needs assessments in the absence of a stable central government; decipher and interpret territorial markers; accommodate irrational security concerns in planning strategies; and accept bigotry as a baseline condition for planning. The effectiveness of design professionals in the context of a divided city is limited by the extent to which their training and original assumptions bar them from operating under social conditions they perceive to be distasteful and dysfunctional. Until the dilemmas that result are addressed by reforming their professional education and providing them with wider consultation, wasted potential and disillusionment among planning professionals are likely to predominate.

Despite all the disadvantages stacked against them, built environment professionals still retain a significant and mostly unrealized potential to shape policy and assist in the broader process of coping with the negative impacts of urban partition. It seems probable that their lack of onsite training and preparation constrains their effective involvement more than any

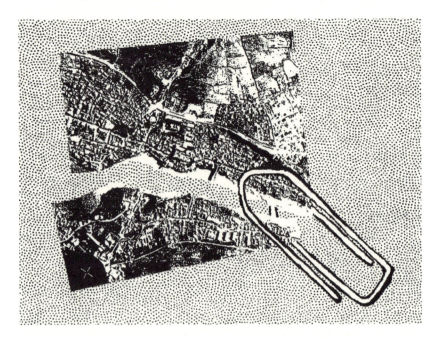

Figure 9.1. One Mostarian urban planner expressed his frustration with a torn photo and a paper clip. Tihomir Rosic, used by permission.

other single factor. The field of urban planning has been slow to acknowledge postconflict scenarios as part of its repertoire, leaving that domain undertheorized and without a professional literature supporting the development and critique of strategic approaches to ethnic division.

Some experts attempt to rise above the fray, like the sewage engineer in Nicosia who cleared paths through the political minefield in which he works:

Both sides are working the benefits of human beings. We are not working for the Turkish, or for the Greeks, or for the Muslims, or for Christians. We are working for the human beings. If you say, "Hey I am Turkish" or "I am English," there is no chance to work. You say, "I am a human being. And I am an engineer, and I have to work for the benefit of human beings." (Öznel 2001)

But in most divided cities the notion of public welfare, an anchoring concept for most urban planning strategies, is called into question. Once this moral compass is demagnetized, even veteran practitioners feel the vertigo. For some, the common good becomes difficult to define:

In divided cities it's waste, it's ugly, it's cruel, it's unfair, it's disharmony. The whole thing can be defined as a disharmonious situation. You come to a place, and you say: "Okay, so what am I going to do to rectify the situation, to ameliorate the situation, to do something positive?" And people look at you and say: "What do you mean by positive? Positive for whom?" And you say: "What do you mean for whom? For the good of humankind." They say: "Humankind? You mean Jewish, or Arab?" And then you say, for instance: "There is a common good!" And they say: "Oh . . . you are a philosopher!" (Benvenisti 2003)

Because professional engagement with divided cities is fraught, most experts avoid it or continue to work from within discredited political mechanisms, as if conditions were normal. In choosing their course, a dilemma is unavoidable: to participate is inevitably perceived as to be partisan, while inaction squanders opportunities to assist traumatized communities. Neither option presents clear prospects for satisfaction and success.

The neutrality and objectivity that is so much a part of the professional's ordinary mindset cannot be sustained. Professionals attempting to avoid taking sides often find that a political affiliation has been assigned to them, since noncommittal behavior can be viewed by both rivals and critics of the state as a tacit affirmation of the status quo or as "instrumental in the exercise of state repression and coercion" (Bollens 2000: 14). In highly dichotomized circumstances, indifference to sectarian concerns is often equated with callousness and complicity in the minds of local antagonists. One police officer in Belfast observes

you can't just stick a Catholic into a Protestant estate or a Protestant into a Catholic estate—they won't survive. The house won't survive, they won't survive; so, though it seems sectarian, it's actually common sense. You don't do that. You know, you don't put a cat into a kennel of dogs—terriers—it just doesn't make sense. (Edmund S., 2001)

It follows that the patronage of public municipal institutions, generally a mainstay for urban designers and planners, is often absent in the divided city due to the steady erosion of trust in local government that generally accompanies physical segregation. The lack of reliable and satisfactory political patronage eliminates a major prerequisite for coordinated professional involvement.

As a result, solutions are sometimes made hastily in response to emergencies and often without the benefit of professional input, as with Belfast's publicly funded barricades: "Security walls; peacelines, are not designed within a scheme. They come as a consequence of the conflict, and it arises on the ground" (Fred J., 2000).

The majority of built environment professionals choose to wait for political solutions and the return of working conditions with which they are familiar:

Thinking about that and talking with colleagues who have been working in the area of urban planning for twenty, thirty years, I must say that I am disappointed. I am disappointed by those colleagues' way of thinking and their vision of the city. (Ziad T., 2000)

Local professionals become marginalized as whole sections of their cities are destroyed and partitions offend many of the basic principles underlying progressive urban development. This approach leaves the divided city without expert assistance at junctures characterized by extreme vulnerability and volatility. It is exactly at these moments—when the traditional patrons of design and urban planning are weakened, and when faith in public institutions is at a low ebb—that thoughtful and balanced physical interventions are most needed. Without such interventions, politicians are left to manage the physical segregation of cities alone, without the practical or theoretical tools required to do the job well. Bad decisions and hasty solutions create walls that generate new sets of problems and antagonisms, even while they extinguish some immediate and localized brushfires.

There is thus a lack of a systematic response to the dilemma of partition among built environment professionals. They are typically absent from the political discourse regarding physical segregation as a solution to inter-ethnic disputes. It may be that they simply mirror the general public's distaste for partition lines that carry so many negative and painful associations. When both citizens and politicians would prefer to dismiss this subject, there is generally little likelihood that professionals, who are often paid with tax dollars, will press independently for critique and evaluation.

Given the enormous costs of urban partition, the consequences of this kind of professional acquiescence can be grave. New roles need to be carved out by built environment professionals in order to improve their effectiveness under conditions of abnormal stress, violence, and discord in a segregated urban environment. Meanwhile, external observers might wonder when an urban crisis is unfolding: where are the experts? Why are comprehensive responses so rare? A pursuit of satisfactory answers leads the observer to explore more carefully the fundamental relationship between built environment professionals and politics.

The divided city is a physical crisis nestled within a political crisis carried forward by a raft of social ills. Previous chapters have shown that urban division occurs in incremental and patterned ways that reveal the logic of partition. If the problem is governed by patterns, it follows that systematic professional responses are also possible. A range of professional strategies, some to be avoided and some to be repeated, can be identified by examining responses to urban partition in Beirut, Belfast, Mostar, Jerusalem, and Nicosia.

In what follows, postures of compliance and avoidance supported by a mantra of neutrality are not considered successful professional approaches to a divided city, while engagement and advocacy, supported by a firm sense of professional responsibility, are. A number of these strategies will be explored in the pages that follow, allowing for some final speculations about optimal professional engagement in the context of extreme urban segregation.

Strategies of Compliance

Many built environment professionals avoid or ignore divided cities because they appear inscrutable, hopeless, and corrupt. Foreign experts look on with detached amazement, while many local experts depart if they have the means to do so. Those who choose to become involved are confronted with an array of problems. These relate to their institutional affiliation, to political patronage, access to information, publicity, and collegial cooperation—all of minor significance under normal working conditions.

Training and prior experience in healthy cities are not always relevant. Resources are at a minimum, or alternatively, well-funded municipal projects are heavy with political baggage. These debilitating factors confront professionals with a series of dilemmas: To stay or to leave? To work or abstain? To tone down the effects of bad policies or attempt to influence new, better ones? To assist side A or side B? Each decision leads to a new series of complications and risks.

Planning professionals generally assume that problems generated by sectarian conflict and interethnic violence are beyond the scope of their expertise. It seems clear that this assumption stems more from faulty suppositions embedded in their training than from the nature of the actual problems presented by urban partition. The core issues of the divided city can be described using a vocabulary of form, space, movement, and association that is neither exotic nor unfamiliar; but to grasp the grammar and syntax of urban partition calls for an appreciation of social dynamics that is frequently lacking.

Architects, urban planners, and cultural-heritage conservators are similarly constrained by the conventional attitudes toward individual sites and structures cultivated in them in school. This educational system has generated a class of highly competent professionals that is generally unprepared to assist the citizens of cities that have been partitioned by ethnic conflict.

Conventional professional training for architects and planners instills faith in the transformative powers of design where a harmonious social context is taken more or less for granted. It typically does not provide the tools needed to cope effectively with planning in a divided city, where a practitioner must address social needs in a political labyrinth where values and expectations are frequently distorted.

In accordance with this training, planners generally take a "five-mile-high" view of urban dynamics that fails to incorporate the contradictory, idiosyncratic, and microscale territorial conflicts that characterize physical partition between rival groups. They are "trained to be above partisanship" (Boal 2000), but neutral space is typically not available for occupancy when you arrive in the divided city.

One Lebanese scholar observed that orthodox architectural education "doesn't give you the political or the philosophical depth to deal with situations" (John S., 2000). A Cypriot urban planner went farther: "There are no decisions that are not political . . . so whatever architect thinks that he is not politically involved doesn't understand his role" (Pavlos A., 2002).

The first hurdle that must be cleared by built environment professionals seeking a substantial role in the divided city context is an attachment to neutrality. Orthodox training links the quality and credibility of professional contributions with nonpartisan engagement. In circumstances where neutral ground is scarce, this orthodoxy directs the professional to identify the public and commercial spaces in the city where social mixing once occurred as the only appropriate sites for intervention. This approach remains faithful to the idea that urban apartheid "is political and has nothing to do with architecture" (Malek G., 2000)—a view that is reasonable and appeals to common sense, but is incorrect.

A more circumspect view of this issue leads to the conclusion that "divided cities are results of political struggles, so any urban planning in the cities cannot be dissociated from political directives and urban physical issues are the translations of political options" (Marwan T., 2000). Leaving aside the broader question of whether spatial interventions in normal cities can ever be considered apolitical, it appears that neutrality is unachievable for professionals hoping to operate in an environment polarized by internal sectarian conflict. This leaves the built environment professional in a tricky position, stuck between impotent orthodoxy and effective heresy.

Efforts to maintain professional neutrality, though usually well intentioned, tend to undermine professional effectiveness in the divided city. This truism is illustrated by examining a fundamental challenge encountered by professionals active in any divided city: how to ensure that the benefits of planned development are shared. The obvious course is to ignore intercommunal disputes and attend to the most pressing social ills, but this approach is treacherous.

To insist on nonpartisan professional engagement is to invite irrelevance. The feigned ignorance of political pressures and liabilities can produce effects opposite of those intended. This kind of reversal occurred when, for example, urban planners in Belfast attempted to allocate new housing in an impartial manner at Unity Flats, Twinbrook Estates, and along Alliance Avenue. They discovered that many families prioritized security and solidarity above material improvements in their living conditions. One urban planner in Belfast began his career working on nonsectarian housing schemes but later observed: "People always settle in familiar ethnic-cultural groups. You could say it's a natural thing to do. So why not plan for it?" (Richard S., 2000).

Such disappointments and failed experiments in nonsectarian urban planning demonstrate the difficulty of adopting a color-blind approach to a color-bound problem: "a policy approach that seeks neutrality creates a gap in community connectedness that is filled in by conspiratorial theories on both sides of the ethnic divide" (Bollens 2000: 282).

But the conscientious professional would like to confront the difficulties of ethnic segregation in a fair and rational way:

[The urban planner] views "politics" as the cause of the conflict, rather than its outcome. He tends to ignore the conflict by defining policy problems in noncontroversial terms such as "land and order," "inequalities," "rational allocation of resources." His justification for ignoring the conflicting perceptions is that official recognition would perpetuate them. (Benvenisti 1982: 198)

This logic is tidy but rarely supports successful interventions. A plausible political interpretation must be given to professional interventions or else a much less flattering one is likely to be automatically assigned. The professional's need to remain above the fray interferes with the development of optimal development strategies in a divided city because it assumes the false separation between technical and political concerns, allowing for the possibility that physical interventions could be developed in isolation from a balanced and thorough understanding of fundamental social crises.

In practice, the divided city offers little hospitality for the professional who would like to be welcomed as an "involved, objective outsider." This individual must either step back onto the margin or engage the urban development process according to the terms and timetables of a political patron. Frustration and ineffectiveness inevitably result. This frustration is evident in all five divided cities examined here, but it is especially clear in Belfast, where the Housing Authority long refused to incorporate ethnicity into its allocation schemes, to the detriment of its constituents, who did not have the same luxury:

The planners would argue: "These houses are for no particular religion, anybody can come and live in them." But if they're in a certain area, say they're in a Green area, well, you're not going to get Protestants coming to live in them. Because the first thing that's going to happen is that they'll be petrol-bombed out, and forced out, since you'll get local people living in the area coming around and saying, "You're a Protestant? No, you better leave. That house is for a Catholic. You don't live here." (Stephen N., 2001)

An Israeli urban planner acknowledged that "we know we're not doing the best service for the Palestinians as things stand" (Ari C., 2003). A Belfast architect expressed similar disappointment with the weak stance of his colleagues in the face of ongoing physical segregation and social malaise:

You know, I'm surprised that nobody came out of the woodwork and started making philosophical noises. But nobody did, that I'm aware of. It's a difficult one, that. It's a fact though. (Richard S., 2000)

It appears that in all these cases many otherwise capable scholars and practitioners have been unwilling or unable to lend assistance to their native cities. Inadequate training and timidity in the face of political compromise contribute to the problem, but a host of other factors deserve examination.

Not content to remain on the sidelines, many professionals become directly involved with the processes of urban partition where they are undertaken by the municipal government, as in Belfast, Jerusalem, and Beirut. This presents them with another pitfall of the neutrality desired: a willing-

Figure 9.2. Blighted space near Belfast's peacelines, c. 2002, points to the high costs of this approach. Authors.

ness simply to follow the orders of political masters and thus to take an active role in the design and implementation of ethnic partitions. To justify these actions, so out of keeping with their practical and ethnic training, built environment professionals tend to characterize themselves as trusting technicians hired to make manifest the government policies handed down from above.

Central to this characterization is the notion that to question the substance of those policies would be to overstep the scope of their expertise. But several divided cities professionals have noted that urban planning and design "cannot be dissociated from political directives" (Salaam 2000), pointing to the conclusion that the relationship between physical interventions and politics is especially intimate in the divided city context:

you are telling [urban planners] that the land is shifting, so they are planning on quicksand. If this is what they need to do, you have to teach them. I am not so sure that many of them are interested in this, because they are in the service of the politicians. Though they hate it and they think they are above that, they are paid by politicians and they are paid to implement political planning. The more the situation is political, the more their planning is political and the greater their need to find excuses. (Benvenisti 2003)

As long as they remain beholden to these authorities, the talents of built environment professionals are routinely commandeered for the implementation of poorly coordinated projects undertaken in the interests of damage control and alleviating popular anxiety. In the absence of more comprehensive strategies with which to accommodate ethnic violence in the urban environment, short-term security concerns typically rise to the top of political agendas for municipal governments attempting to cope with physical segregation. Architects and planners find themselves committed to combating an endless series of brushfires on behalf of political authorities that typically cannot claim to serve the interests of all urban residents with equal vigor. Professional activity under these conditions ensures that localized concerns are addressed individually according to their urgency, and rarely harnessed by a unifying philosophy or higher set of priorities.

Hired professional technicians are typically prepared to duck responsibility for lackluster or harmful outcomes, while policymakers are typically pleased to see their projects described by seemingly disinterested professionals as impartial and untainted by politics. An urban planner in Jerusalem acknowledges that he has some qualms with the political goals of the municipality that he serves, but he does not think that they interfere with his effectiveness as a professional:

I believe no matter what your political views or perceptions may be, there's so much room, there's so much to do. . . . I, for example, hold different political views than my mayor, and we work together in an excellent way. We work together, I do think, in a superb way. Which demonstrates that you could hold different views on the big picture and still conduct an ethical way of designing and planning, without compromising your own ethics. (Ari C., 2003)

This depiction of amicable employee-employer relations in a city where the public sphere is drastically tailored around a favored ethnic group sidesteps a number of important contradictions. It suggests that the sheer number of projects undertaken by the city dilutes or renders meaningless the problem of complicity with segregationist policies, though the hierarchy governing municipal departments of this kind undermines the idea that there is room for difference. It also implies that urban planning done in an ethical manner can somehow be considered distinct from any ethically troublesome agenda it may be serving. Such faulty logic is major obstacle for professionals attempting to play a constructive role in the ongoing development of divided cities through official, bureaucratic channels.

Sometimes just being a technician is tricky, all philosophical concerns aside. When even technical solutions appear to fail, secondary rationales can be provided. Describing his firm's engagement to design and build partitions in Belfast, one architect notes that lack of precedent makes the evaluation of alternatives difficult: "You are dealing with a form of construction in which really there just are no experts around. There are no design guidelines for these problems" (James L., 2000).

Taught to assist urban development processes in a nonpartisan manner, built environment professionals may bristle when political motivations are ascribed to their proposals. They may point to their marginal status with respect to policy formulation and express pessimism and a growing conviction that any efforts to generate consensus and identify joint concerns are futile. These frustrations were felt by an urban planner in Mostar, who observed that

planning is always a compromise between a profession and the politics—50 percent approximately . . . however, today's politics outweigh the profession. Its share in deciding today is 95 percent and above. (Nezad M., 2000)

Practitioners and theoreticians frequently recognize the futility of their position as public servants in a divided city. A Bosnian planner in Mostar lamented:

I thought I could work, do something, without them, [by avoiding] politicians. I was a little naïve. I said to my Croat colleagues, urban planners, that we should work together and not pay attention to the politicians, to make plans. However, we have done nothing. Simply, they forbade them over there to attend meetings with us, here. (Nezad M., 2000)

A common result is that both the public and their own colleagues perceive built environment professionals in the divided city context as "absolutely bloody useless" (Richard S., 2000), augmenting a sense of helplessness that is often widely felt.

Strategies of Avoidance

The process of demoralization leads many built environment professionals to pursue strategies of avoidance even when social and physical transformations in the urban domain become severe. Many urban design and planning experts in divided cities are chronically frustrated people. Denied the professional resources, institutional support, governmental patronage, peer support and clear mandate taken for granted in an ordinary practice, multiple incentives compel them to disengage. Two fundamental arguments regarding non-engagement allow them to refrain from discussions regarding social justice while keeping a tent staked on moral high ground.

1. No engagement, no complicity

Most common, perhaps, is the assertion that any form of involvement in the physical development of a divided city amounts to a kind of complicity with ethnic segregation. It has been noted previously that in the divided city there is generally no neutral territory, literal or figurative, available to the professional. Any position perceived by planners and architects as impartial is most often transformed into a hostile posture in the minds of at least one constituent group.

In Belfast, for instance, many urban planners have maintained an official disengagement from the question of ethnicity while incorporating sectarian concerns actively in their daily work. For some professionals in Northern Ireland and elsewhere, this kind of common sense seems too close to social engineering. They prefer not to practice at all in areas affected by ethnic conflict—those often most in need of their expertise—rather than work in a way that seems repugnant or hypocritical. Reluctance to perpetuate prejudice has probably cost Belfast the input of many talented professionals. Their absence may have left the field more open to exploitation by policymakers eager to whitewash segregationist strategies or validate postponement of essential reforms.

This kind of professional disengagement is evident in most divided cities. Even as the built environment continues to generate new forms of suffering, planners wait for a reliable political client to emerge from the maelstrom. Such passivity and quiescence follow naturally from the conventional underpinnings of urban planning practice. Orthodox interventions are predicated on the existence of a stable state and legitimate sources of local power. These prerequisites are rarely found in the divided city. Professionals intent on withholding the benefit of their participation until clear and permanent political outcomes are achieved automatically exempt themselves from the most urgent and important stages of constructive involvement.

In the whole time I've been involved with this, I've never heard of someone sitting down and saying: "Let's have a conversation about what this would look like, or how we can make this a mixed community, or how we can possibly devise ways of ensuring that people can live together." I've never heard of that conversation taking place by politicians or by anyone else, because it's too politically sensitive to deal with. (Philip J., 2001)

One urban planner in Nicosia refused to wait for a political settlement before getting involved, and was subsequently criticized by her colleagues for cooperating with representatives of a government not recognized by Greek Cypriot authorities:

Critics of the cooperation wondered how we could work with Turkish Cypriots on the other side of the city. My answer was: the city belongs to both of us. They said to wait for a solution. My answer was: that would be very late. It is not late just because in waiting we would lose a lot of buildings, rather that we gain the most by building relations through this physical architectural planning process. For me, the "Turkish Cypriots" are something completely different than they were before we started this project. (Petridou, 2001)

This logic is compelling, but rarely deployed. The desire to plan in advance of a political settlement is the exception rather than the rule among professionals who are qualified to make positive contributions to the ongoing development of divided cities. Mostar provides a good example of a city where political obstacles have proved to be overwhelming for many experts. One urban planner there noted the growing gap between spontaneous development and professional involvement:

I cannot see that [planners] have done anything . . . the professionals are afraid. They keep saying, "There is a lot to do on the subject," or "We don't have time for that," and so on and on. But we cannot stop the life and stop building. (Ziad T., 2000)

A planner in Belfast planner laments the absence of built environment professionals from major decisions related to the physical partition, where he and his colleagues contributed little to the problem despite having ample time and opportunity to design comprehensive strategies:

So [this is] what has defeated me all the way along the line. . . . I can't understand how policymaking and planning have stepped aside from all this . . . how all the policy statements have ignored the conflict. (Richard S., 2000)

These voices, and those defending disengagement from the process of physical negotiation between rival ethnic groups, were heard in every city examined. Momentous personal and ethical liabilities are frequently cited. But if the risks and uncertainties of engagement are high, so is the cost of remaining aloof.

2. No complicity, no responsibility

By avoiding the perils associated with professional involvement in the lose-lose dialectic of the divided city, nonpolitical professionals bear no responsibility for the process of policy formation. Yet in this way they are absent from the discussions and debates where their expertise is most germane. If they are invited to address any physical problems, these tend to be of secondary significance in relation to the thorny impacts of urban apartheid. Their projects then siphon resources away from core problem areas and "risk being lipstick on the gorilla," sometimes employing the rhetoric of systematic urban rehabilitation in a way that "combines elements of denial and farce" (Neill 1995: 69).

Even if they were willing to strike out more assertively, architects and planners are rarely asked to apply their analytical skills to the problem of physical partition. At the same time local politicians, who lack the incentive to assess or confront the negative implications of their own policies, rarely attempt to deal with spatial segregation in a systematic way. One politician in Belfast confirmed that top-down approaches have yet to link up with bottom-up solutions:

I don't think there is any overall planning or direction in relation to how we are going to fundamentally tackle the problem of division within our city. . . . We as politicians, as planners, as architects, as everybody, we haven't really attempted to tackle the problem of sectarianism except in a fairly piecemeal fashion. . . . We've concentrated our energies on the superstructures of politics, we haven't gotten down to the reality on the ground. (Maginness 2001)

Few models exist for successful long-term interventions, in part because there is no consensus on how to measure success. Still, the outlook is not uniformly bleak. Some professionals do choose to engage in the problems of the divided city prior to a full political settlement. Some of the most prominent strategies they have employed are described in the following section.

Strategies of Engagement

Engagement Through Centralized Planning

Many professionals active in the divided city context rely on the municipal authorities who issue policies and salaries. These authorities themselves may owe allegiance to only one party to the conflict. In this instance, urban planning naturally becomes lopsided.

Jerusalem provides an informative example. The municipal government still maintains a large in-house urban planning department ready to implement projects according to political directives from above. Israeli architects and planners responded to both political and military authorities when they constructed or erased ethnic partitions in the Jerusalem, since urban territory was commonly viewed "as a military asset, not as a planning asset or as normal space where people can live" (Benvenisti 2003).

The same professionals working on behalf of the municipal government in Jerusalem were obliged to "manipulate jurisdictional boundaries" (Bollens 2000: 29) on paper in order to consolidate the control of contested territory. These actions contributed to a process of prejudicial demographic engineering, though it can be assumed that few of these professionals would have chosen to view their efforts in this light.

Engagement Through Collaborative or Parity Planning

A cooperative approach was pursued in Nicosia with more favorable results, thanks to relatively balanced political representation in that city. Politicians initiated an innovative communal master-planning project that brought together architects, urban planners, economists, sociologists, and policymakers from both sides of the city to share ideas and coordinate projects that were often undertaken in a simultaneous and symmetrical fashion on both sides of the Green Line. This process, too, was oriented around emblematic places and largely symbolic benefits, but it differs from the Mostar scenario discussed below in several important respects.

First, local rather than foreign professionals were involved in cooperative planning and consultation exercises of their own design. If the process was influenced by idealistic or lofty ambitions, those ambitions were the product of a native, shared optimism rather than a remedial program imposed by external actors. Second, projects in Nicosia's historic core focused not on landmark structures but on schemes for neighborhood revitalization in the areas near the center of the Old City that are separated by the partition line but were adjacent to each other prior to its construction. Third, emblematic projects in the historic core of the city were complemented by cooperative infrastructure projects of a highly pragmatic nature.

These low-profile initiatives are exemplified by the shared sewage treatment system linking southern and northern sectors of Nicosia, completed during a period of high political tensions between the two communities. The explanation for its success has nothing to do with symbolism or highmindedness: two sewage treatment networks simply were not affordable, and a cooperative scheme was necessary despite unfavorable political and diplomatic circumstances. During the lengthy implementation period politicians and professionals came together in the buffer zone without titles or institutional affiliations. Mayors were simply citizens, agency directors were simply engineers, and chief planners were simply architects.

One Turkish Cypriot civil engineer who played a vital role in these proceedings saw a kind of triumph in the cooperative sewage system project:

The Turkish people are using the treated water from the south in their farms to grow crops and make money to survive. The south side residents also benefit because their wastewater gets treated, which is important for health. Symbiosis. You don't have to talk about nationality. You just have to say, "I am a human being and I love my country. I love my environment." (Öznel 2001)

Cooperative master planning, historic preservation, and infrastructure projects do not appear to have changed the course of segregationist politics in Cyprus. Still, these efforts demonstrate a few essential facts often forgotten by rival ethnic communities sharing a divided city: that collaboration is possible in the absence of a comprehensive political settlement and that cooperation can be advantageous even while bitter resentments and suspicions persist.

Built environment professionals in Nicosia created a diverse portfolio of cooperative projects based on "social objectives" (Petrídou 2001). These included the shared sewer system, uniform architectural rehabilitation guidelines for the segregated historic core, "twin team" research and survey exercises, collaborative master planning, coordinated repair of the city walls, joint study tours to Baltimore, New York, Bonn, Banja Luka, and Rome, and regular meetings to discuss progress and share information at United Nations offices in the buffer zone. As they were able to recruit capable politicians to support these efforts, their mediating strategy succeeded where superficially similar efforts in other divided cities like Mostar and Jerusalem did not.

In Belfast, where municipal authority is stronger and more autonomous than in any other divided city examined here, many professionals seek to implement reconstruction projects in an even-handed way. Although this approach is entirely consistent with the training and philosophy of most built environment professionals, attempts at nonpartisan planning in the divided city context usually backfire. This failure often results from a tendency to ignore the tensions and conflicts that created the need for imaginative intervention in the first place. The example of Craigavon, a new suburban development designed for working-class Belfast residents, demonstrates the obstacles to nonpartisan planning.

An outside observer would have called Craigavon the right project executed for the right reasons, but it fell on barren social ground:

The feeling was that this was a vast mistake. . . . The architects awarded themselves prizes, gave themselves medals, and then they went away . . . and the roofs leaked and the people moved out. . . . It seemed at first it couldn't get any better; the result is that it couldn't be any worse. (Boal 2000)

The Craigavon experiment gave physical form to an ideal of social reform that was not yet supported by the urban contract. Another urban planner directly involved noted: "You can't have a bridge where there isn't a willingness to cross. You can't have a flag when there isn't any unity" (Richard S., 2000). Again, concerned professionals were left frustrated and confounded.

In Belfast, balanced urban plans are frequently derailed because urban planners are beholden to policymakers who have deep investments in sectarian issues and are tied directly to constituents in need of short-term security guarantees. Under such circumstances, professionals involved in the problems of divided cities become complicit with policies that may often run afoul of their academic training or consciences.

Confronted by a double imperative—immediate threats and directives from municipal authorities—local experts are left with few alternatives. Those who remain active are frequently forced to rationalize their actions as the lesser of several evils in an inherently dysfunctional municipal system.

Engagement Through Privatization

What happens when there is not even a dysfunctional local government to provide a platform for professional intervention? When municipal authorities are severely weak or disorganized, active professionals must turn to other institutional frameworks. An interesting surrogate for municipal authority is private investment. Deference to market forces allows experts once again to view their involvement as neutral and nonpartisan—guided by the invisible hand of the market rather than a political agenda.

A near perfect example of this approach is found in Beirut, where the creation of a private company as a guiding force for postwar urban reconstruction marked the symbolic abandonment of government agencies in favor of private enterprise. It attracted the best foreign and native professional talent to the city with a clear set of objectives, ample funds, and an innovative business model—in sharp contrast to national and municipal offices, which appeared demoralized, disorganized, and decrepit by comparison. This ambitious undertaking provides a model for market-driven interventions that provides another set of insights regarding how built environment professionals can intervene in the divided city without appearing to give up their impartiality.

In the spring of 1994, a red line was drawn around the core of Beirut's ruined central business district and the entire parcel—including the most valuable real estate in the city—was put up for sale on the international market. The process was engineered and managed by the Lebanese Company for the Development and Reconstruction of Beirut Central District (Solidere) with anchoring capital investment and a blessing from prime inister Rafiq Hariri.

This tax-exempt, joint-stock corporation was made up of property rights holders and investors holding stock in the downtown area. Eligibility for shares was determined by prewar property ownership in the development area or a cash subscription in U.S. dollars. Solidere's shares are also traded on the secondary stock market under the supervision of the Bank of Lebanon and in conjunction with thirty-two Lebanese financial restitutions. From 1995 onward, physical reconstruction in Beirut would be largely synonymous with the activities of Solidere, which was given sole proprietary authority over all decision making related to physical reconstruction inside the red line.

Relinquishing highly contested urban territory to the vagaries of market forces was unprecedented. The ultimate success of Beirut's experiment has yet to be determined. It is certain that Solidere is an interesting hybrid of tradition and innovation. Drawing on Beirut's reputation as the entrepreneurial and secular capital of the Middle East, this investment-driven model for postwar reconstruction is in close keeping with the character of

Figure 9.3. The downtown area largely destroyed during the civil war and designated by Solidere for privately funded reconstruction. Solidere, used by permission.

the city and appears aggressively pragmatic. Opportunity and risk are distributed across a wide international spectrum of investors and a lengthy implementation timetable generated by a comprehensive preliminary plan. Largely bypassing local favorites and rivals, all major architectural design commissions were tied to international competitions intended to attract unimpeachable professional talent and raise the profile of the project as a whole with celebrity designers.

By tying Beirut's physical recovery to the profit motive and the unit value of widely held Solidere stock, incentives were distributed in a manner that minimized local political influences. For exactly the same reason, responsiveness to the concerns and expectations of local residents was dramatically reduced. While the central business district received the lion's share of investment and attention, the remainder of Beirut—the vast majority of the city and its residents—remained relatively stagnant.

Determined to maximize return on investment for Solidere shareholders, a team of in-house urban planners, architects, and conservators designed a utopian enclave tailored primarily to the expectations of an international corporate elite.

Critics of the project grew bolder and better organized throughout the late 1990s, lamenting the replacement of the Green Line separating ethnic factions with Solidere's red line separating economic classes. Advocates cited their confidence in the trickledown economic benefits of concentrated institutional investment and asserted that the complex incentives propelling private investment allowed revitalization to proceed in a fraction of the time and cost that would have been required if the job had been left to Lebanon's crippled public institutions.

More than a decade after its first stock offering on the open market, Solidere's achievements, from the standpoint of physical rehabilitation in the central business district, are nothing short of astonishing. New construction proceeded at a rapid rate and in accordance with exceedingly high standards of design and infrastructure. The technical dimensions of project planning and coordination have been largely impeccable, a fact demonstrated by the consistently high quality of new buildings and public spaces. The design professionals responsible for this work emphasize that they have created an economically viable downtown that will lead the revitalization of Beirut as a whole, and upon which the fortunes of the country largely rest.

Spokespeople for Solidere claim to have reconstructed a multiethnic social arena, physically and symbolically reconnecting pieces of the city that were severed during the course of interethnic hostilities. Though downtown Beirut has now been transformed into an enclave for corporate tenants, its engineers promise that substantial benefits will accrue to all Beirutis once the rehabilitation project is completed and full tenancy has been achieved.

When judged according to strictly cosmetic and economic criteria, and when simultaneously limiting our view to the city's historic core, Solidere's daring open-heart surgery in Beirut has been successful. No hint of infection is visible in the largely rebuilt downtown, which sparkles with rehabilitated nostalgia and an undeniably youthful vigor. A handful of historic landmark buildings have been meticulously preserved, along with the permanent exposure of an archaeological site that may date to the Phoenician period. Beirut's central business district presents the image of a fully recovered financial capital ready to do business in the international arena.

Inside Solidere's project boundary line, conditions for continued investment and prosperity are optimal. Advocates argue that full-scale reconstruction needed to start somewhere, that ripple effects will be substantial, and that no similarly viable alternate scheme was offered by Solidere's critics. This trickledown model is alluring, but yet unproven and perhaps simplistic.

There is little doubt that some of its well-heeled tenants are poised to guide the city toward a prosperous future. But critics are quick to point out that these tenants bear little resemblance to the diverse array of occupants living and working in the downtown area prior to the war:

I'm not taken by the great effort for physical beauty and the renovation of Allenby Street. I don't accept the city without its people. There were 130,000 people living there from all confessions and all classes of society, which is equally important: from craftsmen to very rich professionals. It was a bulging society. (Marwan T., 2000)

Just over the threshold of Solidere's investment zone, the portrait of postwar Beirut appears quite a bit more complicated. Thousands of buildings and tens of thousands of residents remain untouched by the benevolent hand of organized rehabilitation, and no comprehensive strategy has yet been developed to address them. Though these observations are consistent with Solidere's long-term strategy, difficult questions about the overall merits of the market-driven investors' model of urban rehabilitation in the divided city context remain: How and when will the benefits of elite investment reach typical Beirutis? Will all citizens feel welcome and comfortable in the new downtown, formerly a shared commercial zone?

Until the collateral effects extolled by Solidere spokespersons take effect, the central business district increasingly appears to be a different city altogether from the remainder of war-torn Beirut, resulting in recriminations from local critics who claimed that Solidere had replaced ethnic boundaries with economic ones:

Now if you go to the Green Line, you would still find destroyed buildings. [Solidere] didn't think about rebuilding Beirut, they thought about taking the part of downtown Beirut that is near the sea, destroying it, and building this small, closed enclave for the big bourgeoisie. (Khouri 2000)

Sidestepping comprehensive public consultation in pursuit of a reconstruction project that appears to benefit only the social elite could have unanticipated negative repercussions. One social worker active in Beirut's Palestinian refugee camps notes that, while less fortunate citizens wait for the benefits of focused investment to reach them, disenchantment and cynicism grow:

I feel [Beirut] is still divided socially and morally. People talk to each other, exchange information, but when it comes down to give-and-take services, it's not that hospitable on both sides . . . the majority of the people who turned out to be from [non-Maronite or non-Christian] religions didn't have access to such jobs or rights concerning the state of Lebanon. So I certainly feel that it's not a war between rich and poor, but between people who don't want to share their rights with others [and those others]. (Nora H., 2000)

Other critics believe that excessive demolition accompanied Solidere's renewal scheme in order to meet density and revenue benchmarks, underscoring the tension built into "the logic of Solidere" between historic preservation and real-estate development on the open market: "The more they destroy, the more they make a profit. The more they throw people out, the more they make profit" (Marwan T., 2000).

In no other divided city considered here was comprehensive physical reconstruction initiated so decisively and implemented so quickly according to such high technical standards. The efficiency of this rapid and highly organized process can be attributed to the virtues of market-driven real estate development and the willingness of Beirut's municipal government to give up control over such a prominent and vital project. The near total divestment of Lebanese policymakers and built environment professionals from the reconstruction process in the downtown area is striking.

Beirut is distinguished among divided cities for projecting a postwar image of itself far out of keeping with its prewar character. Though no-one questions the fact that Solidere has adapted the "heart of the city," opinions vary regarding whether it was made stronger or weaker in the aftermath of this reconstructive surgery:

[Solidere's planners] have taken the heart of the capital, pushed the people out of it and forced them to lose ownership of the land . . . they ended up by dividing the city more than ever. (Marwan T., 2000)

Solidere's leaders contend that they have done Beirut a favor by improving a downtown area that was, in the aftermath of the war, "a slum, a destroyed area with no infrastructure" (Malek G., 2000). Solidere's critics meanwhile complain about the unnecessary demolition of a historic fabric that did not meet the high-density requirements specified by Solidere in its master plan, and yet others have suggested that postwar reconstruction following a national crisis of such vast proportions should never have been chained to profit motive.

It is counter-productive for these people who live in shanty towns to see this money dispatched in such a manner while they're still living in dilapidated conditions. It has immediate social implications when the money is not looking after them, when it is developing the whole area for the capitalists and neglecting their issues . . . it is shortsighted for the government to come and waste so much money on nonproductive issues when social differences are still great in Lebanon. (Marwan T., 2000)

It was inevitable that such an unorthodox and focused rehabilitation strategy would leave many observers dissatisfied, especially since it was undertaken in the absence of political and social consensus in Lebanon as a whole. Is not at all clear that what Solidere's urban revitalization project lacks in terms of social inclusion and relevance can be compensated for in terms of the architectural allure and capital investment in downtown Beirut—both of which are likely to benefit well-heeled stockholders long before they benefit the average Beirutis who continue to bear the brunt of partition's negative impacts. Though the reconstruction efforts undertaken in Beirut's historic core have met many of their prescribed objectives, from the outset those objectives did not include many of the most glaring, important, and difficult challenges facing the city's underserved and traumatized residents.

Engagement Through Private Investment in Cultural Heritage

The response of built environment professionals to urban partition is not always harnessed to local political agendas, the free market, or potentially unreliable public institutions. Foreign patronage often shapes the character and scope of physical interventions.

A useful example is found in Mostar, where residents relied almost exclusively on foreign donations and expertise to jumpstart the process of postconflict recovery. As in Jerusalem and Belfast, concepts of evenhandedness, balance, and neutrality remained inapplicable for years following the end of hostilities. Because municipal authorities on both sides of the city generally refused to cooperate, political consensus long remained an imaginary concept feebly maintained for public relations purposes. The burden of postwar revitalization lay most heavily on eastern Mostar, where grossly disproportionate physical and psychological punishment had been meted out to the Muslim residents living in the historic Ottoman core centered on the Old Bridge.

Bifurcated since the city's physical division in 1993, the two halves of Mostar functioned as separate, autonomous and redundant cities throughout the first decade of post-conflict rehabilitation. Physical reconstruction activities would have proceeded in a similarly bifurcated manner if municipal authorities in the eastern sector had possessed the human and material resources required to complete such an undertaking alone, but they did not. This fact forced the city to solicit foreign support and led to a dilemma.

On one hand, lingering resentments between rival ethnic communities made even superficial acts of cooperation across the city's ethnic boundary very unlikely. These odds grew worse in relation to the physical revitalization agenda, since most buildings in urgent need of attention were on the eastern side of the city. On the other hand, external funding agencies and foreign experts insisted that all projects relying on foreign subsidies should be undertaken in a balanced manner and with shared responsibilities.

Foreign implementation agencies obliged to demonstrate impartiality in their local political relationships found it difficult to accept the fact that relatively strict functional and administrative divisions persisted long after the regional conflict was ended by the Dayton Accords in 1995. Pleased by the prospect of contributing to a lasting peace, foreign donors expected their contributions simultaneously to provide material support for physical rehabilitation and to catalyze vital processes of social and political reconciliation in Mostar.

Accordingly, almost every foreign agency to invest in the city's physical reconstruction made its involvement conditional on the demonstration of interethnic cooperation in the municipal government. Local protocols were developed to provide these assurances to foreign donor agencies, and their purses gradually opened as Mostar's rival politicians learned to shake hands and assert their commitment to partnership with increasing persuasiveness.

Support materialized from quasigovernmental and nonprofit organizations like the European Union, UNESCO, War Child, the Aga Khan Trust for Culture, the World Monuments Fund, the World Bank, and others. Encouraged by the ease of this initial progress, many of these agencies went on to focus their efforts on the grandest and most historic architectural landmarks located in the Ottoman core.

Though a number of rehabilitation projects undertaken in the historic core addressed structures of secondary historical importance and of primary and functional value—such as schools, libraries, banks, and office buildings—most foreign investment was poured into highly emblematic and monumental structures. The natural centerpiece for these efforts was the facsimile reconstruction of the Old Bridge, completed in early 2004 and formally dedicated that July.

Among Muslim residents of eastern Mostar these efforts were initially greeted with enthusiasm and approval. As economic reforms failed to materialize in the wake of more symbolic projects, however, dissatisfaction became discernable at the local level. Repairing emblematic historic sites dominated postwar rehabilitation efforts because professionals were hoping to kill two birds with one stone: repair physical damage and at the same time provide encouragement for the beleaguered residents of the city by replacing the structures that had been most inspiring prior to the outbreak of hostilities.

This can be characterized as a motivational rather than a functional revitalization strategy, and it relied heavily on the idea the physical projects can have edifying social consequences. The product of this strategy in Mostar was a kind of virtual rather than actual recovery. Some divided city residents resent projects that dwell on landmark structures damaged during periods of conflict, preferring a more pragmatic approach to reconstruction:

All the money that has been coming here which hasn't been invested into something which can be profitable may be lost in the sense that there will be no one to live in the city . . . there might be no one to cross the Bridge. . . . Not until some firms or some factories are rebuilt where those people could work will we need the Old City . . . if only the eyes are full and the pockets empty, then there is nothing. (Sead A., 2000)

Without significant revenue and having compromised its own capacity to undertake large-scale urban renewal projects, the city of Mostar was left with few appealing options in the aftermath of the war. Its decision to embrace foreign contributions from private nongovernmental organizations resulted in high-profile physical reconstruction projects detached from major gains for social development. This type of compromise is typical for divided cities beholden to an array of uncoordinated private donors, because their funds often come with an inadequate understanding of the needs of urban residents and with multiple incentives to invest in landmark structures.

When confronted with the problem of divided cities, a common instinct among built environment professionals is to attempt to correct the damage, and to repair what was broken, on the assumption that a divided city should not remain divided. This notion has been addressed in Chapter 8. The physical repair of severed urban fabric is one of the most straightforward and seemingly uncontroversial approaches that can be adopted by a built environment professional. The desire to erase the remnants of partition, both physical and psychological, is strong among experts convinced that "as long there is the division line, a visual division line, it is really difficult to achieve unification" (Demirovic 2000). Their conviction rests on the premise that thoughtful physical interventions can bring about positive social change and that the benefits of rejoining neighborhoods separated in a violent and involuntary manner appear obvious.

The symmetry of this logic is compelling. It is tempting to believe that the harmful forces unleashed by physical destruction and division can be reversed, turned on their axis, and harnessed for constructive purposes through physical reconstruction projects. Faith in such a reverse gradient seems reasonable in light of the high costs that invariably accompany spatial segregation in an urban environment, discussed in detail in Chapter 8. The importance of symbolic projects is affirmed by many divided city residents seeking signs of positive change: "[The partition] is really one awfully ugly picture that reminds us of the past on a daily basis whenever one passes by in their car, and is, thus, really a big obstacle" (Ziad T., 2000). Many urban development projects aimed at the reclamation, erasure, or gentrification of partition scars provide local politicians with signs of systemic change but fail to deliver promised social benefits. A prominent example is Israeli architect Moshe Safdie's Mamilla rehabilitation project, including the "David's Village" luxury apartment complex. This project was sited just outside the Jaffa Gate, in a no-man's-land of the former Green Line that contained a dense, middle-income neighborhood prior to the city's partition. Safdie's design was intended in part to demonstrate Israeli resilience and prosperity following the Six-Day War, and also provided an opportunity to invest conspicuously in West Jerusalem while the eastern sections of the city languished.

Likewise, in Mostar, misguided metaphors of reconstruction shaped the planning process and ensured that the lion's share of foreign postwar investments poured into the heavily damaged Ottoman core—with special emphasis on reconstruction of the Old Bridge—despite the fact that many residential structures along the Boulevard had been destroyed and housing in the city remained at a premium. In the minds and imaginations of foreign donors, it was widely believed that a facsimile reconstruction of the fallen Old Bridge would heal social wounds. This would happen, it was assumed, when the landmark bridge physically reunited former antagonists by stitching together Croatians from the western side and Bosniaks from the eastern side.

Unfortunately, few local citizens found much solace in the realization of this project, which was underwritten with a special World Bank loan and monitored by UNESCO, since, as shown above, the Neretva River spanned by the Bridge does not divide Mostar's two rival communities. As a result, the international fixation on the Old Bridge as an emblem of recovery has been of limited relevance with respect to the real nature of the social conflict, its actual manifestations, and the process of long-term social reconciliation in Mostar. Such a process would have been better served if destroyed housing along the Boulevard had been rehabilitated.

External agencies involved with post-partition planning frequently ignore the difficulty and promise of slow social recovery in favor of positive public relations gestures. Regarding the limitations of this approach, one Belfast planner observed:

> The urban scar of sharp ethnic division demands a serious response that must move significantly away from the surface "Band Aid" approach characterizing much of the image-based planning in the city. (Neill 1995, Murtaugh's "Image making versus reality": 224)

The oversimplification of the conflict and its remedies can appear insulting to local residents who will never fully recover, and who can easily envision ways of spending millions of dollars that are beneficial in practical rather than merely symbolic ways. In Mostar a local architect pointed out that the historic core of the city had received most of the attention during the reconstruction process while the functional dividing line was largely excluded:

> in my opinion, the reconstruction should have been more focused on the area where the heaviest fighting took place, the Boulevard area. Almost no work has been done on the reconstruction of the Boulevard. (Ferhad D., 2001)

In Beirut the Solidere project area was chosen for its symbolic character as shared urban territory and encompassed only a fragment of the city's

Figure 9.4. Ruined apartments and "dragon's teeth" along the length of Mostar's Boulevard and former front line, c. 2002. Aida Omanovic, used by permission.

lengthy dividing line. Reflecting on why Solidere addressed only the city's most historic, valuable, and emblematic public space without providing solutions for vast areas of desolation straddling the Damascus Road, one planner observed, "people don't like to remember this dividing line." A decision to dwell exclusively on the emblematic urban core was made despite the attempts of some local architects to focus early efforts on a linear project area defined by the Green Line:

Many times people have suggested to me the need to work on the Green Line—somehow stitching Beirut together along its wartime line of division, the Rue Damas corridor—as a means of healing the city. I still think the Green Line idea is a bit cliche. We need to focus on something that is more interesting and important. It's not the Geen Line that we have to stitch, but the city center. (Gavin 2000)

Project designers characterized the formerly partitioned downtown as challenging but vital to the process of reconnecting the city while Solidere founder and Lebanese prime minister Hariri later reasoned, "you can't leave the heart of the city, because if the heart is destroyed it means the body is not functioning" (Hariri 2000). Solidere's urban planners also intended their efforts to echo on a national scale:

(Solidere) has to work for Lebanon. It has to reconstruct the notion of the multi-ethnic city center as the meeting point of the capital, its social arena and the place where major cultural and ceremonial events take place. . . . To me the project will have to reconstruct the common ground for all the Lebanese. This has to take place in the city center. I don't think it can be done anywhere else. I believe this is a much more important idea than stitching the city along the Green Line. (Gavin 2000)

Confirming that Beirut's historic downtown had been shared prior to the city's partition, one observer lamented the alterations to the city's historic core:

Now I do not identify myself with it because it is empty and there is nothing there. I take my children there and I show them where the major monuments were. The Amin Mosque, the Martyr's Square: everything was so lively, but now it is not the same. (Ali W., 2001)

Another Beiruti critic goes farther to suggest that Solidere's open-heart surgery transformed Martyrs' Square from a shared to an exclusive zone, undermining its healing function in the wake of conflict: "They have taken the heart of the capital, pushed the people out of it, and . . . ended up by dividing the city more than ever" (Marwan T., 2000).

It cannot be surprising that misdirected intentions like these often accompany emblematic reconstruction projects in the divided city context. The physical and social convulsions of interethnic violence shake traditional associations loose from their foundations, limiting the relevance of prewar iconography to postwar planning efforts. Architects and planners who use nostalgia for a compass, seeking to turn back the urban clock to a time when now-hostile neighbors once mingled freely, routinely find themselves shunned by uncooperative and unrepentant divided city residents. Most attempts to heal social wounds with physical reconstruction projects in the aftermath of urban partition are ultimately unsuccessful. While the disintegration and fragmentation of urban communities is commonly accelerated by the purposeful destruction of stabilizing landmark structures, the reconstruction of those same structures does not, in itself, guarantee a return to the prewar social condition.

Engagement Through Advocacy

Some of the most successful architects and urban planners active in divided cities do not gauge their success in terms of physical projects and sites. They confront the political processes that gave rise to the conflict or the political obstacles standing in the way of reconciliation. Their aim is not to mend and their engagement is not contingent upon political settlements. Their interventions address the costs of partition and the burdens of walls on those residents who are forced to negotiate them regularly.

Firmly committed to the social development needs of divided city residents, they help policymakers to prioritize political alternatives by developing and applying sound criteria for development. They act as advocates for good ideas, watchdogs for bad ones, and studious auditors of the costs and benefits associated with a wide array of plausible interventions.

In Nicosia this approach was used by local planners to derive the maximum benefit from the process of cooperative master planning. Joint planning exercises undertaken by Greek and Turkish Cypriot urban planners and architects began in the late 1970s, when there was only a small likelihood that their ideas would be implemented. This does not appear to have deterred the Nicosia Master Plan team from its work. Its existence alone hastened a thaw in diplomatic relations between the two municipalities.

In addition, the team looked carefully and methodically at the future development of the city with and without a comprehensive peace settlement, facilitating the exploration of concrete responses to both the logistical concerns associated with unification and the lost opportunities associated with continuing partition.

They were able to undertake a rudimentary cost-benefit analysis for each scenario and articulate their findings in terms that made sense to local decision makers: improved property values, expansion of real-estate development opportunities, decongestion of vehicular and pedestrian movement, and brightened foreign perceptions of their city.

When political decisions appear faulty, these professionals also mobilize in a political fashion so that their criticisms can help to broaden public debate. A good example is the mobilization of grassroots opposition to Solidere's long-term plan for downtown Beirut. In 1995 vigorous and constructive public debate was orchestrated by a small group of architects and intellectuals led by Jad Tabet and Elias Khouri. They were joined later by many of the most prominent built environment professionals in Lebanon.

Alarmed by the massive spatial and social implications of Solidere's scheme, local experts successfully applied pressure on the company to re-think controversial elements of their project. This opposition movement was created by concerned professionals on behalf of ordinary Beirutis who were generally unaware of how such large-scale decisions might affect them.

Successful professional advocacy in the divided city context relies on public consultation, empirical research and energetic local needs-based assessment. A handful of local urban planners and architects in Mostar have demonstrated the merits of this approach, while fulfilling their obligations to foreign donors to repair individual structures regardless of the public opinion in the city.

Prior to beginning restoration work on individual monuments, the entire historic core was surveyed to obtain physical and social data regarding the occupancy and function of the buildings there. The information collected shaped the selection criteria used to identify high-priority projects that anchored international fundraising efforts. Locally, the door-to-door survey process established between the research team and local citizens a familiarity that generated many positive dividends.

This meant that local perceptions of the post-conflict rehabilitation process were good despite the involvement of offshore managers, and many residents could connect the urban planning process with a name and face whenever problems arose. One Mostarian urban planner active in cooperative projects emphasized the paramount importance of an open, transparent approach:

I believe that the way I handle the job—my professional attitude—will make big contribution regarding the unification and will influence a lot of people. People need someone to lead them to the other side. (Ziad T., 2000)

Anticipating the imminent departure of foreign agencies from positions of leadership in Mostar's rehabilitation, plans for a new nonprofit agency were drafted by local professionals and policymakers. This organization assumes responsibility for fundraising and project management in relation to all physical rehabilitation projects in the historic core for which local capacity is still lacking.

Apparently insignificant when compared to the astonishing reappearance of the Old Bridge on the banks of the river, the Stari Grad Foundation may be the most important product of ten years of reconstruction activity. It provides a permanent framework for cooperation based on common concerns between former rivals. This type of joint social institution is very rare in Bosnia-Herzegovina and constitutes a more reliable indicator for the success of the broader reconciliation process than the reconstruction of any building.

Playing the role of advocate can be a highly effective way to influence urban development in the context of ethnic partition. This approach calls on the expert to become a political actor, abandoning the notion that built environment professionals must implement political directives in an unquestioning manner. It points to an urban development agenda that accommodates social antagonisms, acknowledges political influences, and exposes shortsighted policies to careful and persuasive arguments. In the politically dichotomized environment of a divided city, the professional advocate's job is to isolate, explore, and articulate options corresponding to a wide array of circumstances based on credible, data-driven analysis. In this way professionals can contribute to a healthy climate of skepticism, inquiry, and evaluation.

Linking the Social and the Spatial

Spatial crises call for the involvement of spatial thinkers and problem-solvers. In principle, this involvement should be broad, encompassing all stages of policy formation related to urban partition. It would require dramatically expanding the current scope of professional responsibility. Attempting to define this broadening process while recognizing the extraordinary difficulty of solving interethnic problems directly, Benvenisti offers the following advice to urban planners and others:

Don't make the mistake of saying, "I am just a physical planner." Say, "I am ready to participate in a political process. I am going to define that political process, I am going to do something about it, and physical planning is one aspect of it." Physical planning itself is not going to change the situation. It is the interpretation of good value judgments of politicians, of courageous efforts of politicians to affect change, which later on can be used by physical planners to implement the ideas. (Benvenisti 2003)

Occasionally this process results in the creation of new partitions, as described by one architect in Belfast whose firm was contracted to respond swiftly when violence was anticipated in the Shankill enclave:

[Municipal authorities] heard something and knew that a conflict was coming up. We were fairly far advanced with [plans for an interface area comprised of commercial structures and a road] when during one of the meetings a couple of people from the Northern Ireland Office came to say, "drop all the other plans and build a wall as fast as you possibly can." There was no point in arguing. They know best; they are in charge of security. We diverted equipment onto the site the very next day, got all the information about what kind of infrastructure runs under the road on a Friday, and we were in there the same day with a digger doing the exploratory work. On that Saturday was the big Shankill Road bomb. (James L., 2000)

In this instance, architects were called upon to build a new barricade in anticipation of a single episode of interethnic violence. The resulting peace-line may have reduced damages caused by the bombing, but it also left behind a permanent barricade placing measurable psychological and functional burdens on local residents, as documented by Belfast's remarkable Cost of the Troubles study discussed in Chapter 4.

Misguided approaches to post-partition rehabilitation generally result from a failure on behalf of built environment professionals to accommodate to the complexity of the divided city condition. Neutrality and impartiality are admirable notions that lead most often toward mutual agreement and compliance in the divided city. Postconflict rehabilitation projects fail when problems and solutions are conceived in terms of broken spaces and structures alone.

Effort and investment alone are unlikely to revitalize a divided city because healthy cities thrive on "a general uniting atmosphere in which you feel like a citizen wherever you are" (Marwan T., 2000)—the product of social institutions rather than physical ones. An urban planner from Mostar, active in the city's postwar rehabilitation, offered identical observations:

Physically, there is no division. I can go anywhere, to any restaurant. Nobody will take or tell you anything. But I am telling you, they don't have any economic joint project, they don't have any social joint project because all this social structure is divided. (Pašić 2003)

The most effective architectural projects are rationalized in terms of these social agendas, subordinating projects that strengthen physical structures to those that strengthen social ones. All boats rise with the tide when divided city residents are given a tangible demonstration of the fact that "times have changed, things are improving" (James L., 2000).

The most successful professional interventions in divided cities recognize the linkages between urban planning with politics, spatial crises with social crises, and ethnic partition with long-standing institutional prejudice.

They will accommodate the notion that "society creates the city and not vice versa" (Tueni 2000), without failing to account for the harmful and beneficial impacts of the built environment on social dynamics.

Reflecting on the litany of errors associated with conflict mediation in Belfast and Jerusalem, Benvenisti concludes that even mitigating ethnic conflict can be considered an excessively ambitious objective for nonpolitical professionals seeking to play a useful role in the divided city. He proposes a "problem-sharing" approach in which "success is not measured by approximation of results to a desired goal, but by the degree of agreement, no matter how trivial the issue seems" (Benvenisti 1982: 11). As for architects and planners, Benvenisti recommends a dose of humility regarding the difficulty of affecting positive change amidst endemic ethnic hostilities and meanwhile proposes two useful role models:

Policemen and social workers deal with the symptoms of social malaise, not with its underlying causes. Street-level and life-support officials know only too well that their efforts would at best alleviate hardship, but will not cure society of its endemic malaise. They are not discouraged by that realization as they are trained to operate within the constraints of existing social conditions. They view their input as incremental, and their success as relative. They reconcile ideological imperatives with the necessities of daily life, therefore they are not confused by its contradictions. (Benvenisti 1982: 11)

When urban planning and design are viewed as tools of social development, a new array of professional approaches to the divided city condition emerges. To embrace these alternatives, the notion that ethnic conflict can be resolved or eliminated must be discarded. In addition, many of the most basic assumptions related to public service and benefits must be amended in light of attainable outcomes:

There is no one public good, because the question is not "What is good?" The question is "What is the public?" The people are behind the cause of the division of the city, it's not the monuments . . . what divides them is not the demarcation line but people living on the other side and people living on this side. If you want to reunite the city, you have to reunite the people and do everything possible to make them come back and there are certain mechanisms to do that. (Benvenisti 2003)

A revised professional mandate might then be centered on discovering and developing these mechanisms, together with the need to cope with the everyday challenges of urban partition. This approach forfeits grandiose city-wide impacts and invites professionals to take pride in the small successes generated by relatively modest strategies. These successes accrete incrementally in response to shared, pragmatic concerns defined by local residents. A Beiruti living near the former Green Line confirmed this approach: "I feel that a gradual encounter between us will resolve these superficial hatreds or limitations that people impose on each other" (Nora H., 2000).

As traditional assumptions are overturned, the order of precedence is reversed: symptoms over causes, relative good over absolute remediation, recognition over denial, and pragmatism over postponement. Such a mandate, rarely encountered in the divided city context, expands the professional repertoire to accommodate contradictions and discord rather than treating them as obstacles.

This shift in assumptions and objectives is potentially disruptive. Even cultural heritage conservators, though more accustomed to viewing the built environment in its social context, often forfeit the opportunity to engage the problems of ethnic partition directly in their work, as observed by one Beiruti urban planner:

Here the tradition has been that even physical planners tend to see the city as a big architectural problem and . . . those who tried to oppose the reconstruction in the name of memory and heritage rarely knew what memory is. It was for them the nice old buildings but not what people think about the city or what they're reminded by. . . . They don't have the depth or the knowledge to play the role of social reformers. (John S., 2000)

The challenge of achieving reforms by balancing symbolic and pragmatic projects was likewise emphasized by a resident of Mostar:

A lot of things have been done and everything is useful, any kind of reconstruction. When I said to reconstruct, not maybe to reconstruct [historic monuments] but to build those factories, I was thinking about new job places, you know, to give people opportunity to work and earn money from their own work, you know. (Lejla C., 2001)

One way for built environment professionals to address this challenge is to formulate plans that respond to a spectrum of political outcomes, providing a firm basis for the discussion of development alternatives by municipal authorities and their constituents. It has already been seen that this kind of political contingency planning was undertaken with notable success by urban planners from both sides of the ethnic divide working jointly in Nicosia. Though only a handful of major projects were implemented during two decades of planning, the mollifying effects of this ongoing dialogue on communal relations in general were probably high.

The urban planning processes and physical interventions undertaken by the communal Nicosia Master Plan team did not provide solutions to the problem of partition but did develop viable future scenarios, putting them a large step ahead of many of their counterparts in other divided cities. One senior team member noted, "Some [cooperative master plan] implementation can make you ready for the solutions. It is another way of approaching the solution, I think" (Özen 2001).

Finding a balance between technical and political constraints was not simple or straightforward. Team members in Nicosia acknowledged the most likely political obstacles, without allowing their plans to dictate political outcomes:

We were always ready to find the best technical solutions regardless of politics. If the circumstances did not allow the optimal solution to be implemented, then we could describe the next best solution. I believe that master planning is a technical issue, and should stay a technical issue, but we must be ready for any alternative from the political sphere. (Özen 2001)

This approach allows the built environment professional to play an active role in all stages of urban partition and post-partition planning by helping policymakers to interpret the crisis in pragmatic, creative ways. The development of contingency plans according to the Nicosia Master Plan model does not hinge upon formal commissions and does not rely on a single political outcome for feasibility. It is based on the idea that experts in urban planning and design can provide valuable translation services to help policymakers convert good ideas into sound physical interventions.

One scholar noted: "Generals and diplomats are in the business of resolution. You are in the business of coping. You are a social worker, that is your role . . . I mean, you know that the situations like Jerusalem, Nicosia, or Belfast will not go away. But then there must be some optimism" (Benvenisti 2003).

As indicated previously in this chapter, many aspects of the existing relationship must be called into question when the peculiarities of a divided city are considered. A strategy of tackling problems on a case-by-case basis in which the planners are beholden to governmental authorities falters when the problems themselves are symptoms of much larger dilemmas, or when issues of sovereignty and jurisdiction themselves are part of the dispute.

Although these circumstances are exceptional according to everyday standards, they are the baseline conditions most often confronted by built environment professionals operating in a divided city. Politicians seeking progressive solutions in the context of ethnic apartheid need assistance from nonpolitical actors, as confirmed by a Member of Parliament from Belfast:

It would be great if we could sit down as politicians across the table and do all that, but there's no meeting of minds on the subject. Maybe some day it will happen. I hope it will. But for the moment I'm still a fireman: not an architect, not a planner. I'm a potential architect. (Maginness 2001)

Into this breach the built environment professional may step, with no small degree of trepidation, in order to complement firefighting with balanced, incremental solutions to social needs on both sides of the partition line.

Chapter 10
Patterns

These five cities are linked by similar episodes of development in similar sequences. The patterns are easily discerned and characterize a class of cities violently impacted, and ultimately reshaped, by involuntary ethnic partition. Recognition of the patterns may require concurrent recognition of a moral obligation to confront the problem of urban apartheid in increasingly effective, creative ways. The careful observer is compelled to wonder about the conditions under which partition typically occurs, and the extent to which those conditions might appear in divergent cultural environments. Some citizens of divided cities do not consider themselves special, as noted in a Beirut resident's wartime memoir:

They speak of Beirut as if it were an aberration of the human experience: it is not. Beirut was a city like any other and its people were a people like any other. What happened here could, I think, happen anywhere. (Makdisi 1990: 20)

A similar observation was made by a Belfast police officer:

If you solve this here, then there are communities over here that would want it and over there that would want it . . . if you get the model, you can transfer it. But I don't think there's anyone out there watching, like a shark-watcher. Looking for patterns, issues and patterns. (Edmund S., 2001)

The point was clarified by a Belfast politician:

unless you move to manage your society, any area of conflict or area where there is potential conflict will end up exactly the same way as us. The reaction to fear—it's the same the world over. . . . The reaction to the need to have space, and comfort, and—what shall I say?—peace of mind. It doesn't matter where it is, people want to live in the area where they feel safe, and they constantly, it seems to me, keep looking for a ghettoization—for safety. Is that not how divided societies begin to be divided? Once you have a population that believes that it's not safe to live among the other side, well then they begin to look for other ways to live with the other people; I mean, they don't take the risk. Why take the risk? I can afford myself peace of mind. Is that not a human thing? Rather than a Belfast thing or a Beirut thing or a Mostar thing? It's a human thing. (Ervine 2001)

The lessons drawn from Beirut, Mostar, Nicosia, Jerusalem, and Belfast relate to other, less polarized cities that exhibit symptoms of deepening physical segregation. It is not difficult to recognize spatial segregation as "a coping mechanism tied to specific threats" (Benvenisti 1982: 173) that exist to some degree in every city. The spectrum of division spans

from those which show only relatively mild and normal micro level conflict over allocation of public resources, through those which show some macro level dichotomy, to those cities in which polarization resulted in complete physical partition. (Benvenisti 1982: 5)

Several patterns that bind divided cities together into a meaningful urban class have already been examined. Chapter 2 suggested that urban partition can be a legitimate and unavoidable response to the breakdown of collective security. Chapters 3 to 7 showed that all five cities exhibited similar combinations of stress and insecurity prior to division. Chapter 8 showed that cycles of violence and internal partitioning are tied to the breach and renegotiation of a social compact binding urban managers and urban residents. This chapter consolidates these observations into a more concise portrait of the divided city and its typical developmental pathways.

Standard Sequence

The events that pushed Belfast, Beirut, Jerusalem, Mostar, and Nicosia up to and beyond the threshold of ethnic apartheid have much in common. Hindsight illuminates the shared phases of urban development that presaged violent episodes of partition. A number of standard prerequisites to partition have been identified in the comparative analysis of the five divided cities scrutinized in this book. Not all are found in each city, but they can be considered reliable indicators of a propensity toward physical segregation for ethnically diverse societies under stress while undergoing a major social transition.

1. Politicizing ethnicity

The path leading to urban partition is paved with the merging of political and ethnic identity on a mass scale. In the five cities examined here, ethnicity is the dominant determinant of political affiliation and inherited affiliation is the primary criterion for social organization.

Urban partition along ethnic lines typically appears where public resources have been allocated in a lopsided manner for a generation or longer. Before involuntary segregation disrupts normal social exchange, managers and residents in such cities grow accustomed to the idea that access to key urban amenities is automatically limited for certain minority groups.

A good example is found in Mostar. Former Yugoslav president Tito enjoyed unprecedented political and popular success largely because of his ability to balance and neutralize ethnic rivalries. His political heirs exploited the same rivalries with much less acumen in the decade following his death, ultimately encouraging confrontation. This strategic reversal brought

resentments, suspicions, and belief in one's own collective intrinsic rights to resources solidified ethnic identity, weakened loyalty to the central government, and reinforced the dominant logic of identity politics at the federal level. (Crawford and Lipschutz 1998: 15)

The political manipulation of foreign powers has often generated similar results. Britain's divide-and-rule strategy during its Mandate period set a lasting precedent for institutionalized discrimination. It tended to activate ethnic fault-lines and leave cleavages exposed following the the British departure. Nowhere was this pattern more prominent than in Jerusalem, where the British maintained a long, uneasy, and artificial stalemate among lopsided local rivals. In the early 1950s, one eyewitness in Palestine predicted the dangers bound up in this approach:

Until the balance of justice athwart the frontier is adjusted, it is as foolish to expect tranquility, either in Jerusalem or in Palestine as a whole, as it is to try to open a lock gate before equalizing the water level on either side of it. (Perowne 1954: 107)

The question of "justice athwart the frontier" is central in all divided cities. The historic record suggests that neither erection nor demolition of physical barriers will bring lasting public benefit until that question is adequately confronted. The deleterious harmonization of political structures with structural partition was noted by a Belfast politician commenting on the longevity of the barricades:

We've just institutionalized [a long-term problem]. Because the "short-term", eighteen foot wall is thirty years old. It hasn't gone away, you know. In that respect, I think even our formula of politics almost confirms our difference. It doesn't celebrate our difference, that would be different, if we were celebrating our diversity, our difference . . . I think it's a tragedy that this is the way we have to function in our lives. The peacelines institutionalize, virtually, the concept of difference. For a start, the peacelines went up to solve an initial problem, but beyond that we have not dealt with the core problems that created the peaceline in the first place. So the longer the peaceline is there, the more we confirm, or reaffirm, our incapacity to live together. (Ervine 2001)

In this way urban partitions can contribute to the self-fulfilling prophesy of mutual incompatibility while tending to draw energy, resources, and attention away from the deeper crisis of institutionalized discrimination.

2. Clustering

If pressures multiply, catalytic events occur, and avenues of political redress appear blocked, then members of a threatened urban community may seek out smaller, more ethnically homogeneous clusters for protection. Anticipating that forced separation might bring tranquility, municipal authorities often assist this process of voluntary homogenization with laws, incentives, and relocation programs. In Mostar during the war, uprooted Muslims even received free one-way transportation to the eastern side of the city. Detractors frequently refer to this process as demographic engineering, while advocates of it point to the diminution of local violence, the affirmation of group identities, and the strengthening of a sense of psychological wellbeing in well-defined social enclaves.

Chronic insecurity creates an atmosphere in which discrimination and fear flourish (Benvenisti 1982: 15):

The defense mechanism of clustering around your own kind was a natural reaction, but it was also rooted in [each group's] fundamental perception of . . . itself as a besieged and threatened group, and of the other side as cruel, ruthless, and demonic. (Benvenisti 1986: 87)

Strained relations between minority and majority ethnic communities are routinely complicated by a lack of consensus regarding relative group status. Benvenisti's "double minority syndrome" effectively characterizes group relations in all five divided cities.

A good example is Nicosia. Here, for decades prior to the formal and physical partition of the island, Greek Cypriots could view themselves as members of a national political majority and a regional demographic minority while, in symmetrical fashion, Turkish Cypriots assumed that they lacked adequate and fair political representation, but turned to neighboring Turkey for backstop protection during times of crisis.

Both sides feel victimized. Both sides compete with the iconography of pain. . . . [The Double Minority Syndrome] very much holds here too, because the Greek Cypriots see themselves as a minority, given Turkey, while the Turkish Cypriots see themselves as a minority on the island. . . . The game was: who is the victim and who is the minority? (Papadakis 2002)

Likewise in Belfast, the Catholics in Northern Ireland have long maintained a dual membership in Irish majority and Northern Irish minority communities.

Because both groups typically view themselves as a beleaguered minority, both feel entitled to take extraordinary measures to secure their sense of collective well-being and compensate for disparity of needs, power, opportunity, and access to important resources. As these compensatory systems grow in sophistication and effectiveness, they contribute to a self-fulfilling prophecy of enmity while faith in conventional mechanisms of public justice and allocation simultaneously erodes.

The social costs of these deepening animosities can rise to the point where they nullify the benefits attributed to urban segregation. The persistence of prejudice and violence following physical partition underscores the complexity of cost-benefit calculations in the context of coercive ethnic segregation. Segregated enclaves call into question the minimum size of a viable urban unit from both a functional and a social perspective. Ethnic enclaves created and defended by threatened urban residents may offer solace in the short term, but their reduced access to municipal services, roads, schools, places of employment, medical facilities, and the like, undermine their long-term prospects for prosperity.

The Short Strand enclave in Belfast, with a population of about 4,000, is one of the smallest clusters considered in this study. It is an island that would probably function very poorly the without ongoing infusions of federal funding and nonprofit subsidies it receives due to its highly tenuous position as an isolated Catholic neighborhood in east Belfast. Despite the seemingly unsustainable nature of its existence, the walls girdling the Short Strand remain popular:

You can throw blast bombs over the wall, or petrol bombs over the walls: they're not high enough to really stop that. So they're more to make people feel psychologically secure than really physically secure, if you know what I mean. It hasn't really eased the intercommunal tensions, but it makes people feel a little safer, since at least there's a wall there, and it must be a little safe. (Charles D., 2001)

At the same time, the inward pull of cultural homogeneity in dense urban enclaves compounds solidarity. The power of camaraderie felt by living in an enclave even in moments of greatest peril was described by a British journalist in Belfast observing the outbreak of the Troubles in 1968:

And they sang. There on the street corners with the gunfire in the background from the men on the rooftops, and the rocks and petrol bombs crashing and shattering, they sang. They have good songs, the Protestants—"Derry Walls" sung by a thousand voices in the shambles of the Shankill would have graced a Hollywood spectacular: "With heart and hand, and sword and shield, we'll guard old Derry Walls!" (Hastings 1970: 184)

Hardships may justify and reinforce special social cohesion, as in Belfast: "It's not great. Like, when we look at these areas, it's pathetic. But it's where we're known and it's what we're used to. That's what you have, and you don't want to lose it" (McAtamney 2001). The ambivalence of these sentiments leaves open many questions about the potency and value of urban partitions in general and ethnic enclaves in particular.

The isolation of ethnic enclaves in a partitioned urban environment often intensifies until they are "too small with too few residents to become economically viable as self-supporting units, even at rudimentary subsistence levels" (Grundy-Warr 1987: 73). This fact is important, since it underscores the serious practical disadvantages of strict ethnic segregation in a mixed and interdependent community and shows that external actors have a key role in providing subsidies for these social contortions.

3. Political up-scaling

Just as ethnic clustering tends to decrease dramatically the operational circumference of personal interactions and loyalties in the larger urban environment, it also commonly extends the field of political interactions. This happens when formerly nondescript enclaves assume emblematic significance in a political dispute of national or international prominence. Because "intense communal conflicts are usually perceived in their macropolitical contexts" (Benvenisti 1982: 326), divided cities are the product of struggles much wider in scope than the urban environment in which they are enacted. The tug-of-war between these two forces—the concrete inti-macies of the enclave and the abstract associations with a sweeping political conflict—often stabilizes urban thresholds despite the hardships generated by functional segregation at the local level.

Divided cities function in part as emblems of larger political struggles in which individual enclave residents are enlisted to fight battles not directly serving their personal interests. For this reason, rival ethnic communities comprise a sort of insulating or sacrificial layer in a much larger contest. Divided cities are often located at the epicenter of violent contests concern-ing national identity and sovereignty. They are a beachhead for sovereignty struggles grounded in irredentism and ultranationalism.

One observer in Beirut noted that urban violence "was partisan, eco-nomic, and national . . . it was a war for others: it was a proxy war" (Tueni 2000). In Belfast the dynamic is described by residents in similar terms:

what [interface residents] do is, we break the tide. We take all the hits for political instability, we take the hits for weak leadership, we take the hits for bad planning, we take the hits for sectarianism across the community; interfaces take the hits. . . . Sectarianism is not pockets of Prods and Taigs on interfaces. Right? It's all across our community, but it manifests along interfaces. (McGlone 2001)

Restricting the worst of the violence to urban interface areas, broader politi-cal struggles can simmer on indefinitely. Because the chaos and duplication of the divided urban scenario are profitable in so many measurable ways, discussed in Chapters 3–8, vested interests on both sides of a conflict gener-ally desire to stabilize and prolong the battle.

Local political entrepreneurs flourish, foreign mediators prove indis-pensable, cultural traditions are rejuvenated, paramilitary groups gain prominence, intragroup conflicts are muted, smugglers acquire steady pa-tronage, and formerly ordinary neighborhoods earn infamy. In Belfast, the exploitation of partition led one native to observe:

it makes no economic sense, and it doesn't make any religious sense, and it makes very little political sense, but the hatred is there, and that is a very difficult thing to weigh in the balance, and you've got generations of vendettas. That's the back end of it. The forward end of it is that it's turned into this drugs barony business; all these mafias have crawled in under the blanket of this divide . . . it's a very serious propagator, this is one of the things that keeps it on the simmer. (Richard S., 2000)

Each divided city presents a stalemate model in which political upscaling and social downscaling occur simultaneously.

In the case of Belfast, it has been noted that rival claims to Northern Ireland held by Ireland and Great Britain are assumed to hang in the balance, precluding many locally tenable compromises. This stalemate model demonstrates that one kind of equilibrium can be achieved when a weak but regional nationalistic agenda is pitted against a stronger one pursued by a foreign government.

In Beirut, the control of terrain in the capital city corresponded very nearly with control over Lebanon as a whole, since all administrative power has traditionally been concentrated in the capital. Within this destabilized and symbolically weighty environment, rival ethnic factions were able to establish by military means zones of influence in which their constituencies were compelled to gather for protection. Because these violent rivalries would have produced a clear local hierarchy if they had been of a purely local nature, this model demonstrates how the influence of interested third-party nations like Syria, Israel, and the United States complicated the long process of reaching a popular configuration for national governance.

In Jerusalem, both parties to the urban conflict represent much larger political constituencies simultaneously seeking sovereignty over the disputed territories of Israel and the West Bank. Stalemate in this case was achieved when a powerful expropriating government claiming the moral authority to annex territory butted up against compound resistance from traditional inhabitants who lacked political organization, from weaker regional governments lacking clout, and from international authorities unwilling to grant legal sanction.

In Mostar, two young secessionist states tested their capacity to forge and defend new nations defined in terms of ethnicity. This experiment resulted in a violent contest for symbolic urban territory straddling a traditional cultural boundary. Serbia and Croatia vied for Bosnia, the land into which they each hoped to expand in order to improve their prospects for survival. Both expected the Bosniak population to succumb to the victor(s). In the end, the conflict resulted in a stalemate characteristic of all divided cities. Physical division marked an unstable and unanticipated equilibrium of strong military forces attempting hostile acquisition with weak civilian forces holding ground.

In Nicosia, the cultural history of the city made it an emblem of Cyprus, and in turn Cyprus became a symbol of Turkish and Greek irredentism. The lives of many Cypriots were shattered due to the unfortunate and largely incidental correspondence between local demographics and international political rivalries that split a formerly unified, independent, nonaligned country into two ethnic factions. The Greek Cypriots were transformed into defenders of Greek soil and the Turkish Cypriots into their enemies. In this stalemate, the tether binding local and international echelons of political activity proved durable. What could not be settled among foreign nations around the negotiating table would not be resolved on the ground.

4. Boundary etching

Once threatened ethnic communities have retreated into homogeneous clusters and the urban terrain has been converted into political territory, it remains for the battle lines to be formally drawn. Physical etching energizes and activates ethnic interfaces among local communities psychologically entrenched according to the forces of stalemate described above.

The first stage of etching happens gradually and is largely outside the sphere of major political disputes. The importance of physical legacies in the development of divided cities has already been discussed in Chapter 2. These legacies take the form of roads, rivers, valleys, historic quarters, parish boundaries, political districts, and all the other thresholds that traditionally organize social life without forcibly constraining it. Under normal conditions, such fault-lines embedded in the fabric of the city present few burdens because they are permeable or dormant.

Several of these incremental etching processes are of special relevance and should be described in greater detail. The natural topography and landscape of the city often play an important role in the determination of social boundaries, which is to say that the physical legacy of many interethnic partitions is often both arbitrary and long-standing. Rivers and hills have traditionally divided urban space in natural ways, providing effective forms of passive protection from attack and augmenting architectural fortifications. This is evident in the siting of castles and small urban complexes in Europe before and during the medieval period, when the high ground was exploited by city planners in order to achieve a military advantage over attackers.

When elevation corresponds to a mountain range or ridge, high ground often corresponds to the boundary between two watersheds, or between fertile and nonfertile areas. Because the politics of water have increasing significance in many cities, geography remains a potentially contentious issue in the large framework of territorial contests. An excellent example is found in Jerusalem, where the city not only occupies high ground linked symbolically to sovereignty and spirituality, but also straddles the gravitational and economic threshold between wet and dry land.

Elevation has always influenced the physical and political development of Jerusalem, beginning with erection of the Temple Mount on the highest and most symbolically powerful location in the city. The Valley of Kidron makes a natural border between the walls of the Old City and Palestinian East Jerusalem, while Jewish settlements at and beyond the outskirts of the city typically occupy hilltops that allow residents to look down on Palestinian villages oriented around cultivated land, olive groves, or water resources.

Likewise in Nicosia, the earliest settlement in the capital gravitated toward the Pedeios River, functioning simultaneously as a spine and a natural border defining two distinct sectors of the city. This later corresponded in a general way to the Turkish and Greek enclaves in the north and south respectively, as shown in Figure 8.1.

As shown in Chapter 7, the Pedeios would later be diverted and its path through the city filled in to create the primary commercial corridor. The section of the city north of the corridor became defined as a traditionally Ottoman or Muslim enclave, while the area to the south could be characterized as predominantly Greek or Orthodox. The former riverbed remained a traditionally shared public area where Cypriots of all ethnicities routinely interacted. Because this area was never firmly imprinted with a single ethnic identity, it cannot be surprising that it was later to become the de facto, and then the official, partition between rival groups with the onset of violence in the mid-1950s. Inscribed first as a river, then as a commercial artery, then as a functional divide, and finally as a physical partition, one line etched by the natural course of water has governed social and political dynamics in Nicosia for centuries. There is no better example of the typical evolution of ethnic boundaries—at once incremental, arbitrary, and emblematic—than the Nicosia Green Line.

All examples of commercial arteries evolving into partition lines are listed in Table 10.1. The seams and rings of regular urban growth also exert a powerful influence on the fabric of the city, shaping the life of urban residents and the demographic character of the enclaves defined by them. Aggressive urban development schemes, especially those implemented in the nineteenth and early twentieth centuries, often resulted in the sharp delineation of old and new urban sectors. Typically, the new area bears the cultural imprint of its political sponsor. In this way, growth and ethnic segregation can sometimes coincide, leaving one group in a more progressive

TABLE 10.1. COMMERCIAL ARTERIES CORRESPONDING TO PARTITION LINES

City	Corresponding arteries
Belfast	Shankill and Falls Roads
Beirut	Martyr's Square, Damascus Road, Hamra Street
Jerusalem	Jaffa, Mamillah, and Nablus Streets
Mostar	Boulevard of the National Revolution
Nicosia	Paphos and Hermes Streets

and another in a relatively retrograde environment while still sharing the same urban address. Jews in the new Jerusalem and Croatian Bosnians in west Mostar, both enjoying considerably higher standards of living than their Muslim counterparts, illustrate this pattern well. Where the new fabric connects to the old, the etched boundaries are susceptible to reactivation under special conditions of social instability and intergroup rivalry.

Mostar provides an excellent illustration. As with other cases of its kind, the Old Town was for many centuries coterminous with the city itself, and beyond it the agricultural use of the land intensified incrementally the farther one got from the urban center. When Austro-Hungarian provincial authorities began planning a major scheme for northwestern expansion of the city around 1878, Mostar consisted of two halves cleanly separated by the city's widest and most impressive traffic artery, the Boulevard of the Revolution.

Formerly the city's western periphery, this invisible boundary became central when it was converted into a residential and commercial thoroughfare catering to inhabitants of the new sector and used freely by all Mostarians. Though the city remained demographically mixed during these stages of growth and development, residents of Croatian descent felt a stronger affinity with Bosnia's post-Ottoman administrators and so came to dominate the recently constructed portions of the city. In this manner, a line with a political and social character was unintentionally etched into the city over a previously innocuous border between the city and the countryside. While social circumstances remained favorable, this line exerted no obviously negative influences upon the city and was associated with no campaigns related to ethnic segregation. The same line would become activated later when conditions changed for the worse.

The Mostar example shows how the boundary between urban and semi-urban or rural land-uses retained a functional and symbolic significance throughout many phases of urban development.

Jerusalem offers an even more vivid illustration of how land-use patterns can shape the boundaries of ethnic segregation. Because the Palestinian population claims a cultural hinterland in the Judean desert to the east of Jerusalem, Jerusalemites not living in the walled city traditionally resided in villages immediately to the south and east, such as Silwan, Sour Baher, Beit Safafa, and al-Tur. These villages are part of the area conventionally called East Jerusalem. The city sits at the crest of an important ridge so that the nearby areas of West Jerusalem are green and fertile by comparison. Because most Israelis emigrated from temperate climates, they settled most naturally on the western side of the city. These trends left a strong demographic stamp on both sides of this geological boundary long before the outbreak of violence between Jerusalem's rival ethnic communities.

Patterns of gentrification in the urban environment also introduce boundaries and thresholds that harden when collective security is threatened. It was shown in Chapters 3–7 that ethnic antagonisms often have their roots in class-based rivalries. Even when questions of economic exploitation are eclipsed by violence, the influence of thresholds inscribed by purely economic distinctions is often prominent. Israeli and Palestinian communities in Jerusalem demonstrate how class and ethnicity can overlap in a divided city, deepening rather than multiplying urban boundaries.

Belfast offers an almost ideal example of the interplay and ultimately of the divergence between class and ethnicity in the context of longstanding intergroup antagonism. There, the degree to which Catholic and Protestant enclaves are distinguished appears to decrease with wealth. Among middle- and upper-middle-class residents of the city, ethnic distinctions operate in a relatively benign and uniformly nonviolent way. It is exclusively in working-class sectors that ethnicity is routinely associated with violence, intimidation, and physical partition.

It follows that class-based difference is a primary organizing factor in Belfast; though there is a stereotypical rivalry between Protestants and Catholics, most observers would agree that the adjectival phrase "working-class" should be appended. Such dominant and sublimated dichotomies are found in most divided cities and contribute mightily to the confusion that surrounds them.

Infrastructure also generates lines that take on a nonarbitrary significance when social and political tensions flare up. Every city is etched by conduits for people, information, power, water, and waste. Under special circumstances these pathways become boundaries. Roads are most commonly transformed in this way because they give shape to neighborhoods and regulate the movement of their residents. Roads can be used as thresholds that organize or stem the forces running perpendicular to them. Few lines are more obviously or conveniently inscribed in the physical urban environment, and their importance as boundaries grows as competitive social tensions arise.

The Boulevard of the Revolution in Mostar has already provided a good illustration of the relationship between the preexisting cleavages created by prominent traffic arteries and the seemingly spontaneous emergence of interethnic boundaries. The activation of the Damascus Road in Beirut from the Martyrs' Square to the farthest suburbs further demonstrates the importance of infrastructural boundaries in the context of violent competition between resident groups. Many factors determined the exact position of the Green Line between the Christian-dominated eastern portion of the city and the Muslim-dominated western sector, but most struggles were enacted along Beirut's traditional north-south axis. This axis touches the oldest shared portions of the city, tracing the locations of medieval fortification walls that formerly defined the Place du Canons and the western perimeter of the urban nucleus.

The strong linear presence of the Damascus Road along that axis provided an ideal front line and visual corridor for snipers stationed along its length. These functional advantages, in addition to the enormous symbolic importance of the corridor, made the conversion of a shared public roadway into the city's primary military interface almost inevitable. It became, in this way, the most dominant of many fault-lines that preexisted, by decades or centuries, interethnic conflict in Beirut, and it ultimately defined the physical parameters of the conflict.

5. Concretizing

The awakening and transformation of these inscribed boundaries from permeable into impermeable thresholds separating neighboring resident groups is a process that relies on purposeful design and execution. Chapters 3–7 examined the actors and strategies employed to this end, tracing the steps by which informal lines become official and invisible ones become physical. In incremental and predictable ways, ethnic enclaves that once provided a social mooring for beleaguered residents can become stultified, isolated, and dysfunctional. Because the consequences of this process are routinely unfavorable for urban residents living and working near ethnic partitions, it is worth looking closely at the typical steps leading to a hardening of formerly benign urban boundaries.

The most familiar and important factor affecting the hardening process is the loss of physical security. When threats, episodes of violence, and shifts in political power leave one or more groups feeling vulnerable, they will eventually seek new forms of protection. Alternate systems of policing and justice must be created when traditional systems fail, as in Beirut and Mostar during the worst periods of partition, or become biased against a minority group, as in Belfast and Jerusalem. Evidence of the great effort and discipline used to construct these surrogate systems is found in paramilitary organizations, the informal policing of common crime in ethnic enclaves, vigilante networks, rituals of territorial marking and the systematic intimidation of rival group members. The construction of barricades along interethnic boundaries is one of the most forceful and emblematic expressions of a desire to counteract the vulnerabilities that have been inadequately addressed by the municipal government.

These barricades are generally intended to be temporary. They are created as stop-gap measures pending a negotiated settlement. Many urban partitions that were erected hastily in anticipation of diplomatic intervention have, however, remained in place for decades. Their construction has consumed large sums of public land and funding, and their maintenance has called for the creation of entirely new military and paramilitary entities that were formerly unnecessary. This frequently suits the political aims of key participants in the ethnic conflict. The British Mandate administrations of the twentieth century provide a good example, as they

failed to decide whether partition would be a temporary or permanent byproduct of devolution, deferred the issue of boundaries, population movement, compensation . . . resulting in [boundary disputes in] Kashmir, Ulster . . . that remain still unresolved. (Schaeffer 1990: 114–15)

A sort of controlled ambivalence with regard to regions shaped by ethnic conflict was a fundamental component of their divide-and-rule/divide-and-quit strategy.

Most major interethnic partitions that were intended to be demolished at the conclusion of a peaceful settlement have exceeded their life expectancy. As the staying power of urban partitions becomes increasingly obvious, it has become common for the physical character of the barricades to change. In Belfast, for example, the peacelines constructed by the municipality have become more sturdy, more sophisticated, and more visually attractive over time. These changes have accompanied the recognition among policymakers that the peacelines have evolved from interim measures pending toward the solution itself:

The ugly ones are called Mark I's . . . the Mark I wall was actually put up very quickly. They used the steel stanchions and dropped the precast concrete units in them. It was done—it was only meant to be temporary, but it's been there literally thirty years now. So that was the early attempt at it. Later on they realized that these were not just going to be taken away in a matter of one or two years' time. That they were going to be permanent, or semi-permanent. And therefore the designs changed accordingly. (James L., 2000)

Fred Boal noted this progression at the peaceline on Cupar Street in Belfast:

In September 1969 they started putting iron in the streets, and by the end of September there were burnt-out cars and trucks, since the locals too tried to make sure the violence didn't spread. The first peacelines were vehicles, replaced by the army's barbed wire fencing, then the wire was taken down and a fence 2 to 2.5 m high was put in, corrugated as a temporary divide [and] intended to be used for not more than six months. But things got worse rather than better. The fence was not high enough. So they doubled it. . . . People thought of them as just a device to regulate behavior a bit until everybody cools off, and then we just take them away again. Go back to how we were living before, before all the nonsense started. (Boal 2000)

Walls continue to be built on the standard premise that they are temporary measures pending full, fair political settlement. A wealth of experience, along with the findings from all five cities examined here, shows this premise to be false. Political actors who consciously rely upon it appear to demonstrate willful ignorance, self-serving misanthropy, or both.

Another useful observation regarding the emergence of physical partitions is their tendency to appear first and most prominently in places where rival community members traditionally mingled or coexisted in unusually close proximity. Mostar as a whole was one of the most integrated cities in the former Yugoslavia, yet it became the epicenter of interethnic violence with the onslaught of civil war. In Beirut, the Green Line passed through residential and commercial zones where the highest levels of prewar intergroup mixing took place. The best examples are the neighboring suburbs of Chiyah and Ghobeire and the central market zone occupied by Martyrs' Square. The same patterns holds true for Nicosia.

These zones represent the viability of interethnic cooperation, and so it stands to reason that they are the first to disintegrate during periods of violent instability. Their elimination also satisfies the self-fulfilling prophecy of mutual antipathy between rival ethnic groups by blotting out tangible alternatives. These observations make it increasingly difficult to claim that physical partitions in formerly mixed areas are the necessary byproduct of compromised security alone. The motivations of political actors who seek faits accomplis in relation to a vision of ethnic apartheid must also be considered.

6. Consolidating

Once ethnic boundaries have been etched and concretized in the urban environment, the political climate determines whether municipal authorities will augment or counteract the process of division. The consent of governmental authorities, whether direct or tacit, to a long-term ethnic apartheid spurs vigilante and paramilitary organizations to complete the basic engineering and maintenance of inter-urban boundaries. Support for such enterprises, or a lack of resistance to them, is generally a byproduct of the weakness and instability of the authorities. Where power vacuums exist, local warlords, profiteers, and self-appointed civilian leaders typically fill the gaps. It is in their interests to generate the conditions of anxiety and suspicion that make their leadership seemingly indispensable.

Sanction from national or municipal authorities is irrelevant where government has collapsed completely, as in the Bosnian and Lebanese cases. These conditions place responsibility for the support or censure of ethnically segregated institutions in the hands of external, third-party political administrators. The official acceptance of ethnicity as the primary criterion for political affiliation was a fundamental part of the larger strategy, and it is a tactic that has been seen in many colonial nations since the disintegration of the British empire.

Ethnic partition, part of a stabilized and incremental process of urban apartheid, results in retrograde urban development. The duplication of infrastructure, institutions, and commercial activities leads often to forms of sprawl and expansion that undermine municipal functions that are typically already inefficient. The conventional logic of shared spaces and services is turned upside down; in a segregated city, each antagonistic ethnic community insists on the possession and control of its own streets, airwaves, currencies, utilities, schools, hospitals, and housing to whatever extent possible, on the assumption that those apparently belonging to rival groups could prove dangerous to them. As if these functional redundancies were not burdensome enough, they are commonly compounded by the symbolic and physical bifurcation of one city into two, each with its own name, history, and destiny.

It has been noted previously that barricades spontaneously erected are often rebuilt in a more permanent fashion when the broader process of ethnic segregation has been sanctioned and stabilized. The resulting disfiguration of the physical urban environment takes place in several and predictable ways. Unofficial partitions (those created and managed by local community members) are typically monitored according to a schedule that corresponds to the dates and times when confrontation is most likely. Often children are recruited for this purpose since they are somewhat more immune to arrest, are easily indoctrinated, and have the time to spend on such purposes during afternoon working hours.

Circulation patterns in ethnic enclaves experiencing high levels of vulnerability to attack are commonly reengineered so that quick entry and exit for strangers is difficult. These changes sometimes include the construction of cul-de-sacs in residential areas or the conversion of through streets into dead ends. At a broader scale, divided cities frequently function as regional cul-de-sacs; they become dead ends for the movement of people, goods, and ideas as well as emblems of social stultification in the eyes of external observers.

The resulting contradictions are rife in Jerusalem, which is "the center of the world, but in fact is lost at the end of a cul-de-sac on a violent, socially desolate frontier." This desolation is more literal in the case of Nicosia's northern sector residents, who found themselves "in a cul-de-sac within Cyprus—all exit roads from the city that lead to the West, South and East were cut off and are now blind alleys" (Kliot and Mansfield 1999: 217, 190).

Other forms of visual marking, generally taking the form of graffiti and painted insignia on walls and buildings, complete the decoration of the divided city, so that strangers and natives can be tutored as they walk as to where they do or do not belong. Official partitions often become integrated almost seamlessly with surrounding structures designed in a manner that suggests permanence and legitimacy. Some shelter soldiers, some enclose restaurants, and others are incorporated into small urban parks. In other cases, partitions remain informal, decrepit, and permanently temporary in light of popular or political ambivalence regarding the territorial compromise they signify.

Figure 10.1. Barricades end traffic along streets connecting rival communities in Belfast, where efficiency is routinely sacrificed to the dynamics of partition, c. 2003. Authors.

7. Unifying but not integrating

Due to the burdensome inefficiencies of physical segregation in an environment engineered for cooperation, urban partition is rarely sustainable. When barriers are eventually removed in order to resume normal development, as in Mostar, Jerusalem, and Beirut, the removal and erasure of boundaries often become a pressing issue. Though physical barricades are easily demolished, the social and physical scars that remain are slow to fade. The psychological residue from long periods of violence and intimidation generally prevents residents who lived through the period of partition from occupying formerly forbidden areas. As a result, seam areas along former partition lines often become viable only for socially neutral purposes such as industrial development or infrastructure.

Long after partitions are lifted and free movement is guaranteed by the municipal authorities, voluntary segregation generally continues—just as it

Figure 10.2. The Green Line abruptly severs traditional circulation routes in the historic core of Nicosia, creating lonely cul-de-sacs, c. 2003. Authors.

Figure 10.3. Partitions intersect urban fabric roughly in the south of Nicosia, c. 2003. Authors.

Figure 10.4. Industrial facilities appear in the stigmatized space behind a Belfast partition where houses formerly stood, c. 2002. Authors.

typically precedes periods of violent partition. These lingering anxieties and suspicions point to one the most fundamental disincentives related to the process of urban partition in general: the legacies of trauma and distrust that live on in many forms, both functional and psychological, long after formal settlements are reached. Just as the appearance of physical barricades is the final stage of a long process of intimidation and alienation between rival ethnic communities, their erasure is also a first step along a complicated and treacherous path toward normalization.

During the period of partition and ethnic segregation, municipal politicians with a stake in the conflict tend either to overlook the existence and impacts of physical partitions or discount them as the unfortunate but necessary byproducts of the dispute. They typically assign no special significance to barriers as discrete elements of the conflict, since this association would only invite further questioning about their purpose and legitimacy. Once the conflict is settled or concluded, the significance of these physical partitions in the eyes of the same political actors often changes dramatically. Because physical partitions are the easiest part of the conflict to eliminate, their removal is frequently presumed to herald the end of a bitter era of intolerance and the beginning of a new period of social harmony.

If unification is the product of a one-sided military victory, unilateral political problem-solving, or a negotiated settlement that excluded the primary antagonists from the negotiations, the removal of barricades can be considered neither the cause nor the effect of significant social change. The result in this case is unification without integration, allowing for the functional continuity of social division without the symbolism or solace of structural separation.

Jerusalem provides an excellent example of this phenomenon. The reunification of the city was the result of the Six-Day War. This highly successful preemptive strike against Jordanian military forces changed the landscape almost overnight, brought the city entirely under Israeli control, and significantly dimmed prospects for an equitable diplomatic solution between Israelis and Palestinians. The failed correlation between physical unification and social reconciliation is vividly demonstrated by the disappointing aftermath of the Dayton Accords in Bosnia and the repartition of Jerusalem beginning in 2003.

The typical divided city remains divided as long as the insecurities that led to intergroup violence remain. Though physical partitions generate new problems and intensify interethnic rivalries in their own right, their removal is a necessary but not sufficient condition for the creation of more favorable and equitable social conditions in the urban framework. The invisible thresholds upon which they stood can be reactivated at any time in the absence of Perowne's "balance of justice athwart the frontier."

Standard Negative Impacts

The advantages of urban partitioning for the communities living and working close to them were examined in Chapter 8. While it is essential for the outside observer to recognize the benefits they provide to citizens in both a practical and a symbolic sense, it is difficult to exaggerate the harms generated by ethnic apartheid. All the divided cities examined in this book experienced powerful negative impacts following coercive ethnic segregation. Attempting to calculate the cost of partition in terms of lives, dollars, and lost productivity is only the beginning of a broader assessment.

A politician in Belfast summarized the terrible legacy of prolonged partition vividly and deserves to be quoted at length:

Look: ninety miles long by ninety miles wide, a speck on the map . . . it's only recently that we've been born in the same hospitals. Used to be born in separate hospitals. Go to separate schools . . . and, to add insult to injury, were buried in separate graveyards. They don't know each other . . . everyone in my community is clairvoyant, but it's never good news. My community knows how evil and devious other side is going to be even before the other side has thought about being evil and devious. That's the nature of the distrust that exists. There could be nothing good that they are thinking about, that could be in our interests . . . They know each other's ideology, and they know each other's designs of badness, but they don't know each others loves, lusts, desires, appreciations, I mean they just don't know . . . each side presumes that the other side doesn't live a normal life. The other side lives a life that is calculating, unreasonable, and evil towards us. Whereas the vast majority of people on the other side get up in the morning, hope they have a job, go to their work, raise their kids, do the things that normal people do in abnormal circumstances. But if the abnormality lasts long enough, the abnormality itself becomes normal. (Ervine 2001)

The most common impacts of physical partition relate to personal trauma and deepening cycles of violent retribution. Other impacts take longer to manifest themselves in a measurable way, but are likewise insidious. One example of this delayed reaction relates to second-generation residents of divided cities—individuals born into a physically segregated environment who have taken on the mantle of membership in a besieged community.

Whether or not these second-generation residents spend their entire lives in a physically segregated environment, their understanding of normal social and political relationships is distorted by stressful circumstances. This kind of chronic distortion may constitute a significant and lasting concern.

Compounding this handicap is the interruption of educational and personal development due to the vicissitudes of intercommunal violence, as well as the tendency of public schools themselves to become segregated as the functional redundancy of the divided city spreads. Segregated schooling promotes suspicion between rival groups, whether not this result is intended by administrators or teachers.

For those who depend on conflict for power and influence, settlement is undesirable. One example is the ethnonationalist politician who gained prominent public office by promising to defend the interests of a single ethnic community participating in the larger conflict. Another is the black marketeer who provides food, weapons, or vehicles to a paramilitary organization or unofficial government, for whom prolonging communal violence is a vehicle for its own agenda. A third example is the urban resident who finds unexpected meaning, purpose, and self-esteem in the struggle. Dependency on the divided urban condition constitutes a major obstacle to reconciliation.

Another problem is the duplication of services, institutions, infrastructure, and formerly shared amenities. In the divided city spaces and functions once governed by unconstrained cooperative behavior become politicized. In a kind of diabolical Noah's Ark, each party to the conflict requires a network of its own, resulting in massive waste and redundancy. The city is thus often forced to sprawl out from its traditional configuration as one downtown, one government, one utility grid, and one hospital system become two. The inward result is gross inefficiency with increased expenditures and the outward result is dramatically decreased productivity.

Divided cities generate their own problems. Urban partitions tend to foster fear, and engender suspicion, and intensify habits of discrimination by their presence alone. Insecurities like these are reinforced by physical barriers, since "the more clearly the members of a minority group perceive the universe to be dichotomized, the more likely they are to perceive themselves to be the target of adverse discrimination" (Benvenisti 1982: 309). Observable results include increased mutual avoidance, apathy, a growing conviction that a rival group is responsible for assorted social ills, and a lack of interest concerning the activities of residents on the other side of the partition. Partitions can strengthen dependence on involuntary forms of nonviolent coexistence, preempting voluntary social reconciliation.

Psychological discomfort and inconvenience are not the most important of the negative impacts that follow inevitably from urban partitions for those forced to live and work near them. Economic hardship is another unavoidable consequence of prolonged urban partitioning. In Belfast, empirical studies have demonstrated conclusively that deprivation according to every major index rises with proximity to sectarian interfaces.

Similarly, where there are ethnic boundaries it is clear that poverty, benefit dependency, unemployment, poor health, and low wage-earning potential are found in much greater proportions than the citywide average. For example, 41 percent of households along the interfaces in Belfast receive income support from the municipal government, compared with 21 percent in the province as a whole.

These Belfast statistics highlight three important patterns borne out by other studies and field-based research: that problems multiply along fortified urban boundaries, that both urban managers and urban residents pay a high price for coercive segregation, and that blighting of a similar nature occurs along contested boundaries in other divided cities.

When exposure to members of rival communities is curtailed, chauvinism typically fills the vacuum created by the absence of normal social interactions. The introversion that comes with life in an ethnic urban enclave is often augmented by a persistent fear and hatred of strangers. For some, this misapprehension is grounded in concrete experience, but it is transmitted to subsequent generations through the blind inertia of life behind walls. In a partially sealed environment, cultural norms, traditions, and values are held for their own sake while rival communities—likely to possess nearly identical values—are demonized in a similarly automatic fashion.

The divided city is generally characterized by a suffocating climate of dwindling resources and dimming prospects for peaceful resolution. These conditions incrementally erode whatever remnants of goodwill survive the major episodes of violence between rival communities. An atmosphere of tension and uncertainty provides fertile ground for coordinated acts of violence. Political actors whose careers are grounded in an antagonistic model of community relations tend to meet intercommunal violence with halfhearted, ineffective mitigation efforts. Failed mitigation leads to deepening strife, which in turn justifies coercive policies reinforcing the political relevance of ethnic identity.

Urban partitions tend to create a claustrophobic atmosphere that suffocates normal circulation throughout the healthy city. It is natural that such circumstances create a pall of anxiety, distress, and desperation in negatively affected minority communities. Such psychological effects are compounded by the practical inconveniences introduced by walls and borders of varying degrees of porosity.

Residents of divided cities living on or near fortified boundaries typically discover that otherwise normal activities such as going to work, visiting friends, or gaining access to health services and recreation facilities are fraught with problems and dangers. These hazards are complemented by chronic boredom, resentment, and assorted forms of violent retribution for perceived injustices suffered by the community as a whole.

Loss of property and opportunity accompanies urban partition wherever it occurs. Blighting is an inevitable byproduct of urban partition, as property values near violent interfaces decline along with the median income of residents in the same areas. In many cases, blight takes root in formerly central, vital sectors of the city, since these are the most hotly contested portions of urban territory. As a result, it is possible, for example, to observe mechanics and carpenters in their workshops along the Green Line in the heart of historic Nicosia.

More dramatic was the case of Jerusalem during its first phase of partition beginning in 1948. For twenty years, the walls of the Old City were girdled by a no man's land despite the fact that the wasted real estate can be considered some of the most valuable and sanctified in the world.

Figures generated by the Belfast Development Office show that the public budgetary allocations for thirteen interethnic partitions in the city total approximately three million dollars. This appears to be a quite small price to pay for the protection of thousands of citizens along its dangerous ethnic boundaries.

The efficacy of this approach must be called seriously into question, however, since the construction costs for these partitions is dwarfed by the loss of public revenues that might have been generated through rent if the same land had been used for normal development. Researchers in Belfast determined that the city paid about $750,000 annually in the form of lost revenues for the privilege of maintaining its interethnic barricades, and this figure ignores the additional cost of intensive policing and surveillance along the same interfaces.

Combining these figures with the loss of income by interface residents, it becomes clear that most of the material costs of urban partitioning are

Figure 10.5. The erosion of public security, atmospheric quality and real estate values along interfaces in Belfast appears inevitable, c. 2003. Authors.

dispersed and hidden. Partitions that offer a bargain for urban managers in terms of direct expenditures many not be a good deal for citizens obliged to live and work near them.

The potential for urban partitions to undermine security conditions rather than enhance them is demonstrated well in Belfast, where one community social worker concluded:

Peacelines are there to stop violence. Having the interface doesn't necessarily . . . look at where all the violence is taking place: right around interface areas. You'll find those are the least policed part of that community: people think, "They're up there on the interface, they're not rioting down here—let them go." . . . Kids go for kicks to throw stones and get chased by the police, whatever. Which can escalate. So the fact that you put a peaceline up doesn't necessarily mean, "We're going to have peace." Because it hasn't. (Craig W., 2001)

If the root causes of insecurity are ignored by urban managers, the breakdown of the urban contract and the internal partitions that sometimes follow can provide a foundation for future conflicts within a "great, growing, rootless community . . . that might lie open to sudden gusts of political passion" (Gordon 1983: 40). This is the legacy of the urban partitions, and the most compelling indictment of their usefulness.

The Divided City Profile

The comparative analysis of the five cities examined here points to the following generalizations.

1. Incremental and predictable

The activation of interethnic boundaries in an urban domain is an incremental, slow, predictable process in which the appearance of physical partitions is a very late phase. In the cities examined, initial episodes of intercommunal violence did not lead inexorably to widespread violence and mandatory segregation with physical partitions. Frustration and bigotry were often promoted by sectarian political entrepreneurs, paramilitary organizers and foreign governments with much to gain from territorial redistribution.

The tireless plotting of George Grivas and EOKA in Cyprus provides a good example, as described in Chapter 7. In Mostar, former Croatian and Serbian combatants brokered a secret deal to divide Bosnia in the second phase of hostilities. In Palestine, ardent Zionists and hawkish national politicians encouraged the acrimony between Jews and Arabs, while in Lebanon local warlords gladly seized authority when the central government abdicated.

No matter how unexpected or violent their emergence, urban partitions are never the product of a single cataclysmic event or a sudden shift and political fortune. They are preceded by decades or centuries of segregation and disenfranchisement.

2. Division is context-dependent

The divided city diverges from a normal development track not from an unusual predisposition to violence and bigotry but from the presence of certain catalysts, destabilizing circumstances, and interested third parties. For example, urban partition often accompanies a power vacuum at the

TABLE 10.2. MAJOR CATACLYSMIC EVENTS PRECEDING URBAN PARTITION

City	Proximal catastrophic events	Partition
Belfast	World War I, 1922 Irish independence, Education Act of 1944, 1963 advent of O'Neill's liberal administration, 1960s civil rights revolutions worldwide	1965
Beirut	1948 Israel state formation/Arab war, expectation of United Nations settlement, influx of Palestinian refugees from Israel, 1982 Israeli invasion	1975
Jerusalem	1938–1945 World War II Holocaust, 1948 abrupt abandonment of British Mandate	1948
Mostar	1989 end of Cold War with the dissolution of USSR, 1990 advent of Yugoslav disintegratian, 1992 Bosnian referendum in favor of secession, breakdown of designated United Nations "safe areas" and mass shifts of displaced persons	1992
Nicosia	1958 British pullout with interethnic loyalty split, 1961 Cyprus independence, 1974 Athens-backed coup d'état of Makarios/enosis, breakdown of U.S. regional strategy due to the 1979 Iranian revolution, new alliance with Turkey	1958–1963

regional or national level when fallen governments previously held nationalistic ambitions in check. In the case of Mostar, a vacuum of devastating proportions was created with the collapse of socialist Yugoslavia followed by a hailstorm of ethnonationalist propaganda reminding Bosnians of historic animosities that had long been dormant. In the case of Palestine, World War II and the Holocaust accelerated the development of an international consensus for the creation of an Israeli state in the Middle East, provoking feelings of insecurity that under normal circumstances might have been dissipated through a more incremental process of assimilation.

Several of the most notable cataclysmic events that can be associated with urban partition in the five cities under investigation are summarized in Table 10.2.

While the scale and nature of these episodes differ, they are linked by chronological proximity to the appearance of physical partitions. Violence in Beirut was closely related to the rapid influx of Palestinian refugees fleeing violence in neighboring Israel. Jerusalem was deeply affected by the rapid influx of Jewish refugees from Europe following the Holocaust. In Belfast, Mostar, and Nicosia, declarations of independence preceded the worst phases of interethnic violence as ethnofederalist entrepreneurs scrambled to fill the power vacuums left by larger and stronger political structures that had been recently abandoned.

3. Relative deprivation

Interethnic violence in a divided city generally coincides with conditions of relative deprivation, rather than hardship measured in absolute terms. Legal restrictions on employment, housing and education imposed on disenfranchised ethnic minorities preceded and intensified ethnic tensions in Belfast, Beirut, and Jerusalem. A useful example is the exclusion of Catholic students from secondary schools in Belfast, a policy that automatically disqualified them for substantial political participation and white-collar jobs. Twenty-four years after the Education Act was finally passed in 1944, the first generation of university-educated Catholics in Northern Ireland initiated a campaign of protest leading directly to government backlash and the outbreak of the Troubles. Unfair allocation of resources, combined with a new awareness of the scope of the injustice, contributed to a series of violent recriminations.

4. Weak indigene, strong settler

Divided cities result from territorial disputes between one community claiming indigenous status and another comprising newcomers or settlers in relation to their rivals. This pattern is easily demonstrated with the rapid influx of new urban residents from rural areas, generally prompting feelings of insecurity and bigotry in native residents. Rural immigrants are usually of a single ethnic identity, retain strong provincial loyalties to their villages, and have less exposure to formal education than their urban neighbors. Problems arise from this type of demographic shift when it is accompanied by poor assimilation.

In Beirut, for example, residents of Palestinian refugee camps established in 1948 have yet to be functionally or formally incorporated into Beiruti society. These camps provided numerous recruitment opportunities for the PLO when it settled in Beirut in the early 1970s, leading to a rapid escalation in paramilitary violence throughout the city.

5. Long-term harm

Developmental patterns linking divided cities suggest that the long-term impacts of urban partition are negative and continue to harm residents well beyond political reconciliation and physical unification, if these ever occur.

It is encouraging that the sequence of urban partition along ethnic lines is partially predictable. The value of a predictive model is high because many cities in the world currently appear to be on trajectories similar to those followed by Mostar, Nicosia, Belfast, Beirut, and Jerusalem. Muslim Hausas and Christian Yorubas are reeling from bloody cycles of reprisal in Lagos; the construction of high-security gated communities is on the rise in Las Vegas; Kurdish separatists collide with Arab Iraqis in Kirkuk; French peacekeepers struggle to dampen violence between Serbian and Albanian residents of Mitrovica; impenetrable barricades routinely appear along racial interfaces in Cincinnati; concrete barricades between Sunni and Shiite neighborhoods in Baghdad have been installed by American military personnel over the protests of residents of both sides.

The list is long and expanding. Ongoing attempts to cope with the crippling costs of physical segregation will be strengthened by a sure grasp of the logic of the divided city.

Epilogue: Jerusalem Redivided

Immediately following the conquest of East Jerusalem during the Six-Day War, senior commander Moshe Dayan issued two controversial orders to the Israeli army: relinquish direct control over the Temple Mount and dismantle the Green Line. The social and political utility of the partition, which Dayan coauthored in 1948, had long since expired in the eyes of many Jerusalemites on both sides of the city. It had become an emblem of shame; it offered a bitter reminder of Jerusalem's failure to achieve the social integration envisioned by Israel's early intellectual leadership and idealistic *kibbutzim*.

The barricades came down according to plan on 29 June 1967. This procedure involved the rapid removal of 16 km of barbed wire, several large concrete ramparts, fifty-five fortified guard stations, and hundreds of mines in the buffer zone. True to his military objective and his public promise to extend "the hand of peace" to Israel's Arab neighbors, Dayan ushered in a period of relative peace and cooperation in Jerusalem that lasted until the start of the first *intifada* in 1987.

Thirty-four years after his uncle ordered the barricades of Jerusalem to be removed, the then Israeli national security advisor Major-General Uzi Dayan launched a determined political campaign in support of a new ethnic partition. High-level approval for a "security fence" dividing Israel from the West Bank was secured in July 2001 after six years of research and lobbying in the Israeli Knesset. By October 2002, amid growing concerns abroad regarding security and terrorism, work began on approximately 570 km of wall and fence stretching from north to south and conforming to the former Green Line for about 11 percent of its length, with substantial deviations to the east in order to embrace farflung Jewish settlements in the West Bank. The cost to Israeli taxpayers is approximately $2.7 million per kilometer. The cost to Palestinians living in the West Bank is the loss of about 14.5 percent of West Bank territory formerly east of the Green Line, the dis-

Figure E.1. Palestinians waiting at the Qalandiya checkpoint, c. 2002. Authors.

placement of approximately 875,000 individuals, and separation for thousands from relatives, jobs, schools, and hospitals.

The regional barrier passes through Jerusalem with a 51 km segment separating Israeli Jerusalem from Palestinian suburbs to the east. Construction of this new partition, named "enveloping Jerusalem" by municipal authorities, began in October 2003. The partition severs links between East Jerusalem and Ramallah to the north, passes eastward just south of Rafat to the Qalandiya checkpoint, then moves southward to incorporate the Jewish settlements of Neve Ya'aqoy, Pisgat Ze'ev, and Ma'aleh Adumim while excluding the Palestinian suburbs of Hizma, Anata, and Abu Dis. Near Dar Salah the barricade turns again westward toward Gilo, an Israeli suburb to the south of Jerusalem, bending to incorporate the historic site of Rachel's tomb. Most of the barrier in the Jerusalem area is composed of concrete walls 6 to 8 m high. Approximately 220,000 Palestinians residing in eighteen communities along the barricade route will be directly affected.

Jerusalem, having strained under physical partitions for nineteen years and celebrated a "mutual invasion" with their removal in 1967, divided it-

Figure E.2. The new partition dividing east and west Jerusalem as it passes through the Palestinian suburb of Abu Dis, 2003. Authors.

self again. Prime Minister Ariel Sharon called the barrier "an essential element in securing Jerusalem." Uzi Dayan argued that the barrier is reversible, promotes stability on both sides, and is "linked to Israel's strategic goals"—including maintenance of the nation's "identity as a Jewish democratic state." He pointed to the example of the Gaza Strip enclosure walls to support the assertion that "there is no question regarding the effectiveness of a continuous physical barrier in keeping out infiltrators bent on committing terror." It was claimed that no suicide bombers had emerged from the Gaza Strip in the three years following the installation of fortified perimeter fence.

Though the Gaza fence may have been the nearest example, it was not the most relevant. If predictions about the value of Jerusalem's new partition are desired, Belfast and Nicosia provide closer analogues. Urban managers in both cities promoted walls as a pragmatic, temporary reply to urgent security crises. The walls they built remain after more than thirty years. As the preceding chapters suggest, the benefits of partition in those cities do

Figure E.3. The new partition of Jerusalem even protects a bus stop as it passes through the Israeli suburb of Gilo, c. 2003. Authors.

not affirm beyond question the usefulness of urban walls as anti-terrorism devices. In Nicosia, the Green Line has sealed an ethnic dispute in amber without providing an inroad to the root causes of conflict. In Belfast, peace-lines deepened animosity between working-class neighbors.

These examples suggest that the long-term costs of division, when its social and physical impacts are taken into account, are extremely high. Duplication of facilities and services—as seen in Nicosia, Jerusalem, and Mostar in particular—puts unnatural pressure on municipal budgets. Politicians and residents closely associated with the wall are generally stigmatized. Violence is often displaced but rarely snuffed out, and opportunities for cooperation between rival communities are minimized. Temporary measures often become permanent as the waiting period for comprehensive political settlement drags on and mutual suspicions linger on from one generation to the next.

In the meantime, partition often allows for the preemptive acquisition of urban territory and the flourishing of assorted paramilitary groups whose authority rests on the continuation of local conflict. These concerns would not have influenced decision making in Jerusalem because "no one is thinking about whether walls have worked in the past. It is just: get it up. Put a partition between us" (Nada A., 2003).

The comparisons offered in this book affirm the suggestion that Jerusalem's second partition constitutes an "irresponsible illusion" with respect to long-term security and regional stabilization (Nasrallah 2003). It seems likely that the lessons to be drawn from other divided cities were neglected by the politicians responsible for Jerusalem's latest fortification, either because they were not available or because they give rise to unflattering speculations. Regardless, physical segregation remains a viable approach to urban management in the minds of many policymakers who view past failures as anomalous. The new Israeli barrier—alternately called a "security fence," a "seam line," and a "buffer zone"—demonstrates the need for better spatial solutions to violent interethnic conflict in contested cities. As long as purely spatial remedies are applied to recurrent social ills, it is likely that the promise of durable security will go unfulfilled in divided cities.

In Jerusalem, the failure of partition to secure a more lasting peace between Israeli and Palestinian residents was first realized with the turmoil that followed unification in 1967. It is likely that the second iteration of ethnic apartheid will generate as many problems as it solves. Already, Palestinian students are separated from their classrooms; merchants lose customers; farmers are barred from agricultural land; livestock and olive groves are denied water; families will be unable to share holidays; patients fail to reach the hospital. Israeli scholar Meron Benvenisti observed that the new wall is a "short-term political waste of time, and a waste of money . . . reactionary in its concept, and cruel" (Benvenisti, 2003). The frustration and hardship generated among those that are fenced out will be intense and will provide a compelling pretext for further discord.

The new Israeli barrier was declared illegal by the International Court of Justice in December 2004 after it was rerouted by the Israeli High Court of Justice in February 2004. The courts' concerns included inconsistencies with prior agreements, the confiscation of Palestinian property and negative impacts on livelihood. Meanwhile Colin L. Powell, U.S. secretary of state, observed when asked whether a barricade would assist the peace process: "I don't know if you're going to solve the problem with a fence, unless you're solving the underlying problems of the Palestinians feeling disenfranchised" (NBC *Meet the Press*, 5 May 2002). These official reactions did not significantly alter the intentions of the Israeli government to complete the partition program.

As this book goes to press, Jerusalem enters another phase of development as a divided city while Baghdad devolves into a patchwork of barricaded ethnic enclaves patrolled by foreign troops. These fresh cycles of urban apartheid underscore the need for a candid assessment of partition's benefits and liabilities. The divided cities examined here show that urban partitions are not cost-effective over the long term. If meaningful comparisons had been available to them, Israeli politicians and American military commanders might have made different decisions. There is a need for more energetic, research-driven exchange between urban managers and those familiar with success and failure in divided cities. The lives of countless inhabitants of physically segregated cities depend on better, more strategic approaches to the fundamental problems that weaken the urban contract. This book is intended as a small contribution to that larger effort.

Works Cited

Personal Interviews

Edmund S. (pseud.) (2001). 27 September, Belfast.

Lejla C. (pseud.) (2001). 2 November, Mostar.

Arzuen, K. a. A., Ruthie, and Amran Arzuen. (2003). 11 February, Jerusalem.

Ali W. (pseud.) (2001). 7 June, Beirut.

Benvenisti, M. (2003). 12 February, Jerusalem.

Boal, F. W. (2000). 17 August, Belfast.

Halit O. (2001). 1 October, Nicosia.

Charles D. (pseud.) (2001). 26 September, Belfast.

Fred J. (pseud.) (2000). 18 August, Belfast.

Demirovic, Z. (2000). 15 July, Mostar.

Sead A. (pseud.) (2000). 12 July, Mostar.

Ervine, D. (2001). 28 September, Belfast.

Gavin, A. (2000). 13 June, Beirut.

Pavlos A. (pseud.), (2002). 3 October, Nicosia.

Nora H. (pseud.) (2000). 9 June, Beirut.

Sean R. (pseud.) (2000). 15 August, Belfast.

Nada A. (pseud.) (2003). 9 February, Jerusalem.

Malek G. (pseud.), (2000). 8 June, Beirut.

Maria B. (pseud.) (2003). 10 February, Jerusalem.

Salma T. (pseud.) (2000). 15 October, Beirut.

Khouri, E. (2000). 11 June, Beirut.

Kimhi, I. (2003). 12 February, Jerusalem.

Ferhad D. (pseud.) (2001). 2 October, Mostar.

Lein, Y. (2003). 12 February, Jerusalem.

Maginness, A. (2001). 28 September, Belfast.

James L. (pseud.) (2000). 16 August, Belfast.

Craig W. (pseud.) (2001). 25 September, Belfast.

John M. (pseud., (2001). 26 September, Belfast.

Philip J. (pseud.) (2001). 25 September, Belfast.

McGlone, R. (2001). 27 September, Belfast.

Henry M. (pseud.) (2001). 26 September, Belfast.

Morrison, B. (2000). 15 August, Belfast.

Mustafa. (2003). 12 December, Jerusalem.

Najjar, D. (2003). 10 February, Jerusalem.

Nasrallah, R. (2003). 9 February, Jerusalem.
Nohra, J. (2000). 10 August, Beirut.
David O. (pseud.) (2001). 26 September, Belfast.
Richard S. (pseud.) (2000). 15 August, Belfast.
Özen, G. (2001). 1 October, Nicosia.
Öznel, N. (2001). 2 October, Nicosia.
Papadakis, Y. (2002). 5 April, Nicosia.
Adnan M. (pseud.), (2001). 2 October, Mostar.
Pasić, A. (2003). 14 July, Mostar.
Petrídou, A. (2001). 1 October, Nicosia.
Nazad K. (pseud.) (2000). 18 July, Mostar.
Potts, J. (2001). 26 September, Belfast.
Ziad T. (pseud.) (2000). 13 July, Mostar.
Marwan T. (pseud.) (2000). 9 June, Beirut.
John S. (pseud.) (2000). 8 June, Beirut.
Hakim B. (pseud.) (2003). 9 February, Jerusalem.
Ari C. (pseud.) (2003). 10 February, Jerusalem.
Stephen N. (pseud.) (2001). 26 September, Belfast.
Tueni, G. (2000). 11 June, Beirut.
Marko V. (pseud.) (2000). 12 July, Mostar.
Yaacovy, I. (2003). 9 February, Jerusalem.

Sources Cited

Abboushi, W. F. (1990). *The unmaking of Palestine.* Brattleboro, Vt.: Amana Books.
Abrams, C. (1955). *Forbidden neighbors: A study of prejudice in housing.* New York: Harper.
Abramson, A. J., M. S. Tobin, and M. R. Vandergoot (1995). "The changing geography of metropolitan opportunity: the segregation of the poor in U.S. metropolitan areas." *Housing Policy Debate* 6(1): 45–72.
Adams, T. W. and A. J. Cottrell (1968). *Cyprus between East and West.* Baltimore: Johns Hopkins University Press.
Allen, N. and A. Kelly (2003). *The cities of Belfast.* Dublin: Four Courts.
Anderson, B. (1991). *Imagined communities: Reflections on the origin and spread of nationalism.* London: Verso.
Anderson, B. R. O. G. and G. Kligman (1992). *Long-distance nationalism: World capitalism and the rise of identity politics.* Berkeley: Center for German and European Studies, University of California.
Babcock, F. (1935). "The determination of mortgage risk." *Journal of the American Institute of Real Estate Appraisers* 3(4): 316–23.
Baker, E. (1959). "The Settlement in Cyprus." *Political Quarterly* 30 (3): 244–53.
Banac, I. (1984). *The national question in Yugoslavia: Origins, history, politics.* Ithaca, N.Y. Cornell University Press.
Barakat, S., Calame, J. and E. Charlesworth, eds. (1998). *Urban triumph or urban*

disaster? *Dilemmas of contemporary post-war reconstruction.* York: Post-war Reconstruction & Development Unit, University of York.

Bardon, J. (1992). *A history of Ulster.* Belfast: Blackstaff.

Bardon, J. and H. V. Bell (1982). *Belfast: An illustrated history.* Belfast: Blackstaff.

Barnsdale, D. (2001) *The Unholy Alliance.* Alliance to Defend Bosnia-Herzegovina.

Baroudi, S. E. (2006). "Divergent perspectives among Lebanon's Maronites during the 1958 crisis." *Critique: Critical Middle Eastern Studies* 15 (1): 5–28.

Benvenisti, M. (1976). *Jerusalem: The torn city.* Minneapolis, University of Minnesota Press.

———. (1982). "Administering conflicts: Local government in Jerusalem and Belfast." PhD dissertation, Kennedy School of Government, Harvard University.

———. (1983). *Jerusalem, study of a polarized community.* Jerusalem: West Bank Data-Base Project.

———. (1986). *Conflicts and contradictions.* New York: Villard Books.

——— (1995). *Intimate enemies: Jews and Arabs in a shared land.* Berkeley: University of California Press.

——— (1996). *City of stone: The hidden history of Jerusalem.* Berkeley: University of California Press.

Benvenisti, M., A. Hochstein, and W. Ury (1985). *The Jerusalem question: Problems, procedures, and options.* Jerusalem: West Bank Data Base Project.

Benvenisti, M., and S. Khayat (1988). *The West Bank and Gaza atlas.* Jerusalem: West Bank Data Base Project, distributed by Jerusalem Post.

Berkovec, J. A., G. B. Canner, S. Gabriel, and T. Hannan. (1994). "Race, redlining, and residential mortgage loan performance." *Journal of Real Estate Finance and Economics* 9: 263–94.

Birrell, D. (1972). "Relative deprivation as a factor in conflict in Northern Ireland." *Sociological Review* 20(3): 317–47.

Blackman, T. (1991). *Planning Belfast: A case study of public policy and community action.* Brookfield, Vt.: Gower.

Blakely, E. J. and M. G. Snyder (1997). *Fortress America: Gated communities in the United States.* Washington, D.C.: Brookings Institution Press.

Boal, F. W. (1995). *Shaping a city: Belfast in the late twentieth century.* Belfast: Institute of Irish Studies Queen's University of Belfast.

———, ed. (2000). *Ethnicity and housing: Accommodating differences.* Aldershot: Ashgate.

Boal, F. W., S. E. Clarke, and J. L. Ober (1976). *Urban ethnic conflict: A comparative perspective.* Chapel Hill: Institute for Research in Social Science, University of North Carolina.

Boal, F. W., P. Doherty, and D. G. Pringle. (1978). *Social problems in the Belfast urban area: An exploratory analysis.* London: Department of Geography, Queen Mary College, University of London.

Boal, F. W., J. N. H. Douglas, and J. A. E. Orr. (1982). *Integration and division: Geographical perspectives on the Northern Ireland problem.* London: Academic Press.

Bollens, S. A. (1999). *Urban peace-building in divided societies: Belfast and Johannesburg.* Boulder, Colo.: Westview Press.

————. (2000). *On narrow ground: Urban policy and ethnic conflict in Jerusalem and Belfast*. Albany: State University of New York Press.

Bornstein, A. S. (2002). *Crossing the Green Line between the West Bank and Israel*. Philadelphia: University of Pennsylvania Press.

Boulding, E. (1994). *Building peace in the Middle East: Challenges for states and civil society*. Boulder, Colo., Lynne Rienner.

Budge, I. and C. O'Leary (1973). *Belfast: Approach to crisis; a study of Belfast politics, 1613–1970*. New York, St. Martin's Press.

Burayidi, M. A. (2000). *Urban planning in a multicultural society*. Westport, Conn.: Praeger.

Burton, F. (1978). *The politics of legitimacy: Struggles in a Belfast community*. London: Routledgel.

Byrne, S. (1997). *Growing up in a divided society: The influence of conflict on Belfast schoolchildren*. Cranbury, N.J.: Fairleigh Dickinson University Press.

Carey, R., and J. Sheining, Foreword T. W. Segev. (2002). *The other Israel: voices of refusal and dissent*. New York: New Press.

Cleary, J. (2002). *Literature, partition and the nation-state: Culture and conflict in Ireland, Israel and Palestine*. Oxford: Cambridge University Press.

Cohen, S. B. (1980). *Jerusalem undivided*. New York, Herzl Press.

———— (1983). *Israel's defensible borders: A geopolitical map*. Tel Aviv: Tel Aviv University.

Colafato, M. (1999). *Mostar: l'urbicidio, la memoria, la pulizia etnica*. Roma: SEAM.

Commission on Security and Cooperation in Europe and Carnegie Endowment for International Peace. (1996). *Rebuilding Bosnia-Herzegovina: Strategies and the U.S. role*. Washington, D.C.: CSCE.

Conroy, J. (1987). *Belfast diary: War as a way of life*. Boston: Beacon Press.

Cordell, K. (1999). *Ethnicity and democratisation in the new Europe*. New York: Routledge.

Cottrell, R. C. (2005). *The green line: The division of Palestine*. Philadelphia: Chelsea House.

Coufoudakis, V., H. J. Psomiades, and A. Gerolymatos (1999). *Greece and the new Balkans: Challenges and opportunities*. New York: Pella.

Coufoudakis, V., and S. G. Xydis. (1976). *Essays on the Cyprus conflict: In memory of Stephen G. Xydis*. New York: Pella.

Crawford, B. (1995). *Markets, states, and democracy: The political economy of postcommunist transformation*. Boulder, Colo.: Westview Press.

Crawford, B. and R. D. Lipschutz (1998). *The Myth of "ethnic conflict": Politics, economics, and "cultural" violence*. Berkeley: International and Area Studies, University of California.

Crawshaw, N. (1978). *The Cyprus revolt: An account of the struggle for union with Greece*. London, Boston: Allen & Unwin.

Davie, M. F. (1994). Demarcation lines in contemporary Beirut. In *The Middle East and North Africa*, ed. C. H. Schofield and R. N. Schofield. New York: Routledge.

Demi, D. (1997). *The walled city of Nicosia: Typology study*. Nicosia: UNPD.

Diefendorf, J. M. (1990). *Rebuilding Europe's bombed cities*. New York, St. Martin's Press.

Dillon, D. (1994). "Fortress America." *Planning* (60): 2–8.

Doty, R. C. (1954). Suez Pact alters defense plans. *New York Times*, E5. 1 August.

Dumper, M. (1997). *The politics of Jerusalem since 1967*. New York: Columbia University Press.

——— (2002). *The politics of sacred space: The old city of Jerusalem in the Middle East conflict*. Boulder, Colo., Lynn Rienner.

Dunn, S. (1995). *Facets of the conflict in Northern Ireland*. New York: St. Martin's Press.

Dunn, S., and V. Morgan (1994). *Protestant alienation in Northern Ireland: A preliminary survey*. Coleraine: Centre for the Study of Conflict, University of Ulster.

Dymski, G. (1996). Why does race matter in housing and credit markets? Current research and future directions. In *Race, markets, and social outcomes*, ed. P. L. Mason and R. Williams. Boston: Kluwer Academic.

Efrat, E. (1988). *Geography and politics in Israel since 1967*. London: F. Cass.

Ehrlich, T. (1974). *Cyprus, 1958–1967*. New York: Oxford University Press.

El Nasser, H. (2002). More Americans living behind the bars: Gated communities more popular, and not just for the rich. *USA Today*, December 15.

Elbinger, L. K. and B. Elbinger (1991). Peace in Jerusalem. [S.l.], Elbinger.

Elkins, T. H. and B. Hofmeister (1988). *Berlin: The spatial structure of a divided city*. London: Methuen.

Fay, M.-T., M. Morrissey, and F. Smyth (1999). *Northern Ireland's troubles: The human costs*. London; Sterling, Va.: Pluto Press with Cost of the Troubles Study.

Feldman, A. (1991). *Formations of violence: The narrative of the body and political terror in Northern Ireland*. Chicago: University of Chicago Press.

Finke, B. F. (1973). *Berlin: The divided city*. Charlotteville, N.Y.: SamHar Press.

Fraser, T. G. (2000). *Ireland in conflict, 1922–1998*. London: Routledge.

Gaffikin, F. and M. Morrissey (1999). *City visions: Imagining place, enfranchising people*. London: Pluto Press.

Gavin, A. and R. B. Maluf (1996). *Beirut reborn: The restoration and development of the Central District*. London: Academy Editions.

Geipel, R. (1982). *Disaster and reconstruction: The Friuli, Italy, earthquakes of 1976*. London: Boston, Allen & Unwin.

Geipel, R. (1991). *Long-term consequences of disasters: The reconstruction of Friuli, Italy, in its international context, 1976–1988*. New York: Springer.

Gilbert, M. (1964). *Britain and Germany between the wars*. London: Longman.

——— (1978). *Exile and return: The struggle for a Jewish homeland*. Philadelphia: Lippincott.

———. (1985). *Jerusalem: Rebirth of a city*. New York: Viking.

——— (1992). *The Arab-Israeli conflict: Its history in maps*. London: Weidenfeld and Nicolson.

——— (1996). *Jerusalem in the twentieth century*. New York: Wiley.

——— (1998). *Israel: A history*. New York, Morrow.

Glasson Deschaumes, G. and R. Ivekoviâc (2003). *Divided countries, separated cities: The modern legacy of partition.* New Delhi: Oxford University Press.

Goldring, M. (1991). *Belfast: From loyalty to rebellion.* London: Lawrence & Wishart.

Goode, J. and J. A. Schneider (1994). *Reshaping ethnic and racial relations in Philadelphia: Immigrants in a divided city.* Philadelphia: Temple University Press.

Gordon, D. C. (1980). *Lebanon, the fragmented nation.* Stanford, Calif.: Hoover Institution Press.

——— (1983). *The Republic of Lebanon: Nation in jeopardy.* Boulder, Colo.: Westview Press.

Grant, N. (1973). *The partition of Palestine, 1947: Jewish triumph, British failure, Arab disaster.* New York: Franklin Watts.

Grundy-Warr, C. (1987). "Political division and the peace keeping in Cyprus." In *Boundaries and State Territory in the Middle East and North Africa,* ed. G. H. Blake and R. N. Schofield. Cambridgeshire: Menas. 70–80.

Grundy-Warr, C., ed. (1990). *International boundaries and boundary conflict resolution: proceedings of the 1989 IBRU Conference.* Durham: International Boundaries Research Unit, University of Durham.

Hachey, T. E. (1972). *The problem of partition: peril to world peace.* Chicago: Rand McNally.

Hachey, T. E., J. M. Hernon, and L. J. McCaffrey. (1989). *The Irish experience: A concise history.* Englewood Cliffs, N.J.: Prentice-Hall.

Hachey, T. E. and L. J. McCaffrey (1989). *Perspectives on Irish nationalism.* Lexington: University Press of Kentucky.

Hadžić, K. and H. Cemalović (1995). *Mostar, May 1994.* Sarajevo: ZID.

Haff, J. O. (1956). Barrier to Divide Cyprus' Capital. *New York Times,* A3. 29 May.

Hall, M., ed. (1994). *Ulster's Protestant working class: A community exploration.* Island Pamphlets. Newtownabbey: Island Publications.

Harbottle, M. (1970). *The impartial soldier.* London: Oxford University Press.

———. (1971). *The blue berets.* London: Leo Cooper.

Hastings, M. (1970). *Barricades in Belfast: The fight for civil rights in Northern Ireland.* New York: Taplinger.

Hein, C., J. M. Diefendorf, and Y. Ushida (2003). *Rebuilding urban Japan after 1945.* Houndmills, Basingstoke: Palgrave Macmillan.

Henderson, G., R. N. Lebow, and J. G. Stoessinger, eds. (1974). *Divided nations in a divided world.* New York, D. McKay.

Hillier, A. E. (2003). "Spatial analysis of historical redlining: A methodological exploration." *Journal of Housing Research* 14(1): 137ff.

Hitchens, C. (1989). *Hostage to history: Cyprus from the Ottomans to Kissinger.* New York: Noonday Press.

Hocknell, P. R. (2001). *Boundaries of cooperation: Cyprus, de facto partition, and the delimitation of transboundary resource management.* London: Kluwer Law.

Holland, R. F. (1998). *Britain and the revolt in Cyprus, 1954–1959.* Oxford: Oxford University Press.

Hopkins, I. W. J. (1970). *Jerusalem: A study in urban geography.* Grand Rapids, Mich.: Baker.

Horowitz, D. L. (1985). *Ethnic groups in conflict*. Berkeley: University of California Press.

——— (2001). *The deadly ethnic riot*. Berkeley: University of California Press.

Hourani, A. H., and N. Shehadi (1992). *The Lebanese in the world: A century of emigration*. London: Centre for Lebanese Studies with I.B. Tauris.

Hudson, M. C. (1969). "Democracy and social mobilization in Lebanese politics." *Comparative Politics* 1(2): 245–63.

Husain, Z. (1990). *Rationale of partition*. Karachi: Royal Book.

Inder Singh, A. (1987). *The origins of the partition of India, 1936–1947*. Delhi: Oxford University Press.

Jackson, K. T. (1980). "Race, ethnicity, and real estate appraisal: The home owners loan corporation and the Federal Housing Administration." *Journal of Urban History* 6 (4): 419–52.

Johnstone, R. (1990). *Belfast: Portraits of a city*. London: Barrie & Jenkins.

Johnstone, R. and B. Kirk (1983). *Images of Belfast*. Dundonald Strathclyde: Blackstaff.

Jones, E. (1960). *A social geography of Belfast*. London: Oxford University Press.

Joseph, J. S. (1985). *Cyprus: Ethnic conflict and international concern*. New York: Peter Lang.

———. (1997). *Cyprus: ethnic conflict and international politics: From independence to the threshold of the European Union*. New York: St. Martin's Press.

Kendall, H. (1948). *Jerusalem, the city plan: Preservation and development during the British mandate, 1918–1948*. London: HMSO.

———. (1949). *Village development in Palestine during the British mandate*. London: Crown Agents for the Colonies.

Khalaf, I. (1991). *Politics in Palestine: Arab factionalism and social disintegration, 1939–1948*. Albany: State University of New York Press.

———. (1979). *Persistence and change in 19th century Lebanon: A sociological essay*. Beirut: American University of Beirut.

———. (1987). *Lebanon's predicament*. New York: Columbia University Press.

———. (1993). *Beirut reclaimed: Reflections on urban design and the restoration of civility*. Beirut: Dar An-Nahar.

———. (2001). *Cultural resistance: Global and local encounters in the Middle East*. London: Saqi Books.

———. (2002). *Civil and uncivil violence in Lebanon: A history of the internationalization of communal conflict*. New York: Columbia University Press.

Khalaf, S. K., and S. Philip (1993). *Recovering Beirut: Urban design and post-war reconstruction*. New York: Brill.

Khoury, P. and F. Ragette (1983). *Beirut of tomorrow: Planning for reconstruction*. Beirut: American University of Beirut.

al-Khuri, Fuad I. (1975). *From village to suburb: Order and change in Greater Beirut*. Chicago: University of Chicago Press.

Kinealy, C. and G. MacAtasney (2000). *The hidden famine: Poverty, hunger, and sectarianism in Belfast, 1840–50*. Sterling, Va.: Pluto Press.

Kirapala, S. (1991). *Select documents on Partition of Punjab in 1947: India and Pakistan*. Delhi: National Book Shop.

Kliot, N., and Y. Mansfield. (1999). "Case Studies of Conflict and Territorial Organization in Divided Cities." *Progress in Planning* 52(3): 168–237.

Koppel, T. (1989). *The Koppel Report—DC/Divided City.* ABC-TV. Library of Congress, Vanderbilt Television News Archive Collection.

Kraemer, J. L. (1980). *Jerusalem: Problems and prospects.* New York: Praeger.

Kumar, R. (1997). *Divide and fall? Bosnia in the annals of partition.* London: Verso.

Leonard, M. (1994). *Informal economic activity in Belfast.* Brookfield, Vt.: Ashgate.

Livingstone, R. (1998). *The road: memories of the Falls.* Belfast: Blackstaff.

Lovan, W. R., M. Murray, and R. Shaffer (2004). *Participatory governance: Planning, conflict mediation and public decision-making in civil society.* Aldershot: Ashgate.

Low, S. M. (2003). *Behind the gates: Life, security, and the pursuit of happiness in fortress America.* New York: Routledge.

Lynch, J. and J. Campling (1998). *A tale of three cities: Comparative studies in working class life.* Houndmills, Basingstoke: Macmillan.

Makdisi, J. S. (1990). *Beirut fragments: A war memoir.* New York, Persea.

Mallinson, W. (2005). *Cyprus: A modern history.* New York: I.B. Taurus.

Marcuse, P. and R. van Kempen (2002). *Of states and cities: The partitioning of urban space.* Oxford: Oxford University Press.

Markides, D. W. (2001). *Cyprus 1957–1963: From colonial conflict to constitutional crisis, the key role of the municipal issue.* Minnesota Mediterranean and East European Monographs 8. Minneapolis: University of Minnesota.

Markides, K. C. (1977). *The rise and fall of the Cyprus Republic.* New Haven, Conn.: Yale University Press.

Marshall, M. G. (1999). *Third World War: System, process, and conflict dynamics.* Lamham, Md.: Rowman & Littlefield.

Matthew, R. H. (1964). *Belfast regional survey and plan, 1962: A report prepared for the Government of Northern Ireland.* Belfast: HMSO.

McAuley, J. W. (1994). *The politics of identity: A loyalist community in Belfast.* Aldershot: Avebury.

McGarry, J. (2001). *Northern Ireland and the divided world: The Northern Ireland conflict and the Good Friday Agreement in comparative perspective.* Oxford: Oxford University Press.

McKittrick, D. (1989). *Despatches from Belfast.* Belfast: Blackstaff.

More, T. (1516/1914). *Utopia.* New York: Collier.

Morgan, A. (1991). *Labour and partition: The Belfast working class, 1905–1923.* London: Pluto Press.

Morris, A. E. J. (1972). *History of urban form: Prehistory to the Renaissance.* New York: Wiley.

———. (1979). *History of urban form: Before the industrial revolutions.* New York: Wiley.

Morrissey, M. and M. Smyth (2002). *Northern Ireland after the Good Friday agreement: Victims, grievance, and blame.* London: Pluto Press.

Mumford, L. (1960). *The culture of cities.* New York: Harcourt Brace.

———. (1961). *The city in history: Its origins, its transformations, and its prospects.* New York: Harcourt Brace.

Murray, M. (1991). *The politics and pragmatism of urban containment: Belfast since 1940*. Brookfield, Vt.: Avebury.

Murtagh, B. (1995). "Image making versus reality: Ethnic division and the planning challenge of Belfast's peacelines." In *Reimaging the pariah city: Urban development in Belfast & Detroit*, ed. W. J. V. Neill, D. S. Fitzsimons, and B. Murtagh. Brookfield, Vt.: Ashgate. 209–30.

Nasr, S. (1993). "New social realities and post-war Lebanon: Issues for reconstruction." In *Recovering Beirut*, ed. S. Khalaf and P. S. Khoury. New York: 63–80.

Neill, W. J. V. (2004). *Urban planning and cultural identity*. London: Routledge.

Neill, W. J. V., D. S. Fitzsimons, and B. Murtagh, eds. (1995). *Reimaging the pariah city: Urban development in Belfast & Detroit*. Brookfield, Vt.: Ashgate.

Neill, W. J. V. and H.-U. Schwedler (2001). *Urban planning and cultural inclusion: lessons from Belfast and Berlin*. New York: Palgrave.

Newman, D. (1994). "The functional presence of an 'erased' boundary: The re-emergence of the Green Line." In *The Middle East and North Africa*, ed. C. H. Schofield and R. N. Schofield. World Boundaries Series 2. London: Routledge.

O'Halloran, C. (1999). *Belfast Interface Project: Inner East/outer West: Addressing conflict in two interface areas*. Belfast: Belfast Interface Project.

O'Halloran, C., and N. Jarman (2000). *Peacelines or battlefields: Responding to violence in interface areas*. Belfast: Community Development Centre.

O'Malley, B., and I. Craig (1999). *The Cyprus conspiracy: America, espionage, and the Turkish invasion*. London: I.B. Tauris.

Organisation for Economic Co-operation and Development. (2000). *Urban renaissance: Belfast's lessons for policy and partnership*. Paris: OECD.

Patterson, H. (1980). *Class conflict and sectarianism: The Protestant working class and the Belfast labour movement, 1868–1920*. Belfast: Blackstaff.

Perowne, S. (1954). *The one remains*. London: Hodder & Stoughton.

Polyviou, P. G. (1975). *Cyprus: The tragedy and the challenge*. Washington, D.C.: American Hellenic Institute.

———. (1980). *Cyprus, conflict and negotiation, 1960–1980*. London: Duckworth.

Ragette, F., ed. (1983). *Beirut of Tomorrow*. Beirut: American University of Beirut.

Reed, E., and F. Ajami (1988). *Beirut: City of regrets*. New York: Norton.

Rikhye, I. J., M. Harbottle, and B. Egge. (1974). *The thin blue line: international peacekeeping and its future*. New Haven, Conn.: Yale University Press.

Romann, M., A. Weingrod, and B. Egge (1991). *Living together separately: Arabs and Jews in contemporary Jerusalem*. Princeton, N.J.: Princeton University Press.

Rossides, E. T., and V. Coufoudakis, eds. (2002). *The United States & Cyprus: Double standards and the rule of law*. Washington, D.C.: American Hellenic Institute Foundation.

Saadeh, F. R. (1948). *Plan for the solution of the Palestine problem*. Beirut.

Sachar, H. M. (2007). *A history of Israel: From the rise of Zionism to our time*. New York: Knopf.

Salibi, K. S. (1976). *Cross roads to civil war: Lebanon, 1958–1976*. Delmar, N.Y.: Caravan Books.

Salibi, K. S. (1988). *A house of many mansions: The history of Lebanon reconsidered*. Berkeley: University of California Press.

Scarman, L. (1972). *Violence and civil disturbances in Northern Ireland in 1969: Report of Tribunal of Inquiry.* Northern Ireland Parliament Papers 566. Belfast: HMSO.

Schaeffer, R. K. (1990). *Warpaths: The politics of partition.* New York: Hill and Wang.

Schölch, A. (1983). *Palestinians over the Green Line: Studies on the relations between Palestinians on both sides of the 1949 armistice line since 1967.* London: Ithaca Press.

Schleifer, A. (1972). *The fall of Jerusalem.* New York: Monthly Review Press.

Schnall, D. J. (1984). *Beyond the green line: Israeli settlements west of the Jordan.* New York: Praeger.

Schofield, C. H., ed. (1994). *Global boundaries.* London: Routledge.

Schofield, C. H., and R. N. Schofield, eds. (1994). *The Middle East and North Africa.* World Boundaries Series 2. London: Routledge.

Seaver, B. M. (2000). "The regional sources of power-sharing failure: The case of Lebanon." *Political Science Quarterly* 115 (2): 247–71.

Segev, T. W. (2000). *One Palestine, complete: Jews and Arabs under the British Mandate.* New York: Metropolitan Books.

———. (2002). Foreword to R. Carey and J. Sheining, *The other Israel: voices of refusal and dissent.* New York: New Press.

Segev, T. W., and Arlen Neal (1986). *1949: The first Israelis.* New York: Free Press, Collier Macmillan.

Sego, K., I. Ribarevic-Nikolic, J. Seljko, and V. Kolopic. (1992). *Mostar '92: Urbicid.* Mostar: Hrvatsko Vijece Opcine.

Sennett, R. (1994). *Flesh and stone: The body and the city in Western civilization.* New York: Norton.

Seshadri, H. V. (1982). *The tragic story of partition.* Bangalore: Jagarana Prakashana; Distributors Rashtrotthana Sahitya.

Shammash, Y., and Ori Stendal (1973). *Minority groups in Israel (within the green line).* Jerusalem: Prime Minister's Office, Bureau of the Advisor on Arab Affairs.

Shlaim, A. (1990). *The politics of partition: King Abdullah, the Zionists, and Palestine, 1921–1951.* New York: Columbia University Press.

Smith, H. (2002). "Turkish Cypriot rally calls for end to division." *The Guardian,* Nicosia. 27 December.

Springfield Inter-Community Development Project (1992). *Life on the interface: Report on a conference.* Island Pamphlets. Belfast: Island Publications.

Steinhardt, N. S. (1990). *Chinese imperial city planning.* Honolulu: University of Hawaii Press.

Strand, H., L. Wilhelmsen, and N. P. Gleditsch (2003). Armed Conflict Dataset. Oslo: International Peace Research Institute.

Surridge, B. (1958) *Cyprus: Report of the Municipal Commission, 1958.* Nicosia: Cyprus Government Printing Office.

Tabbara, L. M. (1979). *Survival in Beirut: A diary of civil war.* London: Onyx Press.

Tal, E. (1994). *Whose Jerusalem?* Jerusalem: International Forum for a United Jerusalem.

Tamari, S. (1981). *Building other people's homes.* Jerusalem: Arab Thought Forum.

———— (1999). *Jerusalem 1948: The Arab neighbourhoods and their fate in the war.* Jerusalem: Institute of Jerusalem Studies, Badil Resource Center for Palestinian Residency and Refugee Rights.

Theophanous, A., and V. Coufoudakis (1997). *Security and cooperation in the eastern Mediterranean.* Nicosia: Intercollege Press.

Turok, L. (1994). "Urban planning in the transition from Apartheid—part I: the legacy of social control." *Town Planning Review* 65 (3): 243–58.

United Nations Development Programme (1984). *Nicosia Master Plan: Final report.* Nicosia: UNDP.

Wasserstein, B. (1991). *The British in Palestine: The mandatory government and Arab-Jewish conflict, 1917–1929.* Oxford: Blackwell.

————. (2001). *Divided Jerusalem: The struggle for the Holy City.* New Haven, Conn.: Yale University Press.

White, M. (2003) *Historical atlas of the twentieth century.* N.p.: Matthew White. http://users.erols.com/mwhite28/warstatx.htm

Index

Page numbers in italics refer to illustrations

advocacy, 196–98
Alexandria (African township), 33
Allenby Street (Beirut), 55
Annan, Kofi, 139
anti-Semitism, 29–30, 32, 90
Aoun, Michel, 58
apartheid, 33
Attila (military operation), 135; Attila Line, 135. *See also* Green Line, Nicosia
avoidance, professional strategy, 177–80

Baghdad, 242
Balfour Declaration, 87–88
al-Basta, 48
Beirut, 1, 37–60; assessment, 187–89; civil war, 49–58; downtown area, map, *185*; as emblem of political struggle, 211–12; engagement through privatization, 184–89; map, *40*; political reading of conflict, 150; proximal cataclysmic events, 233; red line, 184, 186; refugee camps; settlement history, 39–44. *See also* Green Line, Beirut; refugee camps
Belfast, 1, 61–81; class conflict masked by ethnic rivalries, 159–60; class and ethnicity, 216; concretizing of peacelines, 218–19; cost of partition, 13–14; double minority syndrome, 209; as emblem of political struggle, 212; ethnic confrontations, 4–5; ethnic enclaves, camaraderie, 210; ethnic partitions, 6; expediency of walls, 149–50; faith in urban barricades, 162, *163*; industry closures, 157; legacy of partition, 227; local advantages of rivalry, 146; new peaceline established, 198–99; obstacles to nonpartisan planning, 183; partition wall, *155*; professional disengagement, 178; proximal cataclysmic events, 233; public housing policy, 165, 173–74; segregated neighborhoods, 70–71. *See also* Green Line, Belfast; Northern Ireland
Benvenisti, Meron, 200; advice to urban planners, 198; double minority syndrome, 153, 208–9; on security fence, 242
Black Saturday (Beirut), 54
Black September, 45
blighting, 230
Bloody Sunday, 73
Boban, Mate, 111–12
Bombay Street (Belfast), 71–72
Bosnia-Herzegovina: annexation by Austria-Hungary, 108; civil war, 110; proposed partition, 108–11
Boulevard (Mostar), 105, *118*, *194*; as interethnic boundary, 104, 108, 114–15, 217
boundary etching, 213–17
Boyne, Battle of, 65
Broz, Josip. *See* Tito, Josip Broz
Bulevar Narodne Revolucije. *See* Boulevard (Mostar)

camaraderie in enclaves, 164, 210
causation. *See* urban partitions, proximal crises
centralized planning, 181
Chamoun, Camille, 43, 45, 47, 49
Charter of National Reconciliation (Lebanon), 57–58
circulation patterns: Beirut, 52, 53; Belfast, 72; in enclaves, 221; Jerusalem, 83–87; Mostar, 114–15; Nicosia, 139, 141
cities, 15–18; scale and group identity, 27–29
class conflict, 159–61; masked by ethnic rivalries, 160
Clerides, Glafkos, 132
clustering, 208–10. *See also* ethnic segregation

collaborative planning, 181–83
commercial arteries and partition lines, 215
compliance strategies. *See* professional strategies, compliance
complicity and disengagement, 178–80
concretizing of boundaries, 217–20; Beirut, 50–52; Belfast, 217–20; Jerusalem, 92–94; Mostar, 113–15; Nicosia, 132–34
consolidation of boundaries, 220–21; Beirut, 54–57; Belfast, 73–74; Jerusalem, 94–95; Mostar, 115–16; Nicosia, 134–39
Cromwell, Oliver, 65
cultural heritage, private investment, 189–98
Cupar Street (Belfast), 219
Cvetković-Maček Agreement, 108–9
Cyprus: achieves independence, 131; British rule, 126–30; class conflict masked by ethnic rivalries, 160; double minority syndrome, 208–9; history, 125–27; quota system for political office, 131, 151; Turkish invasion, 134–35
Cyprus Problem, 130, 135; impacts, 139–42

Damascus Road (Beirut), as Green Line, 38, 217; map, *40*
David's Village, 192
Dayan-al-Tal partition line. *See* Green Line, Jerusalem
Dayan, Moshe, 92–93, 96, 237
Dayan, Uzi, 237, 239
Dayton Accords, 107, 116–17
deaths, 13; Beirut, 13, 58–59; Belfast, 13, 67, 78; Cyprus, 13, 139–40; Israel, 13; Jerusalem, 97; Mostar, 118
demographic engineering, 208
Denktash, Rauf, 133
divided cities: characteristics, 1–18, 205–35; compared with unified cities, 147–48; as emblems of political struggles, 211–13; in history, 21; potential for increase, 7
Dolfin, Zacaria, 30
double minority syndrome (Benvenisti), 153, 208–9

economic conditions in divided cities, 157
economic disadvantage: Beirut, 42; East Jerusalem, 100
Education Act (Northern Ireland), 1947 (UK), 68–69, 234
enclaves. *See* ethnic enclaves; sectarian enclaves

engagement, professional strategy, 181–98
enosis, 126–28, 130, 134
EOKA (National Organization of Cypriot Fighters), 127–28, 232
EOKA B, 134
Ervine, David: on consolidation of boundaries, 207–8; on fear, 1, 4, 205–6; on legacy of partition, 227; on need for multifaceted approach, 158; on voluntary segregation, 1, 4, 205–6
ethnic cleansing, Mostar, 103–5, 114
ethnic discrimination, institutionalization, 28–29. *See also* ghettos
ethnic enclaves, 3–7, 21–22; camaraderie, 210; costs, 220–21; suburban models, 32–34. *See also* clustering
ethnic political quotas: Cyprus, 131, 151; Lebanon, 42
ethnic rivalries, 1–3; masking class conflict, 159–61; related to breach of urban contract, 148–49
ethnic segregation: Belfast, 70–71; Cyprus, 125–26; historic context, 150–52, 162; and reconciliation, 145–46
ethnicity and political affiliation, 3–4, 206–8; Bosnia-Herzegovina, 109–10; Ireland, 65–68, 70–71; Jerusalem, 83–87, 89; Lebanon, 44–45, 48, 55; Mostar, 114–15; Nicosia, 121, 126–32; Yugoslavia, 109. *See also* ethnic cleansing; ethnic segregation

Falls Road (Belfast), 71
Fitzgerald, Sir William, 91
foreign governments. *See* international involvement

gated communities, 34
Gemayel, Amin, 57
Gemayel, Bashir, 45, 57
Gemayel, Pierre, 49
geography, physical. *See* physical geography
Georghadjis, Polycarpos, 132
ghettos, 29–32
Good Friday Agreement, 73
Great Britain: and Ireland, 65–81; League of Nations mandate in Palestine, 88–90; withdrawal from territory, 91–92
Green Line. *See also* partition line
———, Beirut, 9, 38–39, 50–52; dismantling, 58
———, Belfast, 9; impermeability, 158

———, Jerusalem, 8–9, 84–85, 94–95, *101*; dismantling, 85, 96, 237; genesis, 93–94; impermeability, 158
———, Nicosia, 8–9, 122–23, 129, *136*, *137*, *223*, *224*; establishment, 132–33; transit restrictions eased, 139
Griffith, Arthur, 66
Grivas, George, 127–28, 232

Hariri, Rafic, 194–95
high-intensity areas, Belfast, 76–78
Holocaust, 91
Home Rule, 66

industry closures, 157
infrastructure and development of enclaves, 216–17
integration: failure, Palestinian refugees, 33–34; and western city, 16. *See also* voluntary segregation
interethnic rivalries. *See* ethnic rivalries
interface areas, Belfast, 76–78
interface partitions, 3–7. *See also* peacelines
international involvement, 161; Cyprus, 127–31, 133–35; Lebanon, 45–46, 56; Mostar, 112–13, 116; Palestine, 87–88; postconflict recovery, 189–93. *See also* Great Britain, League of Nations mandate
Ireland: history, 65–71; migration to cities, 68
Israel: invasion of Lebanon (1982), 56–57; occupation of West Beirut, 57; partitioning program, 3; raid on Beirut (1973), 46; security fence, 3, 96, 237–42
Israeli-Jordanian General Armistice, 94

Jerusalem, 1, 83–102, 146; centralized planning, 181; circulation patterns, 221; duplication of facilities, 97–98; as emblem of political struggle, 212; informal division, 92; lack of social reconciliation, 226; map, 86; municipal boundaries, 147–48; partition, 91–96, 97–102; physical geography and boundaries, 213–14; proposed internationalization, 92; proximal cataclysmic events, 233; unification, 95–96; urban growth and development of enclaves, 216; urban planners' role, 176–77
Jordan: armistice agreement with Israel, 94; recognition of Israel, 94
Jugoslavia. *See* Yugoslavia
al-Jumayyil, Bashir. *See* Gemayel, Bashir
Jumblatt, Kamal, 45

Karadžić, Radovan, 111
Karami, Rashid, 43
Kata'ib Party, 49
Khatib, Ahmad, 55
Khouri, Elias, 196
Kingdom of Serbs, Croats, and Slovenians. *See* Yugoslavia

Lebanon: civil war, 49–58; impacts, 59–60; quota system for political office, 42
Lebanese Arab army, 55
Lebanese army, 55–56
Lebanese Company for the Development and Reconstruction of the Beirut Central District. *See* Solidere
Lebanese Front, 48
Lebanese National Movement, 48, 55
Lein, Yehezkel, 83
Lloyd George, David, 67
London Agreement, 131

Macmillan, Harold, 127, 129
Madrid Street (Belfast), 61
Makarios III, archbishop of Cyprus, 131, 133–34
Mamilla rehabilitation project (Jerusalem), 192
marching dates (Ulster), 61, 63
Maronites: political leadership, 45, 47; settlement in Beirut, 41. *See also* Mubarak, Ignace
Martyrs' Square (Beirut), 38, 41, 195
Mason-Dixon line, 129–30, 132. *See also* Green Line, Nicosia
Megali Idea, 126
Meouchi, Paul, 49
Milošević, Slobodan, 109
Mladic, Ratko, 113
More, Sir Thomas, *Utopia*, 27–28
Mostar, 1, 103–20; advocacy, 197–98; cost of partition, 14, 117–20; as emblem of political struggle, 212; free one-way transport, 208; industry closures, 157; map, *106*; political obstacles to effective planning, 177, 179; postconflict recovery, 189–93, 197–98; prewar history, 107–9; product of ethnic rivalries, 207; proximal cataclysmic events, 233; role of local politicians, 149; urban growth and development of enclaves, 215. *See also* Old Bridge (Mostar)
Mubarak, Ignace, archbishop of Beirut, 42

Municipal Commission, 130
Muslims: Beirut, 37–39, 42; refuse to join
    government, 57. *See also* Sunni Muslims

National Pact (Lebanon), 42
neutrality. *See* professional neutrality
Nicosia, 1, 121–42; advocacy, 196; circulation
    patterns, 221; collaborative planning,
    181–83; cost of partition, 14; as emblem of
    political struggle, 212–13; habits of segrega-
    tion, 5, 7; influence of public policy,
    150–52; maps, *124, 151*; physical geography
    and boundaries, 214; planning ahead of
    political settlement, 179; political contin-
    gency planning, 201–2; proximal cataclys-
    mic events, 233; sewage treatment system,
    121, 125, 182. *See also* Cyprus
Nicosia Master Plan team, 196, 202
nonpartisan professional engagement. *See*
    professional neutrality
nonsectarian urban planning, 173–74
Northern Ireland, cost of Troubles, 14
Northern Ireland Civil Rights Association, 69

objectivity. *See* professional neutrality
Old Bridge (Mostar): destruction, 116; recon-
    struction, 190–91, 193
O'Neill, Terence, 69
Orange Order, 61, 65–66, 68
Orek, Osman, 133
Owen, David, Baron Owen, 112–13
Öznel, Nevzat, 14, 121, 125, 168, 182

Paisley, Ian, 69
Palestine: British security fence, 89; divide-
    and-rule, 89, 207; Jewish immigration, 89,
    90
Palestine Liberation Organization (PLO), 44,
    45; evacuate Beirut, 56; Israeli raid (1973),
    46; recruitment from refugee camps, 234
Palestinian National Congress, 88
Palestinian refugees, 33–34, 43–45, 234
partition. *See* urban partition
partition lines, Mostar, 9, 104–5
peacelines (Belfast), 62–63, 73–74, *75*
Peel Commission, 89–90
Penal Laws (1697), 65
perimeter walls, 19–21, 22–25, 143–44; demise,
    25–27; Milan, 23; related to vulnerability,
    17; suburban U.S., 34

Phalangist Party, 49; Black Saturday, 54
physical barricades. *See* urban partitions
physical geography, influence on social
    boundaries, 213–14
physical segregation. *See* urban partitions
Place des Canons. *See* Martyrs' Square
    (Beirut)
PLO. *See* Palestine Liberation Organization
political planning, 175–77
political up-scaling, 210–13
population transfers, Beirut, 54
Powell, Colin L., 242
private investment in cultural heritage,
    189–98
privatization, 183–89
professional acquiescence, 170
professional neutrality: difficult to sustain,
    169; impractical, 172–74
professional strategies: acquiescence, 170;
    avoidance, 177–80; compliance, 171–77; en-
    gagement, 181–98
professionals: accommodation to complexity
    of divided cities, 199–200; disengagement
    from ethnicity, 178–79; marginalization,
    169–71; sidelined, 180
Progressive Socialist Party, 45
psychological trauma, 3, 13; Beirut, 60; Bel-
    fast, 79–80; Cyprus, 140–41; Jerusalem,
    98–99; Mostar, 119
public welfare notion questioned, 168–69

redlining, 22
refugee camps: Beirut, 33–34, 43–45, 234; Bei-
    rut, Phalangist attacks, 57. *See also* Sabra
    refugee camp; Shatila refugee camp; Tall
    al-Za'tar
relative deprivation, 234
Rhodes Agreement. *See* Israeli-Jordanian
    General Armistice

Sa'ad, Ma'ruf, 47
Sabra refugee camp, 57
Safdie, Moshe, 192
Sampson, Nicos, 134
Scarman Tribunal, 72
sectarian enclaves, Belfast, 70–71
Shankill Road (Belfast), 66, 71, 198–99
Sharon, Ariel, 239
Shatila refugee camp, 57

Shihab, Fu'ad, 49
Shi'ite Muslims, 41–42, 45
Short Strand (Belfast), 61, 63–64, 209–10
Sidon, 47
Sinn Fein, 66
Six-Day War, 96
social context of rehabilitation, 198–203
Solidere, 184–89, 193–95, 196–97; assessment, 187–89
South Africa, townships, 33
Soweto, 33
Stari Grad Foundation, 197–98
strategies, professional. *See* professional strategies
Suez crisis, 43
Sunni Muslims, 41–43, 47. *See also* al-Basta
Surridge, B. J., 129–30
Sykes-Picot Agreement, 87, 89

Tabet, Jad, 196
al-Tal, Abdullah, 93
Tall al-Za'tar, 49, 55
Tegart, Sir Charles, 89
Tito, Josip Broz, 109; ability to balance ethnic rivalries, 207
training of professionals, 171–72
Troubles (Northern Ireland), 71–74; impacts, 14, 74–81
Tudjman, Franjo, 109

Ulster Volunteer Force (UVF), 67
United Nations, peacekeeping force in Cyprus, 134
urban apartheid. *See* urban partitions
urban contract, 24, 143–66; breakdown, 154–61; consequences, 162–64; erosion, 153–54
urban growth; Beirut, 41–43, 46–47; Belfast, 68–69; and development of enclaves, 214–16; Jerusalem, 216; Mostar, 215
urban partitions, 3–7; camaraderie, 210; consequences, 1–2, 162–64; context-dependence, 232–24; direct involvement of professionals, 174–77; duplication of services, 97–98, 228, 241; efficacy, 5, 35, 164–66, 230–31; emerge in areas of coexistence, 219–20; expediency, 112, 149–50; incremental and predictable development, 232; logic of the process, 15; lost opportunities,

10–11; ; professional response, 167–203; proximal crises, 11–12, 233; rationalization, 159; related to public policy, 149–53; and sense of security, 146–47; social costs, 209; social and economic disadvantage, 229; undermining of security conditions, 231; vested interests, 228. *See also* ethnic enclaves; ethnic segregation
———, impacts, 12–15, 209, 227–32, 235; Beirut, 58–60; Belfast, 73–81; Jerusalem, 97–102; Mostar, 14, 117–20; Nicosia, 139–42
———, nature of boundaries, 8–10, 213–17; Jerusalem, 92–94; Nicosia, 132–33
———, permeability; Beirut, 38; Belfast, 62, 158; Jerusalem, 85
———, sequence of development, 10–11, 232; Beirut, 44–52; Belfast, 68–73; Jerusalem, 90–94; Mostar, 109–15; Nicosia, 127–33
urban planners. *See* professionals
urban walls. *See* urban partitions
Utopia (More), 27–28
UVF. *See* Ulster Volunteer Force

Vance, Cyrus: and Cyprus, 134; and Mostar, 112–13
Vance-Owen plan, 112–13, 117
Venice, ghetto, 30–32
voluntary segregation, 222, 226–27; Beirut, 54; Belfast, 70; Jerusalem, 92, 97; Nicosia, 141
Vučurević, Božidar, 111

walls: and feeling of security, 146–47, 156; and revised urban contract, 144–53. *See also* perimeter walls; urban partitions
War of Independence (Ireland), 67
warning beacons, 2–3
Washington Agreement, 116–17
West Jerusalem: Jewish immigration, 98; urban growth, 94
Woodhead, Sir John, 89–90

Young, Peter, 133
Yugoslavia, 108–9

Zionism, 87–88
zuama system, 44–45
Zurich Agreement, 131

Acknowledgments

Research in support of this book took place gradually over the years 1998–2003. We called upon dozens of strangers in each of the cities we studied—politicians, planners, residents, journalists—and were met with generosity in every instance. These sources addressed our questions with candor and a shared interest in the riddle of partition.

Their voices can be heard in the preceding pages, since our analysis relies on insights gathered from interviews. We were greatly aided by native research assistants in each city who navigated, translated, scoured archives, and helped to conduct interviews: David Russell, Mazor Shlomo, Zeina Halabi, Hajdi Hudec, Lejla Alikalfic, Kirsten Zaat, Talya Kozminsky. We are endebted to them for their insights, energies, and dedication. Special onsite support was provided by Agni Petridou, Arie Rahamimoff, Rami Nasrallah, Angus Gavin, Ross Campbell, Fred Boal, Leontios Geramisou, Meron Benvenisti, and Amir Pašić. Dr. Pašić's encouragement and support were especially vital throughout, since it was his vision and leadership during the "Mostar 2004" summer workshops that framed the questions that prompted this investigation.

The manuscript benefited from the careful scrutiny of many kind readers like Seth Rogoff and Lucinda Thompson along with the expert touch of preliminary editor Carol Pearce. The city maps were created by the thoughtful hand of Aubrey Chandica. We are especially grateful to Peter Agree and Genie Birch at the University of Pennsylvania Press for their steadfast support of the project. Above all, we are deeply indebted to the John D. and Catherine T. MacArthur Foundation, providing kind support through the Research and Writing grant program for Global Security and Sustainability that allowed for first hand observation and comparison.